EVIL
PSYCHOPATHS

EVIL
PSYCHOPATHS

DANGEROUS AND DERANGED

GORDON KERR

Futura

A *Futura* Book

First published by Futura in 2009

ISBN: 978-0-7088-0210-6

Produced by Omnipress Limited, UK

Printed in Great Britain

Futura
An imprint of
Little, Brown Book Group
100 Victoria Embankment
London EC4Y 0DY

An Hachette UK Company

Photo credits: Corbis (front cover)
Getty (inside pages)

CONTENTS

PART FOUR: 20TH CENTURY AMERICAN PSYCHOPATHIC KILLERS

PART FIVE: 20TH CENTURY EUROPEAN PSYCHOPATHIC KILLERS

PART SIX: PSYCHOPATHIC KILLERS FROM THE REST OF THE WORLD

INTRODUCTION

They are different to the rest of us. While we do our level best to maintain the checks and balances that keep us civilised, there are some amongst us who do not, or cannot, have the ability to set loose the monster within with devastating and often shocking consequences. They are narcissistic, ruthless, emotionally cold, cruel, vicious, self-seeking, easily bored men and women who are totally uninhibited in the methods by which they achieve their goals. But at the same time, they can be charm itself, capable, very often, of manipulating people into doing or believing things they would never dream of. What other explanation could there be for the mass hysteria created by Adolf Hitler before and during World War II, when an entire nation took part in horrific acts of cruelty and mass murder? Pol Pot's depraved regime in Cambodia in the 1970s, when hundreds of thousands of Cambodians were killed, provides another example of an entire country being manipulated into carrying out unspeakable acts. Or how do you explain Myra Hindley's chilling compliance with whatever her lover Ian Brady demanded of her – graduating from posing for pornographic photographs to helping him to find children on whom he could work out his depraved fantasies? Gilles de Rais, a powerful man in 15th century France, seems to have had little trouble in recruiting a whole team of accomplices who helped him to find innocent children to be the victims of his cruel games.

The psychopath often does not kill for financial gain or improvement. He or she does it simply because it provides psychological gratification, or, as notorious serial killer and psychopath Ted Bundy put it shortly before his execution: 'I'm the most cold-blooded sonofabitch you'll ever meet ... I just liked to kill, I wanted to kill.' Dr Thomas Neil Cream did not even have to be present when his victims succumbed to the potions and pills he doled out to them. The simple knowledge that they were going to die was enough for him.

Others try to explain their acts away by citing voices in their heads, as in the case of John Lynch, the Berrima Axe-murderer, or attempt to justify their acts as some kind of moral crusade. The Yorkshire Ripper, Peter Sutcliffe, claimed to be 'cleaning up the streets' by killing thirteen prostitutes, while John Wayne Gacy, killer of thirty-three boys and men in the 1970s, described his victims as 'worthless little queers and punks'. There is little doubt that the legendary Jack the Ripper was also on some kind of moral crusade, cleaning up the squalid streets of 19th century Whitechapel in London's East End. John Reginald Christie, the murderous strangler of 10 Rillington Place seemed to be on a mission to exorcise his hatred for women, a mission he shared with the famous Night Stalker, Richard Ramirez, the rapist, sodomiser and gruesome serial killer of women, whose victims died smelling his foul breath, gained from eating an excess of junk food during the neglect of his childhood.

Of course, some do gain from their acts. John George Haigh, the 'Acid Bath Murderer' killed people for their bank accounts or property before giving them a hot bath, but his behaviour was that of a psychopath who belived he was invincible, somehow above the law. Unfortunately for him, he was just not quite insane enough to escape the gallows. Velma Barfield, Nannie Doss and Mary Ann Cotton, the famous women serial poisoners killed in the main to benefit from insurance policies, but there is no denying that they also killed for themselves, because their victims stood in the way of their happiness, something that is unwise around a psychopath.

Some are, however, beyond the pale. How can you account for the sick acts and behaviour of men such as Dennis Nilsen, Robert Black, Ian Brady, John Wayne Gacy, Ed Gein or Patrick Mackay? These are men whose actions place them outside of society with little chance of finding their way back in. For them, killing was an act to be enjoyed, to take pleasure from and to do again and again until they were stopped. Other lives did not matter. For Dennis Nilsen, for instance, killing was all about him and his terrible loneliness. He never at any moment stopped to consider the life he had snuffed out. Neither did Patrick Mackay, very often killing and staying for a while in the house of the person he had killed, listening to the radio or watching television.

Ultimately, their pleasure and gratification is all that matters. Peter Kurten, the 'Vampire of Dusseldorf', as he was known, loved killing and gained sexual gratification from it, achieving orgasm when he poured petrol over one of his numerous victims and set it on fire. Patrick Mackay talked about the erotic nature of a wound he had inflicted on a priest who was dying in front of him. He also spoke about how euphoric he felt after killing, a feeling that would remain with him for several days.

How did they become monsters? Of course, some were just born that way, but it is interesting how many of the killers in this book were born to a life of abuse, anger and neglect. Peter Kurten's father would rape the mother of his thirteen children in front of them; he would also rape his daughters. The step-father of Aileen Wuornos became a psychopathic child molestor who would eventually hang himself in prison. Velma Barfield was beaten by a drunken disciplinarian of a father. Richard Speck had an abusive stepfather and Ed Gein lived in a rigidly disciplined religious household where his mother did not allow him or his brother to cultivate friendships and spent afternoons reading the Bible to them. All of these negative experiences were stored away by these men and women, either to be copied when they got older or to be avenged.

Evil Psychopaths examines the excesses to which some people's demons will drive them and examines the lives of psychopaths, their motivations, their methods and the journeys their lives took to the fatal moment when they found that they enjoyed no greater pleasure than taking another life.

PART ONE

PSYCHOPATHIC KILLERS IN HISTORY

EMPEROR NERO

He was quite simply a megalomaniac from a long line of psychopaths.

His grandfather led the way. Lucius Domitius Ahenobarbus had been savage and cruel. The gladiatorial contests he organised were so bloody and vicious that the Emperor Augustus had to ask him to tone things down a little. His father, Gnaeus, once rode his horse over a small child on the Appian Way, the road connecting Rome with southeast Italy, just for fun. He was also reported to have gouged out a man's eyes for criticising him and killed another man for not drinking as much as he had been ordered to. Gnaeus lived a debauched life, he was a serial adulterer and enjoyed an incestuous relationship with his sister, Domitia Lepida. He was known to defraud bankers and when he occupied the important position of Praetor, Nero made a habit of swindling charioteers, victorious in the games, of their prize money. The great Roman historian, Suetonius, described him as 'despicable and dishonest'.

Nero's mother, Agrippina, great granddaughter of Emperor Augustus, also came from a troubled background. Born during the reign of the tyrannical Emperor Tiberius, she witnessed her two brothers starved to death by order of Tiberius. To make matters worse, not only did she have her first sexual experience at the age of twelve, but it was with her surviving brother, the future emperor, Caligula. In 39, Agrippina and her sister, Julia Livilla were discovered to be involved in a plot to murder Caligula and replace him with their late sister Drusilla's widower, Marcus Aemilius Lepidus. Lepidus was executed and the two women were sent into exile on the Pontine Islands where they had to dive for sponges to earn a living. Nero's first few years, therefore, were spent in relative poverty. Meanwhile Gnaeus died when Nero was three, thus escaping trial for treason, incest and adultery.

Following the assassination of Caligula in 41 CE, Agrippina was recalled to Rome by the new emperor, Claudius, who was her uncle. She married a rich and influential Roman, Passienus Crispus, who divorced his wife, Messalina, for her and when he died not long after – probably as a result of poison administered by his wife – she became a very wealthy widow.

A few years later, she added position to wealth when she became the wife of the Emperor Claudius whose third wife, Messalina, had been executed for plotting to kill him. Agrippina used her influence to persuade her husband to adopt her young son, Nero, as his heir, over his own son with Messalina, Britannicus. Nero also came under the influence of Lucius Annaeus Seneca, the stoic philosopher who had been appointed his tutor. Her next step in the fulfilment of her ambitions was to have the fiancé of Claudius's daughter Octavia falsely accused of having committed incest with his sister. This allowed Agrippina to engineer the marriage of Nero to his half-sister.

The only obstacle that remained in Nero's way was Claudius himself and he had begun to talk once more of his son Britannicus being restored as heir to the throne. Agrippina dealt with this threat in the same way as she had dealt her second husband. She had Claudius poisoned in 54 CE. The following year, Britannicus died in suspicious circumstances at a dinner.

Nero, the fifth and final emperor of the Julian dynasty gained power at the age of sixteen, the youngest emperor until that time. His reign began well. He had the advice of good men – Seneca and Sextus Afranius Burrus, a Praetorian prefect. After around five years in power, however, the habits of his family began to predominate. He began to indulge in debauchery, eating and drinking to excess and he took his servant, Acte, as mistress, arousing the jealousy of his mother, Agrippina who, some commentators have suggested, was involved in an incestuous relationship with her son. This irritated Nero and he banished his mother to a separate residence. However, it was not long before he became bored with Acte and, anyway, he had fallen in love with the ruthlessly ambitious Sabina Poppaea. Around this time, however, he began to take an interest in male companions, probably under the influence of Seneca. He cultivated a favourite, Doryphorus, possibly because he resembled his mother. It did not last long, however. Nero had him poisoned in 62 CE.

He also made several attempts to murder his mother, especially when she began to side with his wife Octavia in opposition to his new love and even began to support the claim of Britannicus to the throne of Rome. An attempt to poison her failed. Then, he arranged for the ceiling of her bedroom to collapse on top of her, but that also failed. He even went as far as having a collapsible boat built. However, following its collapse at sea, she managed to swim ashore. Eventually, he took the obvious option – he sent someone to beat her and stab her to death and dressed her death up as suicide. But in all honesty, no one missed her. The Roman Senate had never got on with her and Nero was glad to have removed her influence from his life.

He returned to his life of fun and games – staging chariot races and athletics at grand festivals. He put on musical contests at which he could compete, and, obviously win. The Senate was appalled. It was considered undignified to perform in public and for an emperor to do it was unthinkable. Nonetheless, Nero loved it, to the extent that no one was allowed to leave the auditorium while he was on stage accompanying himself on the lyre. Women are said to have given birth while he performed, so afraid were they to leave the auditorium and men sometimes feigned death in order to get out of his marathon performances.

In 62 CE, a new and pernicious adviser entered Nero's circle. Following the death of Burrus from illness, two new men took office – Faenius Rufus and the cruel and licentious former lover of Agrippina, Gaius Ofonius Tigellinus. When Nero had come to power, he had stopped the hated treason courts that had blighted Rome for many years. Tigellinus re-introduced them. It all proved too much for the wise adviser, Seneca, who resigned as things began to deteriorate at court. That same year, Nero ordered the execution of his wife Octavia for adultery and life became a vile round of sport, music, orgies and murder. He married Sabina Poppaea but would later kick her to death one night after she complained about him coming home late from horse-racing.

The Great Fire of Rome on the night of 18 July in the year 64 CE was devastating for the city. Many Roman houses were made of wood, helping the fire to spread very quickly. It burned for six days and seven nights, destroying four of the fourteen Roman districts and seriously damaging another seven. Of course, the legend has grown that Nero 'fiddled while Rome burned', an impossible feat as the violin would not be invented until many centuries later. Some have said that he did climb onto the roof of his palace, however, to get the best view of the conflagration and that he sang a song, The Capture of Troy, as he watched. Others claim that he tried to control the fire and afterwards funded the re-building of large parts of the city from his own pocket. However, it does seem suspicious that after the fire he built his 'Golden Palace' on large parts of the city that had been decimated by it. He added pleasure gardens to it, a large artificial lake in the centre and a thirty metre-high statue of himself. If the fire had not destroyed such large parts of Rome, the palace could not have been constructed. The Roman people remained suspicious.

Nero had no doubts. He blamed it on the growing religious sect, the Christians, followers of the recently crucified Jesus of Nazareth. He punished them by crucifying them like their leader or by throwing them to wild animals in the circus. He horrifically used many of them to illuminate his garden at night, tying them to stakes and setting light to them.

There were forces moving against him, however. A plot known as the 'Pisonian Conspiracy' was uncovered. Seneca was amongst the nineteen executions and suicides that followed its discovery. Nero had people executed or invited to commit suicide purely on the basis that he disliked them or was suspicious of them. There were no trials.

Towards the end of the decade, he travelled to Greece to take part in the Olympic Games where he won, naturally – everyone was too frightened to defeat him at anything. He even won the chariot race although he tumbled from his chariot.

Meanwhile back in Rome the treason trials continued. Numerous generals, senators and nobles were put to death merely on suspicion that they were conspiring against the emperor. There was also a shortage of food and the people of Rome were becoming agitated. He was summoned back from Greece but it was too late. In March 68 CE, Gaius Julius Vindex, Governor of Gallia Lugdunensis, a vast swathe of modern-day central France, rescinded his oath of allegiance to the emperor and encouraged others, including seventy-one-year-old Galba, Governor of northern and eastern Spain, to do the same. Nero sent legions from the Rhine and they defeated Vindex at the Battle of Vesontio, following which Vindex committed suicide. Unfortunately for Nero, however, the troops sent from Germany also revolted, refusing any longer to acknowledge his leadership. In Africa, Lucius Clodius Mace followed suit but his defection was altogether more serious as he was able to cut off much of Rome's food supply which came from North Africa. He informed the Senate that he was ready to replace Nero, if required.

The Emperor was helpless, spending his time devising new tortures with which to punish the rebels when he finally defeated them The only man who could have helped him, Tigellinus, was seriously ill and without him, he was lost. The Senate voted to condemn him to death by flogging. But, reluctant to die in this manner, he slashed his own throat as the soldiers approached to take him away. Not quite dead, he was finished off by a servant. 'What an artist the world is losing!' he cried as he prepared for death. His high opinion of himself continued to the end.

CHARLES VI OF FRANCE

What a strange sight he must have been. Wild and unwashed – he had not washed for five months, in fact – and with iron bars in his clothes as supports and protection. The problem was that he had come to believe in recent months that he was made of glass and was terrified of being broken. He had also decided that his name was George and did not have a clue who his wife was when she came to visit him.

Charles VI was very ill. It is suggested nowadays that he suffered from schizophrenia, many of his symptoms being those of a schizophrenic. Porphyria, the disease that blighted the life of Great Britain's King George III, is also suggested. Porphyria is a hereditary illness that results in delirium and visual and auditory disturbances as well as giving its victims painful physical symptoms such as inflammation of the bowels, painful weakness in the limbs and loss of feeling. Porphyria has certainly been diagnosed as existing amongst a number of Charles's ancestors.

Indeed, the French monarchy had its share of mad rulers, the first of which was probably Clovis II, known as 'the Do-Nothing'. His great-grandson, Childeric III was known, for obvious reasons, as 'the Idiot' and Robert of Clermont, an ancestor of the Bourbons, who lived at the end of the thirteenth century, seems to have become a psychopath after receiving several blows to the head during a tournament. The 16th century King Charles IX was mentally unstable with sadistic tendencies and uncontrollable rages. In the 18th century, the sisters, Princess Marie Louise and Princess Louise Elizabeth were sadly deranged.

Of them all, however, it was Charles VI who was worst. He became king in 1380 at the age of twelve and seems at that time to have been a pleasant and agreeable young man. He was unfortunate in his regents however, because his uncles, the Dukes of Anjou, Berry, Burgundy and Bourbon, increased the tax burden on the people for their own gain, plundering a treasury already short of funds due to the cripplingly expensive Hundred Years' War against the English. There was social unrest in France as a result, particularly during the year 1382. Finally in 1388, Charles dispensed with the dukes' services, replacing them with a group of councillors from humbler backgrounds.

He was married in 1385 to a beautiful fourteen-year-old Bavarian princess, Isabeau, with whom he had fallen head over heels in love with the moment he had seen her. To begin with, the marriage was a very happy one, although Isabeau made no effort to learn to speak French. She would turn out to be a spoilt and selfish woman interested only in getting what she wanted.

Charles's life seems to have changed following a mysterious illness he suffered in April 1392 when he developed a fever and his hair and nails fell out. While still not fully recovered, in August of that year he undertook an expedition to punish those responsible for an assassination attempt on one of his advisers. Leading a small army, he was impatient at the slow progress they were making. His bad mood was exacerbated by the fact that he was still suffering from periodic bouts of fever.

While riding through a forest, a barefoot man dressed in rags is said to have suddenly ran out of the trees and grabbed the bridle of Charles's horse, shouting at him to turn back, that he had been betrayed. The man was dragged away from the king's horse but followed the army, persisting in his warnings to the king.

A little later, as the band of knights emerged from the forest, a page, drowsy in the summer heat, dropped the king's lance. It clanged against a steel helmet being carried by another page. This sudden noise seemed to do something to Charles because he shuddered and drew his sword, yelling 'Charge the traitors! They wish to hand me over to the enemy!' He spurred his horse forward into his own men and started to swing his sword wildly amongst them. Eventually, a chamberlain and a number of his men pulled him from his horse and restrained him on the ground where he slipped into a coma-like trance. Around him lay four dead men.

Charles remained in his coma-like state for two days but then began slowly to recover. He was distraught when he learned of the men he had killed and was never the same man again, his bouts of insanity becoming increasingly frequent. On one occasion, his irrational behaviour almost cost him his life. On 28 January 1393, Queen Isabeau staged a masked ball. Charles was a member of a group of courtiers who dressed as wild men for the party, wearing costumes of linen cloth soaked in either resinous wax or pitch to hold a covering of frazzled hemp, giving them the appearance of being hairy from head to foot. This was obviously a great fire risk and the torch-bearers were, consequently, ordered to stand around the walls of the room, far away from the cavorting men who were chained to one another. Unfortunately, the king's brother, Louis de Valois, Duke of Orléans, was unaware of the danger. Arriving late and carrying a torch, he approached one of the wild men to see who it was and accidentally set fire to him. Panic broke out and the wild men desperately tried to escape the flames. One of them was close to the Duchess of Berry who quickly threw the train of her dress over the man to protect him. The man under her dress was the king and she had unwittingly saved him from an ignominious and horrific death.

A couple of months later, Charles was in the grip of another debilitating attack. In an attempt to ease the pressure on his brain, a surgeon drilled a couple of holes in his head and, indeed, he did seem to experience some relief for a while. In 1395, however, he was once again in the throes of insanity. In 1397, believing that he was perhaps the victim of an act of witchcraft or sorcery, priests tried to exorcise him. It made no difference, however, and the attacks began to last longer. Even in his periods of clarity, his mood swings were extreme. When ill, he was delusional, denying he was king and that he had a wife and children. He would run dementedly from room to room in his palace, claiming that he was being pursued by his enemies until he collapsed from exhaustion. He was locked in darkened rooms and would attack anyone who came near him, servants and doctors. He smashed furniture and wet himself and in 1405 refused to wash, shave or change his clothes. They tried a primitive form of shock treatment, a number of men blackening their faces and leaping out at him in his room. It seemed to do the trick and he finally agreed to be washed and to change his clothes.

His relationship with his wife was, of course, very bad. She was terrified of him and he began to hate her. She provided him with a young mistress to divert his attention from her. It suited her, as she had for some time been openly having an affair with the king's brother, Louis. People actually questioned the legitimacy of Charles's children, especially when the heir to the throne, Charles, was born.

Eventually, the king became unable to govern. Even when not suffering from one of his bouts of anxiety, he found it difficult to make decisions or concentrate and a power struggle developed between his brother Louis and John the Fearless, Duke of Burgundy. It had a huge impact on France that was manifested when an English army led by King Henry V defeated a French army five times its size at the Battle of Agincourt in 1415.

Over the years, Queen Isabeau's looks had faded and she became fat and suffered from gout. She had to be pushed around in a wheelchair and became agoraphobic. The interests of the royal children were protected by Bernard of Armagnac who learned that Isabeau was plotting against the king with John the Fearless. Charles, in a period of good health, was furious. He was also angry at Isabeau's dissolute behaviour and decided to do something about it. He, his son and Bernard of Armagnac rode to Vincennes to deal with her latest lover, Louis de Boisbourdon. They seized him, tortured him savagely, strangled him and threw him into the Seine in a leather sack. As for Isabeau, she was banished to Tours. Released in 1418 by John the Fearless, she took her revenge on Bernard of Armagnac, ordering her new lover, Jean de Villiers, to kill him and carve the cross of Burgundy on his chest.

Isabeau did not have a monopoly on mindless violence, of course. When John the Fearless had a meeting with Prince Charles, in 1419, the sixteen-year-old Dauphin hacked him to death. Isabeau responded by disinheriting Charles.

Meanwhile, the king had been living in a condition of neglect at Senlis, near Paris. Following his marriage to Princess Catherine, daughter of Charles and Isabeau, however, and the naming of him by Isabeau as heir to the French throne, Henry V of England brought Charles back to Paris. He was, by this time, very ill, but is said to have recovered somewhat, thanks to a diet of oranges and pomegranates. In the autumn of 1422 he became ill again and this time he did not recover. He died surrounded by strangers, aged fifty-four.

VLAD THE IMPALER

When Vlad III came to power in the Balkan country of Wallachia in the 15th century, life was harsh. They were ruthlessly violent times and members of his family had experienced extreme brutality. His brother Mircea II, for instance, had been captured by dissident boyars – nobles – and had his eyes burnt out with red-hot pokers before being buried alive. His father, Vlad III, had suffered a horrific death on the orders of John Hunyadi, regent of Hungary, by being face-scalped – the edges of his face were cut and the skin was then peeled off, while he was still alive.

Vlad was, himself, not averse to cruel practices in his castle at Târgoviste in order to retain power and control in his domain. In one story, he is reported to have received a group of foreign visitors who slighted him in some way. It may have been that they committed the insult of failing to remove their hats in his presence. He punished them by ensuring that their hats would never come off – he had them nailed to their heads.

Because of his fight to remain independent of the Ottoman Empire, Romanians view Vlad as a great hero and an effective, although often harsh ruler, but it is easy to understand why the writer Bram Stoker turned him into one of literature's great villains, the blood-sucking vampire, Count Dracula. He is said to have killed around 100,000 people in various cruel ways, his brutality extending to torturing, burning, skinning, roasting and boiling, feeding people human flesh – normally their friends or relatives – cutting off limbs and drowning. However, his favourite method of dispatching his enemies and those he, quite simply, did not like, was to impale them.

The victim's legs were each attached to a horse and a sharpened stake was forced slowly into the body through the anus or, sometimes, the chest. When inserted through the anus, it was forced upwards until it emerged from the mouth. The point of the stake was oiled but was not sharpened to a great extent as that would kill the victim too quickly and spoil Vlad's enjoyment. Children were impaled on a stake forced through their mothers' chests.

Death by impalement could take days and was, of course, agonising, the height of the stake indicating the rank and power of the victim. They were often organised in geometric patterns by Vlad and the bodies were left to rot for months.

On one occasion, in 1460, he is said to have impaled 10,000 people in the Transylvanian city of Sibiu. The previous year saw him impaling 30,000 merchants, officials and citizens in Brasov that he claimed were questioning his authority – never a good idea.

Impaling was just one of a menu of horrific punishments used by Vlad. He was also partial to blinding, cutting off limbs, strangulation, cutting off the nose and ears and mutilating the sex organs. Now and then he would also scalp or skin his victims.

In terms of controlling his people and keeping crime down, the cruelty of his punishments seems to have delivered results. One story tells how he left a gold cup in the middle of the street for several days and no one touched it for fear of the punishment they would receive if they did.

Wallachia was Vlad's native land, but his family had lived in exile in Transylvania after losing the throne to pro-Ottoman boyars. His father was a member of the noble Order of the Dragon, a fraternal order of knights sworn to uphold Christianity and defend the Holy Roman Empire against the Ottoman Empire to the east. Vlad's father, Vlad II, enthusiastically adopted the symbol of the dragon and used it on clothing, flags and coinage. In Romanian, the word for dragon is drac and ul is the definite article. Thus, did Vlad's father become known to all as Vlad Dracul – Vlad the Dragon. Vlad himself became Vlad Dracula – son of the Dragon – when he was accepted into the order at the age of five.

Wallachia was caught between the advancing Turkish Ottoman Empire that had in 1453 finally captured the city of Constantinople, the capital of the Byzantine Empire. For centuries, the Byzantine Empire had acted as a buffer between the Muslim east and Christendom and now, with its fall, Wallachia was caught between the Ottomans and the Hungarians to the north, appeasing each and forming alliances with one or the other. When Vlad came to power, the Ottomans were the sworn enemy of him and his people. He had developed a great knowledge of them through spending a part his childhood living amongst them. His father had been forced to hand over his children as hostages in return for the Turks not invading Wallachia. They were harsh times for Vlad. He was cruelly whipped for being stubborn and insulting to his captors and he developed a hatred for the future sultan, Mehmed. He also grew to distrust his father for giving in to the Turks, an act that, to Vlad, was a betrayal of all that the Order of the Dragon stood for. He was a faithful adherent to the principles of the Order, festooning flags, banners and his clothing with its imagery.

When Vlad Dracul did not provide support to the Hungarian leader, John Hunyadi, in the Varna Crusade in the 1440s, he was assassinated and the Turks released the young Vlad III from captivity, putting him forward as a candidate for the Wallachian throne, while John Hunyadi established his own man as leader. In 1448, at the age of seventeen, Vlad briefly seized the throne, but Hunyadi forced him to flee. Then, when Hunyadi's man turned pro-Turkish, Hunyadi turned to Vlad to replace him. In 1456, Vlad succeeded in seizing the throne again. He would reign for six bloody years.

The Ottomans, for their part, were afraid of Vlad, especially as stories grew about his cruelty towards captured soldiers. They told how he cut off their noses and sent them to Hungary to demonstrate how many he had killed.

There is one story, known as the 'forest of the impaled' that horrified the Turks.

Following an unsuccessful attack by a large force under Sultan Mehmed, Vlad took revenge by leading an army across the Danube in the winter of 1462 and laying waste to the lands between Serbia and the Black Sea. His army killed more than 20,000 people.

Mehmed raised an army of 90,000 a few months later in spring, and marched on Wallachia. As they approached Vlad's lands, however, they were sickened by the sight of a forest of stakes on which Vlad had impaled around 30,000 Turkish captives. Nonetheless, they proceeded with the attack and captured Târgoviste, ousting Vlad and forcing him into a guerrilla campaign against the occupiers who had installed his hated brother, Radu the Handsome as a puppet ruler. Vlad was pursued as far as Transylvania where the Hungarian king, Matthias Corvinus, imprisoned him for four years.

Meanwhile, while Vlad's castle at Poienari was being besieged, someone – probably a servant delivering a warning – fired an arrow through one of the windows with news that Radu's army was approaching. Rather than be captured and taken into captivity by the Turks, Vlad's wife threw herself from a tower into the river that flowed past the castle, legend having her say that she would rather rot and be eaten by the fish than be led into captivity by the Turks.

Vlad was imprisoned from 1462 until 1474, but he gradually began to win round the Hungarian king and even married one of his cousins while in captivity. He was released and reconquered Wallachia in 1476 with a force of dissatisfied boyars, some Transylvanians and a force of Moldavians. By this time, Radu was dead and had been replaced by another Turkish puppet king, Basarab the Elder, a member of a rival clan. As Vlad approached, the king and his supporters fled.

His triumph would be short-lived, however. When his allies departed, he was left weakened and the Ottomans returned to restore their candidate Basarab to the throne. The nobles failed to support Vlad and the peasants were sick of his cruelty. He marched against the Ottomans with a force of only 4,000 men.

It is not known exactly how Vlad the Impaler died. Some say he died in the ensuing battle near Bucharest, fighting the Turks. Others report that he was assassinated, like his father, by disloyal Wallachian boyars. Another story has him being killed by one of his own men. One accounts says that he was decapitated by the Turks who sent his head preserved in honey as proof of his death to Istanbul. He may have been face-scalped, however, just as his father had been.

When his tomb was discovered many years later and opened, his face was covered by a piece of cloth, a sign that he had, indeed, suffered the same fate as his father. Unfortunately, it could not be proved, because, moments after the tomb was opened and the corpse was exposed to light and air, it crumbled to dust, as in all the best vampire movies.

THE BORGIAS

According to the diary of Johannes Burchard, Master of Ceremonies to successive popes in the 15th and early 16th centuries, a gang of unfortunate prisoners, shackled at the wrist, would be dragged into St. Peter's Square, in front of the Vatican in Rome, while lines of guards protected every exit from the square. On a balcony high above stood the seventy-year-old pope, Alexander VI, the man who had been Rodrigo Borgia prior to his elevation to the papacy. Beside him stood his beautiful twenty-year-old daughter, Lucrezia. On a balcony to one side of them stood another figure, Alexander's son, Cesare Borgia, accompanied by a servant. In Cesare's arms he cradled a rifle, taking careful aim into the ragged crowd beneath him. Suddenly a shot rang out, echoing round the vast square. A prisoner collapsed to the ground, blood pouring from a wound. The servant calmly handed Cesare another rifle, fully loaded and ready for use. He fired another round and another unfortunate man folded to the ground. This continued until all the prisoners lay dead, blood pooling around them. A wagon pulled into the square and the limp bodies were tossed onto the back of it. His day's sport over, Cesare turned and strolled back into his apartment, his father and sister taking one final look around the magnificent holy square before doing the same.

The Borgias dominated large parts of Europe in the 15th and 16th centuries. From this one – admittedly very wealthy – family came three popes, eleven cardinals, a saint and a Queen of England. They dominated the politics of Europe, especially during the fifty years of the Renaissance, by murder and intrigue, driven by the greed for wealth and power. Many of them were unrelentingly wicked in their pursuit of power, but they are remembered principally for four members of the family – the two Popes, Callixtus III (Alfonso Borgia) and Alexander VI; Cesare Borgia, a byword for evil, a sometime Cardinal, given that position by his father, Pope Alexander, and later a corrupt and ruthless nobleman. Last but by no means least, was Lucrezia, wickedness in woman's clothing.

The Borgias were like the Mafia – a crime family that killed for political gain and for personal wealth. They also killed, however, for pleasure.

Their origins can be found in two Spanish cousins – Domingo and Rodrigo de Borya whose respective children, Isabella and Jofre, married each other. Isabella's brother, Alfonso, meanwhile, became pope as Callixtus III in 1455, the first Spaniard to occupy this position, but not the first ruthless, greedy individual to do so. He was not first choice, however, emerging as a compromise candidate between two rival factions. He was old and gout-ridden, was considered a stop-gap choice and sat on the throne of St. Peter for only three years. That was enough time, however, for him to elevate two of his nephews to the rank of Cardinal. One of these was Rodrigo, who would become Alexander VI.

In those days, popes were very keen on crusades and Callixtus proclaimed such a venture to liberate Constantinople from the Turks who had captured it in 1453. A crusade was not an inexpensive initiative and to fund it, Callixtus sold works of art, valuable books and offered indulgences for a price, including marriage annulments, church positions and grants of papal territories. He also imposed heavy taxes. Of course, none of this was guaranteed to make him popular and when he died, the Spaniards he had brought in to run the papal empire were summarily chased from office and from Rome.

One member of the family who escaped the wrath of the populace was Rodrigo Borgia, as the de Boryas were called in Italy. He remained in Rome and became pope thirty-four years and four popes after his uncle, Callixtus. It was with him that the reputation of the Borgias for nepotism, greed, ruthlessness and murder really began and he is considered the most notorious pope in history. He was elected to the pontificate – seventeen of the twenty-two cardinals voting for him – but those votes had been bought.

Born near Valencia in Spain, Rodrigo de Borya became a cardinal at the age of twenty-five in a flagrant act of nepotism by Callixtus and Vice-Chancellor of the Holy See a year later. In this role, he became extremely wealthy and was openly promiscuous – he would eventually father seven children in spite of his religious status. At one point, Pius II, who had succeeded Callixtus, had to have a word in the young cardinal's ear to advise him to cut back on his participation in orgies as it was 'unseemly'.

Nonetheless, he took a mistress, Vannozza de Catanei, with whom he had four children, including Lucrezia and Cesare, to add to a couple he already had. He then left her and lived with Giulia Faranese with whom he had another two or three children.

When Pope Innocent VIII died in 1492, Rodrigo was elected pope, having won the election with the purchase of the vote of a ninety-year-old cardinal who was lacking all his faculties. Like his predecessors, he embraced the role and the wealth it would bring to him and his family. Innocent had unashamedly openly acknowledged his illegitimate offspring and had lavished riches and titles on them. Alexander VI saw no reason why he should not follow this precedent. Along the way, he would, of course, also use his position to indulge his other passion – women.

He appointed as cardinals his son Cesare, still only eighteen years of age, and the even younger Alessandro Farnese, son of his mistress. He arranged three marriages for his daughter, Lucrezia, annulling the first and having Cesare murder the second when he, too, became inconvenient. When Alexander was away from Rome, she effectively ran the Vatican and church affairs.

Italy in those days was run by powerful families and Alexander made efforts to link the Borgias with one of those. Lucrezia was married, therefore, to Giovanni Sforza, bastard scion of the family that ran the city of Milan. Jofre was married to Sancia of Aragon, linking him with not only Aragon in Spain but also Naples in Italy where the kings of Aragon also held power. Sancia was no angel – she would have adulterous relationships with both Cesare and Giovanni Borgia, Jofre's older brothers.

By 1500, murder was a commonplace part of the lives of the Borgias with Cesare as the chief executioner. However, the tables were turned on Alexander when he dined with Cardinal Adrian Corneto, a man that he planned to kill. At the dinner Corneto, suspecting that they were trying to poison him, surreptitiously switched drinks with Alexander and the pope and Cesare both drank from it. Cesare recovered, but Alexander died, after lingering for a few days. He was seventy-seven.

While his father lay dying, Cesare wasted no time. He ordered his men into the Vatican to steal whatever they could lay their hands on. Meanwhile, Alexander's body had to be guarded to prevent it being taken and desecrated by the populace of Rome who were ecstatic at the news of his death. When Vatican officials came to prepare him for burial, the corpse had become so swollen in the heat of the August Roman sun that they had to remove his mitre – the headgear worn by popes – before they could stuff him into his coffin.

As for the family, it was devastated by his death, but not because they missed him. Rather, they missed the power and wealth his position brought them. Cesare suffered especially in the aftermath.

Alexander was a nasty piece of work but could not hold a candle to the evil wrought by his children. Cesare was the oldest and like his father populated the world with illegitimate children, the oldest of whom was Pedro Luis, the first Duke of Gandia, born in 1462.

Cesare had a stroke of luck in 1480 when Pope Sixtus IV issued a papal bull that allowed him to dispense with the fact that he was illegitimate. He was, therefore, free to enjoy benefices from the various positions to which Sixtus appointed him, under the influence of the future Pope Alexander. As early as seven years old, he received his first appointment, prebend of the cathedral chapter of Valencia. Other offices that he held also provided stipends, or wages. By nine, he was rector of Gandia, provost of Albar and Jativa and then treasurer of Cartagena. Each of these roles brought money flowing into his coffers.

In the meantime, Cesare was being closely groomed for a career in the church, his education in Rome carefully planned by his father. At the age of twelve he was sent to Perugia to be taught by a Valencian tutor who was appointed a cardinal as a reward. He studied law and humanities at Perugia University and then at Pisa he studied theology. On the completion of his studies, aged eighteen, he was made cardinal by his father.

Cesare was said to be very jealous of the success of his brother, the Duke of Gandia and coveted his secular honours and titles. One night in 1493, the

Duke attended a dinner at which his mother, Vannozza and Cesare were present. At the end of the dinner, he rode off with his brother and friends and servants. Some way off, he bade farewell to Cesare and his group, leaving with a groom and an unknown man who was wearing a festive mask. He was never seen alive again. His body was found in the River Tiber a few days later with his throat cut.

Alexander was beside himself with grief and, taking it as a sign from God, declared that he would renounce nepotism and all the abuses he had perpetrated in the Church. His promises were, of course, short-lived and before long he had returned to his old ways.

The convenient death of his brother brought change to the life of Cesare, however. He gave up his positions in the Church and resolved to make his way in secular life. One of the main reasons for his renunciation of his holy orders was the fact that Alexander had arranged for him to marry the daughter of the King of Naples, bringing with her a lucrative dowry of the city of Tarento. Leaving the Church Cesare was proclaimed Duke of Valentois. Alexander was angered, however, by the fact that the Neapolitan king had other plans for his daughter that did not involve a liaison with the Borgias, powerful though they may have been. He would live to regret his decision to turn down Alexander's offer because the Pope simply entered into an alliance with the French who claimed the kingdoms of both Naples and Milan. The French king, Louis XII had a particularly irritating marriage that he wanted to get out of and Alexander obliged by annulling it. By way of thanks, Cesare was given a French princess to marry, Charlotte d'Albert, daughter of the Duke of Guyenne. Following the wedding, Cesare wrote to his father that he had consummated the marriage eight times on his wedding night.

Cesare was now given the position of general in the French army, winning some important victories. In February 1500, he entered Rome, dragging behind him in golden chains Caterina Sforza, ruler of the two cities he had captured, Imola and Forli. He threw her into prison and only the intervention of the French saved her from dying there.

In the Jubilee year of 1500, there were a great many celebrations into which Alexander and Cesare threw themselves with characteristic gusto. Cesare killed five bulls in St. Peter's Square, amusing the crowds. It was also at this time that he shot the unarmed prisoners in the square. On another occasion, Alexander, Cesare and Lucrezia watched as fifty Roman prostitutes had sex with fifty palace servants, prizes being awarded for the best performance.

During this entertainment, one drunk man enjoying himself too much had his tongue and hand cut off for mocking Cesare. Another man who had the audacity to criticise him in a pamphlet was sentenced to drown in the Tiber.

Money continued to flood in, especially when nine new cardinals were created, but the bloodlust also continued. Cesare strangled the already dying second husband of Lucrezia, the Duke of Bisceglie. He was no longer of any use to the family as he was from Naples and the French had taken that city.

The game was up, however, when Alexander died and Cesare was forced to flee back to Spain where he died three years later, in 1506, while giving a good account of himself as a mercenary. He lives on, however, in Niccolo Macchiavelli's book, The Prince, a treatise on leadership, featuring the leader who gets on through strength of will. Macchiavelli was undoubtedly thinking of Cesare when he wrote it.

Cesare's sister, Lucrezia married Giovanni Sforza at a young age but was not short of help on the day – she was attended by 500 ladies-in-waiting. Soon, however, Sforza had outlived his usefulness and Cesare announced to Lucrezia that he was to be murdered. She warned her husband, however – one of the rare kind acts for which she was responsible – and he fled. He was stupid enough, however, to refuse to grant her a divorce. Alexander used non-consummation of the marriage as grounds for an annulment so that Lucrezia could be free to marry again.

First, however, while the negotiations over the annulment were going on, she retired to a convent. Unfortunately, however, she became pregnant following a liaison with the young chamberlain who brought messages from her father, a youth named Perotto. When she was brought before Vatican judges a short while later, obviously pregnant, she was solemnly judged by them to be a virgin. Incredibly the divorce was finalised.

Cesare was not best pleased and attacked the young chamberlain as he knelt before the papal throne. Perotto survived but was thrown into prison. A few days later it was announced that he had 'fallen into the Tiber against his will'. The chambermaid who had helped Perotto and Lucrezia was also made to 'swim with the fishes'.

The child born of the liaison between Lucrezia and Perotto was named the infans Romanus (Roman infant) by Alexander and he issued two papal bulls concerning him. The first said that he was the child of Cesare and an unknown woman; the second acknowledged that he, the Pope, was the father. Some have suggested that Lucezia insisted on the two bulls because Perotto was not, in fact, the father, although she herself was unsure whether it was her father or her brother who had sired the child.

Her next husband was Alfonso, Prince of Aragon and Duke of Bisceglie. One night he was set upon by a gang of armed men in St. Peter's Square. He was brought to his apartments, close to death and Lucrezia knew that Cesare had been behind the attack. As he lay wounded in his room, Cesare arrived, ordering everyone out. When they returned Alfonso lay dead. He had been strangled.

Lucrezia's third husband was chosen by Cesare. The heir to the Duchy of Ferrarra, Prince Afonso d'Este, was twenty-four and a childless widower. In return for the repeal of his papal tax and a huge dowry, he agreed to marry the twenty-one-year-old Lucrezia.

She had four children by the Prince, but this did not stop her having a fling with the poet Pietro Bembo.

She died on 24 June 1519 at the age of thirty-eight shortly after giving birth to a fifth child. In her latter years she had even gained some respect and managed to kick off the stigma of murder, incest and moral turpitude.

COUNTESS ERZSÉBET BÁTHORY

Villages would wait in dread as, in the dead of night, a carriage, drawn by powerful black stallions, would drive noisily past. Inside would be young girls, cowering in fear. They had every right to be afraid. They would enter the huge Castle Csejthe and never be seen again. People living nearby reported hearing horrific screams emanating from behind the castle walls. There was talk of witchcraft, orgies and vile practices.

Nothing could be done about it, however. The beautiful denizen of the castle, Countess Erzsébet Báthory, was as well-connected as they came. Her family included counts, princes, bishops and cardinals. She was a cousin of the prime minister, Thurso, her uncle Stephen had been King of Poland and she had once been married to the warrior count known to Hungarians as the 'Black Hero' due to the courage he showed in battles against the hated Turks.

King Mathias II of Hungary was reluctant to take action against her because if he did and the allegations and rumours turned out to be untrue, the political repercussions would be dreadful. Eventually, however, he decided that it was time to bring an end to the rumours that had been spreading about the Countess. Either that, or bring an end to what was going on behind the forbidding walls of the castle. He sent a party to investigate, a party that included her cousin the prime minister. They had to be careful – she was, after all, said to be a practitioner of the black arts and some even claimed that she used cats as emissaries and to attack people – but in all likelihood, on seeing her cousin's colours, she would open the castle's massive gates to them.

They had heard that she was likely to be holding one of her late-night gatherings where, they had heard, there were all kinds of goings-on. Screams were often heard coming from the castle while she held these events. The king's mind had been made up when he heard that nine girls from good families had gone missing in the vicinity of the castle.

Most of the windows of the castle that they could see were in darkness as they approached, but the party was surprised to find that there was no guard at the open door. They entered a great hall. Immediately they found a young, partly-clothed girl lying on the floor. She was unnaturally pale, as if the blood had been drained out of her body. She was dead and another girl they found nearby was close to death. She, too, looked as if the blood had been sucked from her body and the many piercings that peppered her body seemed to confirm that fact. Further on, a woman was found chained to a post. She had been whipped and her body was lacerated and burnt. Like the others, her blood appeared to have been taken.

As they descended into the dungeons, they could hear screams and moans from below and the smell of decomposition was terrible. They discovered cells filled with women and children who had been beaten and abused. They released them and escorted them from the castle, before returning to continue their grim search.

No one wrote a description of that night's discoveries, so horrific were they. In a large hall, illuminated by torches, they found all the signs of a drunken orgy having taken place. Implements of torture were scattered around. But there was no sign of the castle's owner. She had fled.

Born in either 1560 or 1561, she was the daughter of Gyrögy and Anna Báthory, who had embraced the new religion of Protestantism and she was raised on an estate in Transylvania. Her cousin Stephen, prince of Transylvania, who attempted to unite Europe against the Turks, was known for his savagery and many have claimed that he provides clear evidence of mental instability in the Báthory family, Erzsébet herself suffered from fits as a child, which, it has been suggested, indicate that she may have suffered from epilepsy. It is also said that she was very promiscuous and got pregnant at the age of fourteen by a peasant.

Aged 15, she married Count Ferencz Nádasdy, whose family, while powerful, shared with her family a reputation for being dangerously unstable and ruthlessly cruel. Her husband was a warrior who was rarely at home, giving Erzsébet ample opportunity to indulge in unsavoury pastimes. That was not unusual in her family, though. Her aunt was reputed to be a witch, she had an uncle who was an alchemist and a devil-worshipper and her brother was a paedophile. Her nurse was said to be a practitioner of black magic and was reputed to have been involved in the sacrifice of children.

As if that was not bad enough, her husband had a number of unsavoury habits, many of which he passed on to his young wife. He was partial to beating servant girls to within an inch of their lives or spreading honey on their naked bodies and tying them down in the open, leaving them to be bitten and stung by insects. When he was not doing that, he was freezing girls to death by pouring water over their naked bodies in the icy depths of winter and leaving them to die. His idea of a love token to his wife was a black magic spell brought back from whichever land he was fighting in.

She had begun to practice witchcraft as she got older and is reputed to have carried everywhere with her a parchment made from the caul – the membrane surrounding the baby in the womb that sometimes covers a baby when it is born. The parchment is said to have carried an incantation that would protect Erzsébet.

She moved into her husband's castle and began her reign of terror over her servants. Beatings were commonplace and death was irrelevant to her when it was the death of someone of such lowly status. Her husband taught her the fine art of beating someone to the brink of death. She was vain, too and was known to have at least five changes of clothing a day and she demanded constant reassurance about how beautiful she was and how fine and pale her skin was.

While he was gone, she maintained the regime of cruelty and torture, even sending him letters in which she described her latest grim escapades. In his absence, she also took countless lovers, both male and female. Her entourage was specially selected by her to include people adept at the black arts, sorcery and alchemy. One strange individual arrived at the castle with a reputation for drinking human blood. She urged him to teach her everything about it.

Erzsébet and Nádasdy had four children, but he became ill in 1601 and died finally three years later. She was a widow at forty-four.

She returned to her estates after a spell in Vienna and it was at this point that pretty young women began to disappear from neighbouring villages. She was encouraged in this practice by friends, who joined in her vile activities. The girls were promised that they were going to be taken into service at the castle, but once there, they were subjected to horrific treatment, locked up in cellars, beaten and tortured, often by Erzsébet, herself. Their bodies were then cut up with razors and burned.

She was known to sew servants' mouths shut or force them to eat pieces of their own flesh or burn their genitals. When she was ill and could not indulge in these horrors, she would attempt to bite those who approached her bed, like a wild animal. There was so much blood, that ashes were scattered around her bed to absorb it.

From peasant girls, she shifted her attention to girls of noble families, confident that no one would try to stop her. She offered to teach social graces to them, but when they arrived at Castle Csejthe, she would torture and kill them, as she had done the peasant girls. Even though the girls' families were afraid to speak out against the nobility, it was a step too far and, like many psychopaths, she mistakenly began to think she was invincible. Following the murder of one young woman, whose death she had tried to make look like suicide, the king finally decided enough was enough.

The investigating party found bones and human remains, as well as clothing belonging to the missing girls, strewn throughout the castle's chambers. There were bodies everywhere, their arms and eyes missing. Some had been burned or partially burned and many had been buried in shallow graves around the castle. Dogs ran loose with body-parts in their mouths.

She failed to attend her trial which began on 2 January 1611. Twenty-one judges sat in judgement, with Judge Theodosius de Szulo of the Royal Supreme Court at their head. Countless witnesses testified, many of whom had suffered at her hands in Castle Csejthe or were members of the families of the missing girls. It was her accomplices, however, who provided the most damning testimony. They were each asked the same eleven questions, amongst them whose murders had they taken part in, who had brought the girls to the castle, what types of torture were used? Ficzko, a dwarf who worked for Erzsébet testified that he was uncertain how many women he helped to kill, but he did know that thirty-seven girls had been murdered. He described how if they did not come willingly, they were beaten unconscious and carried to the castle. Describing the types of torture and beatings, he said, 'They tied the hands and arms very tightly with Viennese cord, they were beaten to death until the whole body was black as charcoal and their skin was rent and torn. One girl suffered more than two hundred blows before dying. Dorko, (another accomplice and procurer) cut their fingers one by one with shears and then slit the veins with scissors.' A nurse, Ilona Joo, confessed to taking part in the murder of about fifty girls. She described how she pushed red-hot pokers into victims' mouths or up their noses. She described how her mistress had placed her fingers in the mouth of one girl and pulled hard until the sides split open. Victims were forced to indulge in deviant sexual practices and one was made to strip flesh off her own arm.

The Countess and her accomplices were convicted of 80 murders, although King Mathias wrote in a letter that there may have been as many as 300 victims and one estimate puts the number at 650.

While her accomplices were gruesomely tortured and killed – fingers pulled off, buried alive or beheaded – the Countess was imprisoned for life, proclaiming her innocence throughout. King Mathias had wanted her to be executed, but before he could have such a sentence pronounced, she would have had to be stripped of her royal immunity.

She was kept locked up in a small suite of rooms in her own castle at Cahtice, with the walls and windows bricked up, claiming all the while that she was innocent of all charges, blaming the girls' deaths on a whole range of illnesses from disease to blood poisoning. She lasted only three years in captivity, dying in either 1613 or 1614.

Countess Erzsébet Báthory is fairly unique in the annals of criminal history in being a woman who indulged in cannibalism and vampirism. However, if she did take such an unhealthy interest in the blood of her victims – she was even said to bathe in it – it was more than likely because she thought that by doing so she could somehow preserve her looks.

Whatever the reason, whether she used the blood because she thought she was 'worth it' or merely got a sexual thrill from spilling it, she was one of the most prolific psychopathic women killers who ever lived.

IVAN THE TERRIBLE

Ivan the Terrible did everything to excess – drinking, worshipping, loving, hating and especially, killing.

The 16th century in Russia was a violent time when life was cheap, especially if you were a Tsar, trying to hold power against rival nobles and external forces. Ivan's childhood was traumatic and possibly holds the secret to his later personality. That, coupled with an attack of what was probably encephalitis, an inflammation of the brain that can lead to confusion, hallucinations and altered states of consciousness following the death of his first wife, Anastasia, in 1560 probably contributed to the mood swings, the violent rages and the psychopathic tendencies that he would display throughout his life.

In 1533, when he was aged just three, his father, Tsar Vasili III, died from blood poisoning following the development of a boil on his leg. Ivan's mother became regent for the young Grand Prince of Moscow, as Ivan was titled at the time. As was often the case in those perilous times, however, she was poisoned five years later. It was no great loss to the then eight year-old Ivan, in some ways, as his mother had never been that close to him. What was more of a loss to him was the removal of his beloved nurse, Agrafena, who was forced to retire to a convent. At this point, a powerful Moscow family, the Shuiskys, seized power, reigning until 1544. It was a terrible time for Ivan and his younger brother, Yuri. They were molested and ignored and had to scavenge for food in their own palace, dressed in rags and uncared for.

The Shuiskys were involved in a feud with rival noble family, the Belskys and the fighting would often be brought into the royal palace, gangs of armed men bursting into the young prince's quarters, causing damage and stealing whatever they could get their hands on. The palace seethed with intrigue and murders and beatings became commonplace. Ivan witnessed horrendous sights such as the skinning alive of his loyal advisor, Fyodor Mishurin.

Ivan, retreating into his own world, took out his frustrations on birds – he would mutilate them, pulling out their feathers, gouging out their eyes and dissecting them while still alive.

By the age of thirteen, Ivan had had enough of the Shuiskys and ordered the arrest of Prince Andrew Shuisky. He was thrown to a pack of hungry dogs and the nobles got the message; Ivan was in charge.

He indulged some of his basest instincts over the next few years. He was in the habit of throwing cats and dogs from the high walls of the Kremlin and roaming, roaring drunk, through the streets of the capital with his equally drunk cronies, beating up whoever got in their way and raping any woman unfortunate to bump into them. As if that was not enough, he often hanged, strangled or buried his rape victims alive. If he was feeling particularly adventurous, he would order his men to throw them to bears.

Surprisingly, Ivan was also a voracious reader, devouring historical and religious texts. He was also devout in his worship, although, as in many other things, he was a little extreme. In his worship of religious icons, he would throw himself recklessly to the floor, banging his head and creating a patch on the skin of his forehead.

He was crowned Tsar in 1547, a position that meant he had to get married. To this end, he organised a beauty parade of a kind, at which noblemen presented their daughters to him. He chose the very beautiful Anastasia Romanova for his wife and her influence seemed for a while to have brought his excesses under control. The couple would go on to have six children, but only two survived infancy.

The first years of his rule were marked by significant progress in Russia. He enjoyed the advice of three wise men – Alexej Adasjev, the priest, Silvester and the Metropolitan – head of the Russian Church – Macarius. With their help and council, he introduced reforms in government, minimising the corrupt power of the nobles, or boyars, as they were called. The church was reformed and he created an elite force in the army, known as the Streltsi.

He made territorial gains, too, conquering the khanates of Kazan and Astrakhan. He took several cities on the Baltic and opened important trading ties with England.

He was also seriously ill during this period, almost dying of a fever in March 1553. It may have been pneumonia but some have speculated that he suffered an attack of encephalitis. Around this time, he asked his boyars to swear an oath of allegiance to his baby son, Dmitri. They refused and Ivan would never forgive them, resolving from that day to destroy his enemies.

It was a tragic time. A few months after his recovery, he and his family visited a monastery where they planned to give thanks for the restoration of his health. A nurse accidentally let the baby prince slip from her arms into a nearby river. The baby drowned and Ivan was devastated.

In 1560, he was distraught once again when his wife Anastasia died following a long illness. Ivan seems to have suffered a nervous breakdown as a result, banging his head on the wall and destroying furniture in an emotional fury. It was a fury that deepened into depression and paranoia – he believed the boyars had poisoned his wife. The mood swings, sudden rages and habitual cruelty that he had displayed when he was younger, returned. He ordered the arrest of a number of nobles who were tortured and killed. He lost his three advisors – Adjasev died in prison, Silvester was sent into exile and Macarius died of natural causes in 1563.

There was nothing and no one to restrain him now from his worst excesses.

But, suddenly, in 1564, he abdicated and left Moscow. There was a clamour for his return which was exactly what the manipulative Tsar wanted. He agreed to return on condition that they accept him as an absolute ruler with the power to punish anyone he believed was being disloyal towards him. He also demanded the power to confiscate their estates. The people agreed and he returned even more powerful than when he had left.

In order to impose his will, he created a new military force – the Oprichniki. They consisted mainly of criminals who dressed in black and rode black horses. They instilled terror in anyone seeing them ride past and quite rightly so – they were known to even slaughter priests at the altar.

It got worse. Ivan transformed the Oprichniki into a kind of religious order - the troops were the monks and he was their abbot. Their religious ceremonies were abominations. Depraved masses would be followed by orgies during which women were raped, tortured and killed. Ivan is reported to have used sharpened, red-hot pincers to tear ribs out of people's chests during these events.

But these perversions would be followed by abject repentance on his part. Sometimes he would bang his head on the ground before the altar until it was bloody and bruised.

He led his Oprichniki in horrors. Once he ordered a peasant woman to be stripped naked and used as target practice by them and on another occasion, he ordered them to throw hundreds of beggars into a lake to drown. Another trick was to lash a nobleman to a barrel of gunpowder and watch, laughing, as the unfortunate man was blown to pieces.

One gruesome story tells of the horrific demise of Prince Boris Telupa. He had a stake inserted from the lower part of his body up and out his neck. He remained alive, impaled on the stake for fifteen hours of excruciating pain. Ivan ordered that the prince's mother be brought to see her son and then gave her to a hundred gunners who raped her until she died. She was then thrown to Ivan's dogs who tore her limb from limb.

Nikkita Funikov, Ivan's treasurer, was boiled to death while an advisor, Ivan Viskovaty, was hung before pieces were sliced off his body.

In warfare, Ivan was equally brutal. When he captured the city of Novgorod, the inhabitants were raped, impaled, sliced and roasted and Ivan personally played a full part in the horror. The archbishop of Novgorod was sewn into a bearskin before being hunted by a pack of snarling hounds. So many people were thrown into the freezing Volkhov River that it overflowed its banks.

In 1572, Ivan once again abdicated. This time he named a replacement, Simeon Bekboelatovitch, a Tartar general. For a year, Ivan lived on his country estate, making occasional visits to the city to pay homage to the new Tsar before becoming bored with the charade and returning to the throne.

He married a series of women and made England's Henry VIII look like a saint in the way he treated his wives. In 1561 it was Maria Temriukovna, a beautiful woman from Ciscassia. When she died in 1569, he married the daughter of a merchant, Martha Sobakin. She died two weeks after the wedding and he married Anna Koltovskaya. Tiring of her, he sent her to a convent in 1575 and married for a fifth time, to Wassilissa Melentiewna. She made the mistake of committing adultery and her lover had the misfortune to be impaled beneath her window. She was allowed to live, but as a nun. When he discovered that his seventh bride, Maria Dolgurukaya, was not a virgin, he had her drowned the day after their wedding. He married his last wife, Maria Nagaya, in 1581.

Possibly the worst of the many examples of Ivan the Terrible's rages occurred in 1581, an incident that resulted in the death of his son and heir, the Tsarevich Ivan. The young Ivan was something of a chip off the old block. Aged fifteen, he had been at his father's side, witnessing the barbaric cruelty of the massacre at Novgorod first-hand. He took as much pleasure in the depravity of the Oprichniks as Ivan and once saved his father's life, stabbing to death a Livonian assassin. However, his relationship with the Tsar had started to go downhill towards the end of the Livonian War that lasted from 1558 until 1582. In 1581, Ivan attacked his pregnant daughter-in-law, the Tsarevich's wife, furious that she was wearing tight clothes. As a result, she lost the child she had been carrying. When the Tsarevich confronted him, Ivan accused him of inciting rebellion. The two argued and Ivan struck his son a blow to the head with his sceptre. The Tsarevich fell to the ground with blood pouring from the wound and died a short while later, despite his contrite father's constant prayers for his survival.

Ivan the Terrible displayed all the signs of being a psychopath. He murdered without any emotion apart from enjoyment. He was self-centred, unreliable, manipulative and subject to wild mood swings and unexpected fits of extreme rage. His rages were so extreme, in fact, that he is said to have often foamed at the mouth during them. He was unable to maintain a relationship for very long and, indeed, most of his friends and advisors ended up dead.

It has been said that he probably suffered from syphilis. One treatment for the disease was the ingestion of mercury and it is known that he kept that metal bubbling away in a cauldron in his bedroom. A later exhumation of his body confirmed signs of syphilis and provided evidence of mercury poisoning.

Towards the end of his life, he had to be carried everywhere on a litter. He was in a terrible condition – he became obese, his skin peeled and flaked and a terrible smell emanated from his body.

In 1584, this tyrant who had done so many terrible things in his life, fainted and died during a quiet game of chess. Russia breathed a sigh of relief.

PETER STUBBE

Towards the end of the 16th century, there appears to have been an outbreak of strange hysteria in parts of Germany, at that time a collection of small states and principalities, unlike the homogenous country we know today. Shape shifters – people who could transform themselves into creatures – were believed to stalk the countryside, tearing people and cattle limb from limb, sucking the very blood out of them. Even as late as 1794, a creature, known as the Beast of Gevaudon – a vicious wolf-like creature that could walk on two legs – was said to be attacking women and children and created a widespread panic in France that lasted for three years.

Peter Stubbe was born around 1549 – the date is uncertain as the local church registers were destroyed during the Thirty Years' War – and lived his life in the town of Bedburg, in the Electorate of Cologne. He became a wealthy farmer and an upright member of the community. By the 1850s, he was a widower who lived with his two children, a girl of fifteen, named

Beele, and a son whose age is unknown. He is said to have enjoyed a relationship with a distant relative, Katharina Trump.

He is also believed to have been a serial killer, cannibal and practitioner of incest who had practiced black magic since the age of twelve.

However, some commentators think that he may have been no more than the victim of the religious upheaval that Germany and much of Europe was experiencing at the time. Since Martin Luther had nailed his ninety-five Theses to the doors of the Castle Church at Wittenberg in 1517, announcing the birth of Protestantism, Germany had been a hotbed of debate about the new approach to religion. Sometimes that debate erupted into violence. The period during which the majority of Peter Stubbe's heinous acts were carried out was a period of internal religious warfare in the Cologne Electorate. Archbishop Gebhard Truchess had attempted to introduce Protestantism and failed. He had been supported in this by Adolf Count of Heuenahr von Waldburg, the Lord of Bedburg. There were invasions by armies from each side and these were followed by an outbreak of plague. Some say that in this time of violence and madness an example was possibly made of Peter Stubbe because he was a Protestant.

In 1857, the castle at Bedburg had been taken by

the Catholic mercenaries who were commanded by Bedburg's new lord, Werner, Count of Salm-Reifferscheidt-Dyck and he was determined to re-establish the Catholic faith in the area. Thus, the capture of Peter Stubbe and the ensuing trial may have been no more than a political trial, with trumped-up charges that were designed to persuade the Protestants in the town to return to the Catholic faith.

Of course, through the centuries others have believed what reports from the time suggest – that Stubbe actually did a deal with the devil and was a werewolf.

In a twenty-five year period, from 1564 to 1589, he is said to have murdered thirteen or fourteen children and two pregnant women. For years children disappeared and limbs and body parts would be found scattered all over the fields surrounding the town because not only did he kill his victims, he is also said to have raped them and to have eaten their hearts afterwards. He killed two pregnant women, they said, and ripped the unborn foetuses out of them.

He was accused of having incest with his daughter Beele and that they had a son as a result. This boy was also killed, and Stubbe is said to have scooped out his brains and eaten them, a meal that he is said to have described as 'a most savoury and dainty delicious repast'.

During those twenty-five years, human beings were

not his only targets. He also attacked and ate the flesh of goats, lambs, cows, sheep and any other creatures he could find.

Peter Stubbe is reported to have carried out all these evil deeds while in the shape of a wolf. Stubbe later said under torture that one day he had met the Devil who had given him a magic belt – a 'wolf-girdle' – that enabled him to change into a wolf, or, as it was put at the time, into 'the likeness of a greedy, devouring wolf, strong and mighty, with eyes great and large, which in the night sparkled like fire, a mouth great and wide, with most sharp and cruel teeth, a huge body, and mighty paws.'

The people of the area tried to find the beast, using hunting dogs. One day as they searched the woods around Bedburg, they caught sight of him and set off in pursuit. At one point, they saw him change from a wolf into a man, nonchalantly carrying a staff and walking towards Bedburg. They recognised him as Peter Stubbe and arrested him.

He was tried in the company of Katharina Trump and his daughter Beele, all three being found guilty of murder and incest, a crime almost as bad, to their minds, as killing another human being. They also submitted Stubbe to excruciating torture designed to make him confess to the killings of the women and children he had dispatched over the past twenty-five years. Indeed, it was so vicious that it is likely that he would have confessed to anything they put to him. As he was stretched on the rack, they tortured him with red-hot pincers and stripped the flesh from his body in ten places. Meanwhile, his limbs were broken with the blunt side of an axe-head in order to prevent him from returning from the grave. He was then decapitated and burned on a pyre. His daughter and mistress were forced to watch this before being strangled and also thrown onto the pyre.

The authorities were determined to demonstrate to others what would happen to them if they did what Peter Stubbe had done. They erected a pole with the torture wheel on it, the likeness of a wolf carved into it. On top was spiked the head of Peter Stubbe, the Beast of Bedburg.

PART TWO

19TH CENTURY PSYCHOPATHIC KILLERS

JOHN LYNCH

THE BERRIMA AXE MURDERER

The Berrima Axe Murderer originated in Ireland but was transported to Australia in 1832 on board the convict ship, the *Dunregon Castle,* after being convicted of theft in County Cavan. In Australia he became the country's most prolific serial killer, dispatching nine unfortunate people with his trusty tomahawk and all, he believed with the approval of God.

He was nineteen years of age when he stepped off the *Dunregon Castle*, a short man at five feet three, but solidly built. Convicts were allocated on arrival to farms to work out their sentence before being released to make their own way in this new land. Lynch worked at a number of farms before returning to his old criminal ways and joining a gang of bushrangers, the Australian outlaws who used the bush to hide from the authorities. Alongside the other gang members, he wrought havoc across the territory, robbing and stealing.

Murder inevitably entered the equation. A man called Tom Smith gave evidence against the gang in

1835 and shortly after was found murdered. Lynch and two other gang members were arrested and tried for the murder and it seemed an inevitability that all three would hang for the crime. Astonishingly, however, even though he had admitted taking part in Smith's killing, the jury acquitted Lynch and sentenced the other two men to death. Next day, they were swinging by the neck from the town's gallows.

He returned to a farm where he had once worked and stole a team of eight bullocks. It was his intention to drive them to Sydney, sell them and make a fresh start. Before long, however, his fresh start was forgotten. On the road, he bumped into a man named Ireland who was travelling with a young aboriginal boy. They were also driving a bullock team that was pulling a wagon loaded with goods – wheat, bacon and other produce – that was being taken to Sydney to be sold.

Lynch immediately began to think about killing Ireland and the boy and stealing their wagon. It would be worth a lot more than the bullocks he was driving. Nonetheless, he enjoyed a pleasant evening with them. Ireland made dinner for Lynch and gave him a cigar.

In his later confession, Lynch claims then to have lain awake asking God what he should do. It was not recorded whether God gave him the go-ahead, but Lynch decided to kill the two men.

Next morning he took the aboriginal boy out with him to round up the bullocks that had wandered in the night while Ireland remained back at their camp cooking breakfast. As soon as they were out of sight of the camp, Lynch sneaked up behind the boy and killed him with a blow to the head with what he called his 'tomahawk', which was actually a small axe. Returning to the camp, he told Ireland that the boy was out looking for the bullocks and as Ireland busied himself making breakfast, Lynch brought his axe down on the man's head, killing him. He ate the meal that had been prepared and then dragged both bodies out of sight amongst some rocks, concealing them under a pile of bushes and boulders.

He remained at the campsite for two days and on the second two men driving a team of horses came along the trail. In his confession, he said he had a good time with these men, giving that as the reason he decided not to kill them during the night. Next day, they invited him to travel with them, an offer that he was happy to accept.

Just outside the town of Liverpool, to the south of Sydney, a man galloped up alongside them and asked Lynch what he was doing driving his wagon and bullocks. Thinking fast, Lynch told him that Ireland had been taken ill on the road and had asked him to take the goods to Sydney and sell them. The boy had remained behind at the camp to look after him. The wagon's owner, Thomas Cowper, was taken in by Lynch's glib charm and thanked him profusely, telling him he would ride back along the road to find Ireland. The two men agreed to meet in Sydney in a few days.

Lynch, of course, had no intention of meeting Cowper and pushed his team hard to get to Sydney well in advance of him, driving through the night. He knew that when the farmer failed to find his missing employees, he would come looking for him, possibly in the company of the law. Arriving in Sydney, he found a drunk to carry out the sale of the goods on his behalf, reasoning that the man would have forgotten in the morning. If he was questioned by the police he would simply tell them that the goods had been stolen off the back of the wagon.

As soon as he had completed the sale, he headed out of Sydney, making his way south towards the Berrima Road. Before long another opportunity arose.

Approaching Razorback Mountain, the area in which he had hidden the bodies of Ireland and the aboriginal boy, he met a father and son called Frazer who were driving a team towards Berrima. Lynch immediately decided to kill the men and replace Cowper's team with theirs. They travelled together to a campsite near the town of Bargo. They had supper with some others who were camped out there and

Lynch crawled under his wagon to sleep. He was just drifting off to sleep when a policeman rode into camp. He looked around and asked everyone if they had seen Cowper's wagon. Frazer said he had not and, amazingly, the police officer failed to spot that very wagon he was asking about in a corner of the campsite with its thief – also a murderer – lying under it. He rode off into the night. Lynch must have truly believed that he had God on his side and that he was invincible. God, of course, now told him to kill the Frazers and steal their team.

In the middle of the night, unseen by the others fast asleep around him, he undid the ropes that held his bullock team and sent them out into the undergrowth. The following morning he told his fellow campers that his team had somehow got free and said he would have to go back and bring another team. In the meantime, he said, he had to hide his wagon. They helped him push it out of sight in the bush and offered him a lift to where he said he lived.

Reaching Cordeaux Flat that evening, they made their camp for the night and ate and slept. The following morning Lynch accompanied the younger Frazer to round up the horses. Under his coat, his axe was stuck in his belt. As soon as they were hidden in the bush, he crept up behind the young man and killed him with his customary blow. The body hidden, he returned to the camp where the boy's father asked where his son was. When he told him he was still looking for one of the horses, the man became agitated, suspecting that something was amiss; his horses had never strayed before. Lynch suddenly pointed into the bush, saying that he could see the boy. When Frazer turned his head to look, Lynch swung his axe, killing him stone dead. As his confession put it, he struck him 'a nice one on the back of the head and he dropped like a log of wood'.

The two men were buried in a shallow grave in the bush after Lynch had delivered a short prayer of thanks to God for his assistance in the murders.

Lynch had been involved in a long-running dispute with a farmer called Mulligan over some stolen goods for which Mulligan owed him money. Mulligan disputed the amount owed, offering to pay only a quarter of what John Lynch believed them to be worth. They had argued bitterly, but Mulligan had held out, refusing to pay a penny more. Lynch had stormed off, cursing and promising revenge.

He now headed for the Mulligan farm, determined to either get the money he thought he was owed or to take the revenge he had sworn. He pulled up at the farm and enquired of Mulligan's wife where her husband was. She told him that he was in the fields working with their son and daughter and asked if she could be of help. Lynch told her he wanted the £30 that Mulligan owed him. She was taken aback and asked him what he was talking about. Becoming increasingly angry, he explained that her husband owed him for the goods that he had stolen when he was a bushranger. She told him that there was only £9 in the house, but Lynch told her he did not believe her. He decided to wait for her husband to return from his fields and confront him then.

He walked to the nearby settlement of Berrima and bought a bottle of rum, reasoning that if he could get Mulligan drunk, he might stand a better chance of getting his money. Returning to the farm, he found the farmer and his wife sitting on the farmhouse verandah waiting for him.

They sat drinking and talking until eventually Lynch introduced the subject of the money. Mulligan asked him to re-consider and possibly be a bit more reason-able about the amount in question, but Lynch was undeterred. In his confession he says that after Mulligan went back to work he sat on a log, consulting with God about what he should do. When Mulligan's son, Johnny, arrived back at the house, Lynch suggested they go and cut logs together. Of course, as soon as they were out of sight in the woods, Lynch pulled out his trusty tomahawk and with his customary single blow to the head, dispatched the boy.

When he walked back to the farmhouse, Mrs Mulligan became hysterical when she saw that he was alone. She was fully aware that Lynch was a highly unstable character and suspected that he had harmed the boy. Her husband, hearing the commotion, came running back to the house, but Lynch swung his axe as the man approached and sent him crashing to the ground, lifeless. He dragged the body into the trees and then when he saw Mrs Mulligan approaching, he attacked her, also smashing her skull with the axe.

There remained only the couple's fourteen-year-old daughter who was inside the house. He ran in to find her standing with a butcher's knife in her hand, terrified. He snatched the knife out of her hand, pushed her into a bedroom and raped her repeatedly before killing her. He burned the four bodies on a bonfire in the bush.

Astonishingly, Lynch now set about getting his hands on the Mulligan farm and becoming respectable. He burned all their personal items and made it look as if the family had moved away. He then placed an advert in the *Sydney Gazette* that purported to be a message from John Mulligan that his wife had left him and he would not be responsible for any debts that she had incurred. Using Mulligan's name, he wrote to all his creditors to inform them that he had sold his farm to John Dunleavy and that Dunleavy was now responsible for any debts owed by the farm. Lastly, he forged a deed of assignment that handed the farm over to John Dunleavy, aka John Lynch. Incredibly, he now owned the farm.

For six months, Lynch lived the good life. He hired a couple to look after the place while he drove his produce to market and he built a good name with both his employees as well as with those with whom he did business.

Then he made a mistake.

Returning from selling produce in Sydney one day, he met Kearns Landregan on the road and offered him a fencing job on his farm. Discovering that Landregan had a criminal past, he suddenly decided to kill him in a fit of moral pique, astonishing in a man with the criminal history that Lynch had. That night, they set up camp at Ironside Bridge. As Landregan sat on a log, laughing at a joke, Lynch crept up behind him and the axe claimed its ninth victim.

John Dunleavy was identified by numerous people as the last person seen in the company of Kearns Landregan and police officers turned up at the farm to take him into custody. The evidence against him was overwhelming, but he persisted in his denials of any wrongdoing. Soon his real identity was discovered to be John Lynch and he was charged with the murder of Landregan. He appeared before the Chief Justice of New South Wales on 21 March 1842 and gradually, his involvement in the mysterious disappearances of a number of other people began to emerge. After an hour of deliberation, the jury found him guilty and the judge sentenced him to die by hanging.

A short while later, the killing spree of the Berrima axe murderer ended when John Lynch was finally hanged. God had, for once, deserted him.

JACK THE RIPPER

The last day of August 1888 was dawning chilly and damp as Charles Cross walked through Buck Row in the Whitechapel district of London's East End at around four in the morning. Suddenly he saw a dark shape lying on the ground in front of the entrance to a stable yard. He was surprised to see, as he approached, that it was a woman lying on her back. Whitechapel was a rough area in which around 1,200 prostitutes were known to work and where most of the inhabitants were poor, unemployed or criminals. Consequently, it was not unusual to stumble upon someone who had collapsed through a surfeit of alcohol or who had been assaulted.

Another man approached on the street and Cross asked him to help. The two men knelt over the woman, failing to notice that she had almost been decapitated. They saw that her skirt had been lifted up over her waist. They pulled it down for decency's sake and went off in search of a police officer. Arriving on the scene, Constable John Neil shone his lantern on the woman and immediately saw that her throat had been slashed from ear to ear and her eyes were wide open and staring. A doctor and an ambulance were called, but it was far too late for them to do anything to help her.

Doctor Rees Llewellyn was first on the scene and he established that she had been dead for no more than thirty minutes and that she had been killed by the wounds to her throat. Her throat had been slashed twice but when they got her to the morgue for further examination, they discovered that she had also been wounded in the abdomen, the killer having mutilated that part of her body. It showed a long, deep knife wound and several other downward cuts. It appeared that she had been already on the ground when these wounds were inflicted.

Within a short while, the woman was identified as Mary Ann Nichols, aged forty-two, who had been living off her earnings as a prostitute under the name of 'Polly'. She had been the mother of five children, married to a printer, but due to her excessive drinking the marriage had broken up, forcing her to take to the streets.

A police veteran, Frederick George Abberline, was put in charge of the investigation but had very little to work on. There were neither witnesses nor clues. No one had heard or seen anything unusual and no vehicle seemed to have transported the perpetrator from the scene.

It was not the first murder in the area in recent times. Just over three weeks earlier, Martha Tabram, a thirty-nine-year-old prostitute, had been found murdered in George Yard. She had died in a frenzied knife attack, receiving thirty-nine stab wounds to her body, neck and private parts. However, her throat had not been slashed, as had happened to Mary Ann Nichols and there was no mutilation of the abdomen. A penknife had been used to deliver the wounds, as opposed to the long-bladed knife that had been used to kill Nichols.

Even some months before that, in April, not far from where Martha Tabram was found, another prostitute was seriously injured in a vicious attack in which a blunt instrument had been rammed into her vagina. It seemed clear to police, however, that these incidents were unrelated to the death of Mary Ann Nichols, even though the locals linked them in their minds. Nonetheless, it was hard to escape from the dreadful conclusion that there was a maniac on the loose.

It was not long before he struck again.

Annie Chapman, known on the street as 'Dark Annie', had had an awful life. She had married a coachman, John Chapman, in 1869 and the couple had three children, one of whom died from meningitis and another of whom was crippled. The marriage came under stress and the couple started to drink heavily. They broke up but when her husband died, Annie lost everything, even the tiny bit of financial security she enjoyed from an allowance with which he provided her. She was forced to earn her living from prostitution when there was no income from her other work – crocheting and selling flowers.

In the early hours of Saturday 8 September, she was thrown out of her lodgings and ordered to earn some money to pay her rent. She was found a few hours later in the backyard of a building on Hanbury Street, across the road from Spitalfields market, by a cab driver. Like Ann Marie Nichols, her skirt was pulled up over her waist. This time, the scene that met investigators was far more gruesome than the last time. The killer had cut out her small intestine and other internal organs and these were lying on the ground beside her right shoulder. Once again, her throat had been cut, this time it seemed, after she had been rendered unconscious by strangulation. Near her feet, arranged in some kind of order, lay a couple of combs and a small piece of cloth that she had been carrying when attacked. Near her head was an envelope of pills. Doctors realised with horror that the uterus, part of the bladder and the upper part of the vagina were no longer inside the body and could not be found at the scene. The killer had taken them with him.

The incisions and the precise nature of the removal of Annie's organs persuaded investigators that the murderer must have possessed anatomical or pathological experience. They began to think that their killer might be a medical man, using the type of narrow, six to eight inch-long knife used by surgeons carrying out amputations.

One thing was certain. The man who had killed Ann Marie Nichols had also murdered Annie Chapman.

Once again, clues were non-existent and witnesses inconclusive. One woman saw a man and woman talking around the time of the murder, but although she was able to recognise Annie, the man had his back to her.

A feeling of suspicion began to grow in the area towards members of the large Jewish community that lived in the Whitechapel area. Local Jewish merchants banded together to create the Mile End Vigilance Committee in an effort to create a neighbourhood watch scheme and Samuel Montagu, the Jewish MP for the constituency in which Whitechapel lay, offered a reward.

The police began to round up suspects – drunks and eccentric characters as well as men who were just downright insane. Each time, however, it came back to the medical prowess that the killer had displayed. The men they were bringing in for questioning did not have it or had cast-iron alibis for the nights in question, sometimes provided by asylums or by police stations in which they had spent the night.

A few weeks passed before the next murder. Forty-five-year-old Elizabeth Stride, known to her fellow streetwalkers as 'Long Liz', was found at one o'clock on the morning of Sunday 30 September in Dutfield Yard, just off Berner Street in Whitechapel. She was not a full-time prostitute, earning a living when she could by doing sewing or cleaning. She was known to like a drink, however, and was no stranger to the magistrates' court. She had left her boarding house early the previous evening.

When she was found, unlike in the other cases, her skirt was not pulled up over her waist. There were no signs of strangulation, but her throat was cut, the knife having sliced all the way through her windpipe. They estimated her time of death to have been between 12.36 and 12.56 am but she had been seen a few minutes before then by a policeman, talking to a man aged around thirty who had dark hair and a moustache. The policeman noted that he wore a deerstalker hat, a black cutaway coat, a white shirt collar and a dark tie. In his hand he carried a bundle. Another witness described a man talking to a woman at 12.45 am. He claimed they were arguing and that he threw her to the ground where she screamed three times. This witness also described seeing a second man standing across the road lighting a pipe, to whom the first man called out 'Lipsky!' The witness said that the second man followed him as he walked away from the argument and that he took to his heels to get away from him. Confusingly, other witnesses came forward to describe other men that 'Long Liz' talked to that night.

The killer had had a busy night, however, because as they examined the body in Dutfield Yard, just a quarter of a mile away, in Mitre Square, the body of another woman was discovered by a patrolling constable.

When he had walked through the square at 1.30 am, Police Constable Edward Watkings had seen nothing unusual, but when he came through the area again fifteen minutes later, he saw something lying in a corner of the square. It was a woman and, to his horror, he saw that her throat had been cut and her innards protruded from a gaping wound that had been made in her stomach. Blood pooled beneath her.

This victim differed in that she had severe mutilations to the face. As with the other victims, it looked as if there had been no struggle. She had probably been surprised and killed very quickly. She had been sliced open from her breast-bone to her pubic hair and her intestines had been cut out. Her left kidney had been removed and taken away by the killer, as had the womb. Her eyelids had been sliced through, the end of her nose cut off and her right earlobe had been sliced off.

Again, no one in the vicinity had seen or heard anything untoward, apart from one witness, Joseph Lawende, who had seen her earlier, talking to a young man at 1.35 am. He had been wearing a deerstalker hat and had a small, fair moustache. There was one significant piece of evidence, however. A constable found a bloody piece of apron lying on the ground at the entrance to a building in Goulston Street. Written in chalk on the bricks above it was the strange message: 'The Juwes are The men That Will not be Blamed For Nothing.'

The piece of apron was from the one worn by the victim and it seemed as if they had at last found something worth investigating. Astonishingly, however, the Commissioner of the Metropolitan Police, Sir Charles Warren, ordered that this vital piece of evidence be washed off the wall. He was concerned that the message would provoke an attack on Jews living in the area.

The officers involved in the case were amazed that the killer could have committed two murders in such a short space of time and escape unseen into the night. They conducted house-to-house interviews and everyone on the streets was questioned, but to no avail.

The Mitre Square victim was forty-six-year-old Catherine Eddowes, known as Kate. She was an occasional prostitute, especially when she had been drinking. This night she had set out to visit her daughter to borrow some money, but failed to arrive. She had found money by some other means and ended up being arrested for being drunk and put in a cell at Bishopsgate police station. They had let her out at 12.30 am and that was the last anyone saw of her alive.

As for the chalked message, no one could recognise the spelling 'Juwes'. There did not appear to be any dialect or language in which 'Jews' was spelt 'Juwes'. The police thought that it was probably a deliberate attempt to put the blame on the Jews and distract Scotland Yard from its search for the real killer.

The case was now hot news and had caught the public's attention. Hundreds of letters arrived at Scotland Yard, at newspapers and at the homes of the investigating detectives. One in particular gave the murderer the name that has gone down in the annals of criminal history for all time. It was sent on 25 September to a news agency, Central news and read:

'Dear Boss, I keep on hearing the police have caught me but they wont fix me just yet. I have laughed

when they look so clever and talk about being on the right track. That joke about Leather Apron gave me real fits. I am down on whores and I shant quit ripping them till I do get buckled. Grand work the last job was. I gave the lady no time to squeal. How can they catch me now. I love my work and want to start again. You will soon hear of me with my funny little games. I saved some proper red stuff in a ginger beer bottle over the last job to write with but it went thick like glue and I cant use it. Red ink is fit enough I hope ha.ha. The next job I do I shall clip the lady's ears off and send to the Police officers just for jolly wouldn't you. Keep this letter back till I do a bit more work then give it out straight. My knife's so nice and sharp I want to get to work right away if I get a chance. Good luck. Yours truly Jack the Ripper. Don't mind me giving the trade name'

At first, the man who received the letter failed to take it seriously but after a couple of days sent it to the police. The night after they received it, Kate Eddowes and Liz Stride were murdered. On October 1, another letter in the same handwriting arrived at Central News:

'I wasn't codding dear old Boss when I gave you the tip. Youll hear about saucy Jackys work tomorrow double event this time number one squealed a bit couldn't finish straight off. had not time to get ears for

police thanks for keeping last letter back till I got to work again. Jack the Ripper.'

The letters were circulated and a copy was placed outside every police station in case the handwriting was recognised, but no one came forward.

A third, and much more gruesome letter, was delivered to George Lusk, head of the Mile End Vigilance Committee on 16 October. Accompanying it was a piece of what turned out to be human kidney. It said, in different handwriting to the other letters:

'From hell. Mr Lusk Sor I send you half the Kidne I took from one women prasarved it for you tother piece I fried and ate it was very nise I may send you the bloody knif that took it out if you only wate a whil longer. Signed Catch me when You can Mishter Lusk.'

It is impossible to say whether the real Jack the Ripper sent these badly-spelled communications. The two ears were never sent and if the killer had had time to carry out his mutilations and organ removals it seemed likely that he could have found time to cut off a victim's ears. But he failed to do so. Some have said that the letter forecast the double killing and must, therefore, be genuine. However, by the time it was sent, on the night of Sunday 31, news was already on the streets about the murders of Eddowes and Stride.

London was now in a state of unparalleled anxiety. The streets of Whitechapel emptied after dark and extra police were put on patrol. Handbills were posted seeking information, butchers and slaughterers were interviewed and bloodhounds were brought in. But still, there were no new developments.

Gradually, as autumn turned to winter, the streets returned to normal and streetwalkers were once more to be seen plying their trade in the area's thoroughfares.

On 9 November, a landlord sent one of his employees to try to get some overdue rent out of a prostitute, Mary Kelly, who rented a room from him at 13 Miller's Court but John Bowyer was unable to obtain a reply to his knock at the door. He went to a window, reached in through its broken glass and pulled aside the curtain that was drawn across. What he saw would with him for the remainder of his life. The small room contained little in the way of furniture, apart from a table and a bed but on the bed lay the body of Mary Kelly, her face horrendously mutilated and her throat cut so viciously that the knife had gone right down to her spinal column. This murder was the most horrific of all the Ripper's deeds. The top layer of her abdomen and thighs had been removed and the abdominal cavity had been 'emptied of its viscera' as the doctor's report put it. The Ripper had cut off her breasts and placed one under her head, along with her uterus and kidney, and the other by her right foot. Her liver lay between her feet, her intestines by her side and her spleen by her left side. The flaps he had sliced off her abdomen and thighs lay on the table.

Her heart was missing. He had taken it away with him.

Panic broke out on the streets of Whitechapel with outbreaks of mob violence directed at any stranger or anyone who seemed at all suspicious. Queen Victoria railed about the lack of lighting in the area and the standard of policing in London.

A man called George Hutchinson claimed to have followed Mary and a man back to the house where she lived and several others had seen her with a man. She had been very drunk by all accounts. All agreed that her companion had been in his mid-thirties, but the rest of the descriptions conflicted with each other and the police were really no further forward.

Mary Kelly's murder is believed to have been the last committed by Jack the Ripper and the file was closed in 1892. That, of course, has not prevented speculation about his identity.

Montagu John Druitt, was one suspect. A doctor, he disappeared around the same time that the murders stopped. Described as 'sexually insane' and believed by his own family to have been the Ripper, he was fished out of the Thames on 31 December.

A Polish Jew named Kosminski who lived in Whitechapel, also became a suspect when he was diagnosed as insane after many years of hating women, especially prostitutes. He had homicidal tendencies and was sent to an asylum in March 1889.

Another asylum inmate, Michael Ostrog, a Russian doctor and a convicted criminal, was locked up because he was found to be a homicidal maniac and rose high on the list of suspects. Furthermore, his whereabouts at the times of the murders were never established.

Other high profile contenders were somewhat more surprising. Prince Albert Victor, Duke of Clarence, known popularly as 'Eddie' was the grandson of Queen Victoria. Amongst a number of theories regarding him it was suggested that he had got a shop girl in Whitechapel pregnant and that she had been taken away to a hospital by the Queen's doctor, Sir William Gull, who had her institutionalised for the remainder of her life. The prostitutes who had been killed had all been friends of the shop girl and knew what had happened. Sir William Gull, it is suggested, killed them and made it look like the work of a madman. The fact that Sir William was seventy years old at the time and Eddie's sexual predilections were slanted more towards the male sex, seem to negate this theory.

More recently, the artist, Walter Sickert, has been put in the frame, mainly, it seems, because he painted prostitutes, although some say that some of his paintings chillingly replicate photographs of the Ripper's victims and the Ripper's letters contain phrases used by the American painter, James McNeill Whistler, who had been Sickert's teacher.

It is unlikely that we will ever discover the true identity of the psychopathic killer known as Jack the Ripper, but, with more books written about him than about all the US Presidents combined, an entire industry carries on around the five murders he committed between the end of August and 8 November 1888.

DR THOMAS NEIL CREAM

He was a sadist, a monster who enjoyed a love-hate relationship with women, a beast who consigned seven of them to excruciatingly painful deaths in Canada, the United States and Britain. He did not even need to be present when they suffered the convulsions leading to their death. He would hand the fatal pills to them, telling them they were too pale or that these would prevent them from contracting a sexually transmitted disease, and walk off into the night. Like his contemporary, Jack the Ripper, the victims he chose to eliminate were prostitutes, although he did take care of a wife as well. In his head, he was cleaning up the streets as well as exercising his psychopathic urge to wield the ultimate power of life and death over women.

He was originally Scottish, born in Glasgow in 1850 but living there only four years before his parents, William and Mary upped sticks and moved to Quebec in Canada in search of a better life for themselves and their children. William worked in shipbuilding and the family prospered. He started his own lumber wholesale business and, apart from Thomas, his sons all joined him there. Thomas was more studious and left to attend McGill University where he studied to become a doctor.

His first real problem occurred shortly after he graduated in 1876. He had made a teenage girl, Flora Brooks, pregnant and her family insisted that he do the decent thing and marry her. The morning after the wedding, however, he was gone, having boarded a ship bound for London where he planned to make a new start without the encumbrance of a young, pregnant wife.

London's medical schools were some of the best there were at the time and doctors were needed to help deal with the appalling disease and sickness that had arisen from the terrible social conditions in areas of the capital such as the poverty-stricken East End. Neil registered at St. Thomas's Hospital in Lambeth, in October 1876, and started the training that he hoped would lead to him becoming a surgeon. Six months later, however, he was disappointed to learn that he had failed the entrance exams for the Royal College of Surgeons. After returning to St. Thomas's for more training, supporting himself by working as an obstetrics clerk, he applied to the Royal College of Physicians and Surgeons in Edinburgh and was accepted. He obtained a licence in midwifery.

A good-looking young man with excellent prospects, Cream had been having a good time in London, going out with a number of well-bred and wealthy women from the better parts of town. But he also saw the seamier side of the city. It was hard to avoid, as women and children put themselves up for sale in places like Waterloo Bridge. He developed a loathing for them, believing them to be the embodiment of evil.

Meanwhile, back in Canada his wife, Flora, died. The death certificate listed cause of death as 'consumption', but it seems likely that Cream may have killed her from several thousands of miles away. Her doctor ascertained that she had been taking medicine that Cream had been sending her. When, on his orders, she stopped taking it, the symptoms from which she had been suffering seemed to dissipate.

In 1878, Cream suddenly returned to Canada, setting up his surgery where he practiced as a physician and surgeon. A year after his arrival, he found himself in trouble when a woman patient, Kate Gardener, was found dead, stinking of chloroform in a woodshed behind the building in which he practiced. She was found to have been pregnant when she died and it seemed obvious that she had gone to Cream seeking an abortion. He confirmed this but claimed that he had refused to help her. He said she had killed herself with chloroform she had bought over the counter from a pharmacist. The examining board thought otherwise as there was no empty bottle beside her body and her face was badly scratched, as if the drug had been administered forcibly. They ruled that her death was murder, but, amazingly, Cream was not indicted. Nonetheless, his career in Canada was over.

In August 1879, he moved to Chicago where he set up shop after passing the Illinois Board of Health Exam. His surgery was located conveniently close to Chicago's red light district, making him handily placed to work as an abortionist outside office hours. He took on an intermediary, a 'midwife', who took a cut of his earnings for putting women in touch with him. He was a bit more proficient than the quacks who operated in these areas but his distaste for women grew, as his need to have sex with them also did. One associate told later of the pornographic photographs he carried around with him and another described his habit of taking drugs – pills made of strychnine, morphia and cocaine. He claimed that they worked as an aphrodisiac.

In early 1880, one of his patients, a prostitute named Mary Anne Faulkner, died and it took a good lawyer to get him off with claims that he had been summoned only after the woman had got into difficulty following an abortion that had gone wrong. Another woman, Ellen Stack, had died after consuming some pills he had given her, anti-pregnancy pills, he had called them. They had contained strychnine. Once again he escaped justice when the authorities could not positively prove that he had given them to her.

It would, ironically, be the murder of a man that would be his undoing. Daniel Stott had sent his wife, Julia, to Cream's surgery to pick up medicine. She had begun an affair with Cream and when Stott became suspicious, Cream had added strychnine to the medicine. It helped that Stott was a wealthy man and Mrs Stott would inherit his money when he died which he duly did in June 1881. Cream seemed to have literally got away with murder, but for some reason created unnecessary interest in the case when he wrote to the coroner accusing the pharmacist of adding too much strychnine to the medicine. Perhaps he was concerned about his reputation, losing a patient in this way, but Stott was exhumed and, sure enough, they found large amounts of strychnine in his body. Cream was immediately suspected and, fearing arrest, he fled to Canada. Unfortunately, Mrs Stott decided to save her own neck by becoming a witness for the prosecution. Cream was arrested in Ontario and sent back to Chicago where he was tried, found guilty and sent to Joliet prison.

He remained locked up for ten years, but his brother succeeded in getting him paroled by judiciously bribing prison and state officials. He was freed in July 1891.

He returned to Canada to stay with his brother and collect an inheritance left to him by his late father. By now, the years of harsh 19th century prison life had taken their toll on Thomas Cream – his face looked older than his years and his hair was thinning. His drug use had also taken its toll and his eyes, watery and yellow, were a manifestation of this. But, once again, he resolved to start again and boarded a ship for Liverpool where he arrived on 1 October.

He travelled to London and was soon established in a first-floor apartment at 103 Lambeth Palace Road in south London, close to St Thomas's Hospital. It was a rough area, teeming with poor children and their mothers clad in dirty dresses and shawls. Death and disease were everywhere and no one worked.

Soon, Cream, now calling himself 'Dr Thomas Neil', and claiming to work at St Thomas's, had resumed his interest in poison. Ellen 'Nelly' Donworth was the daughter of a labourer and had become a prostitute to escape the hard work involved in being a bottle-capper in Vauxhall. She lived in Commercial Street with Ernest Linnell, a private in the army. On 13 October, she went out early in the evening telling a friend that she was going to see a man she had met. Later, she was seen by another acquaintance with a well-dressed man emerging from a pub and then much later she had to be helped home by yet another friend after being seen in an incapable condition in Morpeth Place. The friend, James Styles, put her to bed in her boarding house but by this time she was suffering from agonising pain that seemed to make her body convulse. She claimed, between gasps of pain, that her gentleman friend had given her a couple of drinks from a bottle containing a white liquid. Styles called a doctor who had her taken to St Thomas's but she was dead before she arrived.

The post mortem discovered large doses of strychnine in her stomach.

It was not surprising as poisonous chemicals were relatively easy to obtain in those days. Cream had got it from a chemist on Parliament Street and all he had to do was sign a register. He had lied, saying that he was a doctor attending a series of lectures at St Thomas's. He had bought the strychnine in the first week of October, in the form of *nux vomica* that contained two alkoloids, brocine and strychnine. He must have mixed the poison into the liquid he fed to Nelly Donworth.

Around 10 October, he ordered gelatin capsules that he intended to use on his next victim.

Matilda Clover lived at 27 Lambeth Road with her two-year-old son. An alcoholic, she had been abandoned by the boy's father and had been forced to earn her living on the streets ever since. On 20 October, she left the house to meet a man she called 'Fred' outside the Canterbury Theatre. She returned to her room at around nine that evening in the company of the man who later left. Some hours later, the other occupants of the house heard screams coming from her room. They found her in agony, thrashing about on her bed and unable to breathe. She gasped that 'Fred' had given her some pills and she was sure that they had contained poison. A few hours later, she was dead.

Strangely, her death was not found to be murder, her claims about Fred's pills being ignored. Her doctor stated instead that her death was a result of mixing alcohol with a sedative he had prescribed for her. No one linked Matilda Clover's death with that of Nelly Donworth just a week earlier. The truth was that they were prostitutes and nobody really cared one way or another how they had died.

In November, Dr Cream was summoned back to Canada so that his father's property could be divided up amongst his family. He was sorry to go as he had by now formed a relationship with a Hertfordshire woman, Laura Sabbatini. He escorted Ms Sabbatini with a view to making her his wife on his return. It was an odd facet of his character that while he was intent on killing prostitutes, he was still keen to have a respectable pretty wife. He set her up in a dress-making business and sailed to Canada in the first week of January 1892, returning four months later and taking up residence once more at 103 Lambeth Palace Road. He immediately contacted Laura and asked her to marry him. They became engaged.

Meanwhile, he was stalking the dark and dingy streets of London's less salubrious districts. One night he introduced himself to Lou Harvey, a prostitute who was walking her beat in Piccadilly. He told he was a doctor from America, currently working at St Thomas's.

Lou Harvey was a careful and intelligent woman. Her real name was Louise Harris, for instance, and she gave also gave Cream a false address. She was suspicious of his claim to be a doctor from America and decided to be cautious. Nonetheless, she spent the night with him at a hotel in Covent Garden.

They agreed to meet that night at Charing Cross underground station from where they would go for a drink and a visit to the theatre. They met and went for a drink at the Northumberland public house. As they walked back down to the Embankment beside the river, he told her she looked pale and handed her two capsules, telling her to take them. Louise only pretended to put them in her mouth, however, and when he looked away from her for a moment, she tossed them over the wall into the river. Cream told her he was expected at the hospital and that he would see her later at the theatre. Needless, to say, he did not turn up at the theatre and he would have been surprised to see her there. She was supposed to be dead by then.

He now decided to kill two women in one night, an opportunity that arose when he introduced himself to a couple of prostitutes strolling together. Alice Marsh and Emma Shrivell lived in adjoining rooms at 118 Stamford Street, a dreary thoroughfare close to Waterloo Station. Cream accompanied them to one of their rooms, had his fun with them and left. Several hours later, the two girls were dying in agony.

The newspapers were now in a frenzy, headlines screaming about the 'Lambeth Poisoner'. The police, meanwhile, were nowhere.

Once again, Cream behaved very strangely. He tried to blackmail well-respected men, accusing them of killing the prostitutes. Two famous surgeons received letters and a Member of Parliament and a peer of the realm were also the recipients of blackmail letters. Police immediately recognised that the handwriting on the letters was similar although they were purportedly written by the same man.

His next big mistake was to describe the murders in some detail to a former New York detective that he had become friendly with. He claimed to be only surmising what had happened, but seemed to know more about the killings than had been announced in the media. He also mentioned the names of two women – Matilda Clover and Lou Harvey – one of whom the police did not know had been murdered and the other who was still alive.

The detective became suspicious and mentioned his strange encounter to his friend, Inspector Patrick McIntyre of Scotland Yard. He and McIntyre began to speculate that this Dr Neil was the Lambeth Poisoner. It seemed almost certainly to be the case when they realised that one of the men whom Cream had blackmailed under another name, lived at the same address as him in Lambeth Palace Road.

They began to investigate the background of Dr Thomas Neil. A detective was dispatched to Canada where he uncovered Cream's dubious past. His movements were closely watched and they saw him use prostitutes. Fortunately, these women survived their encounters with him. Two prostitutes that he had met came forward to say that they had seen him in the company of Matilda Clover. Her body was exhumed and they were unsurprised to find that there were traces of strychnine.

Cream was arrested on 3 June.

The inquest into the death of Matilda Clover seemed to be going well for him at first. There seemed to be nothing more than hearsay evidence to support the charges of murder and he appeared to be relatively untroubled by the ordeal. Then, one day, a new witness was called. He looked up in amazement to see Lou Harvey, the woman he thought he had killed weeks ago, enter the court. When they asked if the man who had given her pills was present in court she had no hesitation in turning and pointing at Thomas Cream. He was charged with murder and taken to Newgate Prison.

At his trial, there was little doubt about the verdict and the jury took a mere nine minutes to find him guilty. The judge placed the black hat on his head and sentenced him to death.

Dr Thomas Neil Cream, the 'Lambeth Poisoner' was hanged on 16 November 1892. He left one tantalising mystery, however. In the moment before the trapdoor opened, he began to speak. 'I am Jack...' was all that he was able to utter before he plunged to his death. Was he Jack the Ripper? He had been in prison in the United States when the Ripper had been plying his trade. Or had he? Some suggest he bribed his way out of Joliet earlier than the stated date, or that a double had taken his place. It seems unlikely, but then so was the existence of a man such as Dr Thomas Neil Cream.

H. H. HOLMES

He called it his 'Castle'.

It was built on three stories and boasted one hundred rooms. With soundproof sleeping chambers, complete with peepholes, asbestos-padded walls, gas pipes, walls that slid across, making a room bigger or smaller as necessary, and trapdoors with ladders leading down to the rooms below. It was a maze of secret passages and false doors and a number of the rooms were filled with gruesome torture equipment. Chillingly, there was also a specially equipped surgery. He is thought to have placed victims in special rooms into which he pumped lethal gas, watching their death throes through peepholes. On occasion, he might even set fire to the gas to add a little more excitement. When he tired of that, there was always the 'elasticity determinator', an elongated bed to which a victim was tightly strapped and then stretched. He liked to experiment. Chutes, the sides greased for easier dispatch, led down to a two-level basement with a large furnace burning fiercely. Once he had finished with a corpse, he would slide it down a chute to the basement where he would use vats of acid and other chemicals to get rid of any evidence that it had ever existed. Or, he might remove all the flesh and sell the skeleton to a local medical school.

H. H. Holmes, real name Hermann Webster Mudgett, arrived in Chicago in the 1880s. The city was brimming with excitement as well as visitors, as the World's Fair or Great Exposition was about to take place. Some estimates put the number of visitors to the city at a staggering twenty-seven million for the six months in which the Exposition ran, putting a strain on the forces of law and order, but also offering opportunities for crime and for psychopaths such as Mudgett, now going under the name Holmes. Holmes relished the thought of the countless vulnerable, single women fresh to the big city who would be prey to the charms of a successful 'doctor' with very good prospects such as himself. When he met anyone, he described himself as a well-off graduate of a prestigious medical school.

He found work as a prescription clerk in a pharmacy at 63rd and South Wallace Streets when he first came to town. The female owner of the premises where he worked left town suddenly, or 'went to California', as Holmes said at the time. She and her daughter were never heard of again and it is almost certain that he killed them. He took ownership of the business and bought an empty property across the road, on 63rd Street.

He began to raise money through murder and fraud in order to build his 'Castle' and then let rooms to young women who had come to Chicago to enjoy the fair. Of course, they quickly disappeared – he had tortured and murdered them and sold many of their skeletons to medical schools. The women he employed fared no better and probably proved even more lucrative for him. They were forced to take out life insurance policies as a condition of their employment and he claimed on these as he dispatched the women. He also carried out hundreds of illegal abortions in the Castle's dark rooms and many of the patients did not survive the procedure.

Holmes's finances were in a mess at the end of the World's Fair and, with creditors moving in, he abandoned Chicago and moved to Fort Worth, Texas. He had killed a couple of railroad heiress sisters, but before killing them, had arranged their affairs so that he would inherit property they owned in Texas. He intended to construct another death factory, along the lines of the Castle in Chicago, but the authorities in Texas were not as easy to fool as those in Chicago and he abandoned the project.

He set off on his travels around the United States and Canada and is thought, in all likelihood, to have continued in his murderous ways, although no bodies were found to corroborate this.

It was his killing of a business partner, Benjamin Pitezel and his children that was his downfall. Pitezel and Holmes had concocted a scheme whereby Pitezel would fake his death so that his wife could collect on a $10,000 insurance policy. This would be split with Holmes whose role in the scheme was to provide a body to stand in for Pitezel. But Holmes, who never really liked Pitezel, actually did kill him and used the real corpse to collect the insurance money. He told Mrs Pitezel that her husband was hiding out in South America and persuaded her to allow him to have custody of three of her five children. The three children were killed in various locations as he traveled across America.

But, his luck was finally running out. Pinkerton's detective agency had been on his heels for a while and they finally arrested him in Boston in November 1894. They had long had suspicions about his activities, but it was only when they gained entry to the Castle that these suspicions were confirmed. They found a number of intact skeletons and countless fragments of human bones, including the pelvis of a fourteen-year-old.

When investigators finally examined the Castle, after Holmes's arrest, the media had a field day. 'The

Castle is a Tomb!' screamed the headline in the *Chicago Tribune*. *The Philadelphia Inquirer* called it a 'charnel house'. True crime writers made it a staple of the genre. In Philadelphia, a Holmes Museum opened. As for the narcissistic Holmes, he wrote a memoir, *Holmes' Own Story, in which the Alleged Multimurderer and Arch Conspirator Tells of the Twenty-two Tragic Deaths and Disappearances in which he is Said to be Implicated.* 'My sole object in this publication is to vindicate my name from the horrible aspersions cast upon it,' he wrote, 'and to appeal to a fair-minded American public for a suspension of judgment.' He attempted in the book to make himself seem completely normal and, typical of the narcissistic tendency of the psychopath, saw the book as being of literary merit.

In the book, Holmes, born in 1861, describes being brought up in Gilmanton Academy, in New Hampshire where his lies and pranks resulted in punishment by his father. He also talks about the day that his interest in medical matters began. A gang of boys tried to frighten him by confronting him with a skeleton in a local doctor's office. Rather than terrify him, of course, it made him resolve to pursue a career in medicine. He obtained a medical diploma from the University of Michigan and opened a medical practice. Around this time, he was involved in an insurance fraud, he admits in the book, helping someone to substitute a dead body for his own. Following that, he took a job in an asylum but it proved to be an experience that scarred him and haunted him for many years. Following that, he had moved to Chicago.

He claimed that the women who had stayed at his property had simply left, even going as far as saying that they had benefited from knowing a man such as him.

He told the story of one young woman, Minnie Williams. She had arrived at his door having had an abortion and feeling ashamed. She was suicidal, he claimed, and he took her in, engaging her to work as his secretary for a while. When her sister, Nettie, had arrived, Minnie had become jealous of her because she had fallen for Holmes, and struck her on the head with a stool, killing her. Holmes claimed to have helped Minnie put the body in a trunk, convey it to Lake Michigan and toss it in. Minnie had then left, he claimed and he had burned the items of clothing she had left behind.

He defended himself at his trial, the first murderer in United States criminal history to do so. His performance in court was described as 'remarkable' by one newspaper. He displayed the cool detachment of the psychopath immediately as he questioned candidates for jury service in his case. However, he still made mistakes, becoming too bogged down by detail and showing no emotion following a detailed description of the corpse of his so-called friend and business associate, Pitezel, by asking for a lunch-break. He spent the afternoon trying to prove that his associate's death was suicide, but all the expert witnesses posited that he could not possibly have killed himself. Anyway, the chloroform that Holmes claimed Pitezel used to kill himself, had actually entered his body after death.

That evening, Holmes requested that his two legal representatives be reinstated. He realised, too late, that he was unable to defend the case properly.

In summing up, the Prosecution attorney described Holmes as 'the most dangerous man in the world'.

He was convicted, unsurprisingly of the murder of Benjamin Pitezel and the judge sentenced him to death by hanging.

Holmes now decided to write a confession. It was not from a sense of remorse, however, but because he had been offered $10,000 for it by Hearst Newspapers. It appeared in *The Philadelphia Inquirer*. He claimed to have murdered more than 100 people, attempting it would seem to make his mark as the world's most notorious killer, but swiftly retracting that number and reducing it to twenty-seven.

His first murder, he said, had been of a former school-friend whom he had dispatched with a dose of laudanum, in order to make a claim against an insurance policy he had taken out on him. The second, however, had been an accident. He had killed a man in a fight over money he claimed had been owed to him. Following that, he had killed a few people whom he sold to a man who would then sell them on to medical schools. He was paid between $25 and $45 for each of them. When he lost contact with this dealer in bodies, he would bury the unclaimed victims in the floor of his offices. He explained the various methods he had used – beating to death, gassing in vaults and asphyxia. Many of these people died because there was something in it for Holmes, money or avoidance of exposure and he even had help sometimes. It was a miracle he avoided detection for so long. On one memorable occasion, he had attempted to kill three young women at the same time, using chloroform. They managed to escape and reported him to the police. He was arrested but, unbelievably, was not prosecuted.

He told the truth about the Williams sisters, how he had persuaded Minnie to give him several large sums of money. She and her sister had property in Texas and he wanted to get his hands on it. He persuaded her to get her sister Nettie to come to

Chicago and she was killed immediately. He had told Minnie that her sister had changed her mind about visiting, and persuaded her to sign everything over to him. He then poisoned her and buried her in the cellar of another house that he owned. His efforts to blame her for the murder of her sister and of the Pitezel children he decribed as 'the saddest and most heinous of my crimes'.

Regarding Pitezel, he said that he knew he was going to kill him from the first moment he met him. He won his confidence by showing kindness and consideration for him but meanwhile was showing him forged letters from Mrs Pitezel to her husband. Pitezel had drunk heavily and Holmes killed him while he was in a drunken stupour. While Pitezel was still alive, he lay him on his bed, tied him up, poured benzene over him and set fire to him. Pitezel came to and screamed for mercy, but he suffered an agonising death. When he was dead, Holmes cut the ropes from his body and poured chloroform into his stomach to make it look as if he died accidentally in an explosion. His aim was yet another insurance policy. True to character, Holmes described leaving the house 'without the slightest feeling of remorse for my terrible acts'.

In a macabre aftermath, he is reported to have visited Pitezel's grave some weeks after his interment, in the pretense of acquiring some samples for analysis.

He claimed that he found cutting into the corpse with a knife 'inordinately satisfying'.

His murders of the Pitezel children were even grimmer. He hid them away in a hotel for a week and then began by poisoning Howard. He then proceeded to cut the boy's body up into pieces small enough to be put into a stove that he had purchased for just that purpose.

He took the girls to Chicago, Detroit and Toronto, letting them believe that they would be imminently reunited with their mother. He told them to climb into a large trunk and closed the lid on them, having drilled a small airhole so that they were able to breathe. He then pumped gas through the hole, killing them. He buried them in shallow graves, as ever taking pleasure in killing another human being. He had been like a father to them for eight years, but felt not an iota of remorse.

Even on the gallows in Philadelphia, on 17 May 1896, Holmes changed his story, claiming now that he had only killed two people. He tried to say more, but the trapdoor opened as he was in mid-sentence and this most remorseless of all killers plunged to his death. At least his death was not easy, faint consolation for his victims and their families – it took him fifteen minutes to die. At his own request, to deter body-snatchers, he was buried in cement, so that his body could not be dug up and dissected.

By the time he died, his Castle was no more. On 19 August 1895, a mysterious fire had destroyed it. A U.S. Post Office now occupies the site of the killing factory run by America's first serial killer.

PART THREE

20TH CENTURY BRITISH PSYCHOPATHIC KILLERS

JOHN REGINALD CHRISTIE

It was a small Victorian house, built in the 1860s when the Notting Hill and North Kensington areas were undergoing development. Situated where the elevated dual carriageway, the Westway, runs today, number 10 Rillington Place was located in a row of three-storey terraced houses. The house was split into three flats, none of which had a bathroom. Instead, an outhouse in the garden was used by the occupants of all three flats and a washhouse was also located there for the use of tenants, but it was not always functioning.

Forty-year-old John Reginald Christie was a quiet little man, wth a receding reddish-ginger hair and pale blue eyes. His wife, Ethel, was a plump woman whom friends believed to be frightened of her husband. They seemed aloof as a couple, and many disliked the way they seemed to think they were better than their neighbours. For this reason, they kept very much to themselves.

Christie was originally from Yorkshire, coming from a strict upbringing in which his father was not afraid to beat his children. He would make them go for long walks, which were more like military marches than strolls in the countryside. He was a frail child, disliked by his father, but spoilt by his mother. His emasculation was reinforced by the fact that he had four sisters. He was a very private child with few friends and, while still young, developed a pathological abhorrence of dirt. As he got older, he began to take part in activities at his local church, joining the choir and eventually becoming a scoutmaster. He enjoyed wearing the uniform.

His relationship with his sisters became complex. As a young child he had been disturbed to see one of his sister's legs up to the knee. He became attracted to these women who bossed him about, hating them at the same time for their dominance over him. It is likely that at this time he began to develop an antipathy towards all women, mainly because he felt he could not satisfy them. The nicknames given to him at school when his first attempts at lovemaking ended in failure did not help – 'Reggie-No-Dick' and 'Can't-Make-It-Christie'.

He was a signalman during the First World War and at one point lost his voice for three years following a hysterical reaction to an incident when a mustard gas shell knocked him unconscious. This, however, does not seem to have stopped him marrying Ethel in 1920.

His marriage was blighted by his impotence and he continued visiting prostitutes afterwards, as he had been doing since the age of nineteen. All they served to do, however, was to remind him of his inadequacy with the opposite sex.

His first brush with the law occurred after he became a postman in 1920. He stole some postal orders and went to prison for three months. His life really began to fall apart in 1924, when he was twenty-five. He was put on probation at the post office for charges of violence and there were whispers that he had been using prostitutes. He walked out on Ethel and travelled to London.

In 1928, he was back in prison, sentenced to nine months for theft. When he was released, he lived with a prostitute but when he hit her on the head with a cricket bat, he returned to jail for six months. A few years later, he was arrested again and sent back to prison for the theft of a car. During this time there were police reports regarding his violence towards women, however these could not be proved.

In 1933, he asked Ethel to move back in with him. On the shelf at thirty-five and feeling lonely, she readily agreed, travelling down to join him in

London. Little did she know the kind of man he had become in the ten years they had been apart.

Christie had been an inveterate hypochondriac since he was a child. Following an accident in which he was hit by a car, he began an incredible series of visits to the doctor – 173 over fifteen years. It gave him an excuse to remain at home and complain about his many ailments.

He moved with Ethel into the ground floor flat at 10 Rillington Place in December 1938. They were pleased with the flat because, as it was on the ground floor, they would enjoy exclusive use of the garden. Christie, meanwhile, had signed up as a volunteer member of the War Reserve Police. Incredibly, they asked no questions about his criminal record. He was delighted to pick up his uniform at Harrow police station and served for four years. Unfortunately, however, he became a little too fanatical about the role and was soon known to his neighbours as the 'Himmler of Rillington Place'.

Meanwhile, he continued to consort with other women, one of whom worked with him at the police station. When her husband returned from fighting overseas, he gave Christie a severe beating.

In April 1948, Timothy Evans and his pregnant wife, Beryl, moved into the top floor flat at 10 Rillington Place and six months later Beryl gave birth to a daughter,

Geraldine. Evans was a diminutive, uneducated Welsh lorry driver of limited intelligence who was given to lying and self-aggrandising fantasies. He was a heavy drinker with a very bad temper and he and his wife often engaged in loud and sometimes violent arguments, mostly over Beryl's inability to make ends meet. Evans's low wages barely covered the rent and their bills. Matters were made worse in late 1949 when she informed her husband that she was pregnant again.

Beryl insisted immediately that she wanted an abortion, but Evans, a Roman Catholic, was against the idea. She took pills and did what she could to abort the baby, eventually confiding in Christie who, although he had absolutely no previous experience, told her that he knew how to carry out abortions, having learned how to do it during the war. He persuaded her to let him undertake the procedure, but it ended disastrously. When Evans came home later that day, 8 November 1949, he was horrified to learn from Christie that Beryl had died during the operation. Christie told Evans that he would dispose of her body down a nearby drain and that he would also find someone to look after Geraldine. He ordered Evans to leave London.

Christie later told the police that he saw Beryl leave with her baby around noon and never saw her again. Later, Timothy Evans came home and the Christies went out for the evening. Around midnight, he claimed, he and his wife heard a loud thump from above them. As the man in the second floor flat was away, it could only have come from the Evans flat on the third floor and it was followed by the sound of something heavy being dragged across the floor.

The following day, Christie told the police, Evans told him his wife had gone to Bristol and the day after that, he came home saying that he had packed in his job and was selling up and moving to Bristol to join her.

Evans actually returned to Wales, coming back on 23 November to Rillington Place where, Christie claimed, he told him that Beryl had left him.

What had actually happened was that Christie had gone up to their flat after Evans had gone to work. Beryl laid a quilt on the floor in front of the fire and lay down on it. He may then have tried to gas her and she had panicked and begun to lash out at him. He took out a cord and strangled her. He then tried to have intercourse with her.

It was all too much for the uncomplicated Evans and he eventually went to a police station a few weeks later to tell the police that he had disposed of his wife's body after she had taken something to make her abort her baby. He was afraid to bring Christie's name into it and said that he had obtained the substance he had given her from a stranger. The police did not find the body down the drain outside the front door where he said he had put it, and in fact they could not see how one man, especially a small man like Evans, could have moved the extremely heavy manhole cover that took three of them to shift. They confronted him with this and he confessed that it had been Christie who had administered the abortion pills and put Beryl in the drain. Police searched the house at 10 Rillington Place but it was no more than half-hearted and they even failed to notice the human thigh bone that was being used to prop up the garden fence.

They found a stolen briefcase, however, which gave them an excuse to arrest Evans. Christie was questioned and he emphasised how much of a liar Evans was and how violent his marriage to Beryl had been.

There was still no sign of Beryl and a more thorough search of the property was carried out. Eventually, in the washhouse, they discovered her body and that of her daughter. They had been dead, it was estimated, for three weeks. During lengthy police interrogations Evans inexplicably confessed no fewer than four times to killing his wife.

At the trial, six weeks later, Christie denied that he had agreed to perform an abortion on Beryl and his testimony, plus Evans's poor performance in the witness box, resulted in a guilty verdict. Timothy Evans was sentenced to death and hanged at Pentonville Prison on 9 March 1950.

Christie seemed to have got away with murder.

In late 1952, Ethel Christie suddenly disappeared. Christie told friends that she had moved back to Sheffield and that he was going to join her when he had settled their affairs in London. He gave up his job, sold all his furniture and rented out his flat to a couple. After they had stayed there just one night, however, they learned that the flat was, of course, not Christie's to rent and were thrown out. The landlord rented the flat to a Jamaican immigrant named Beresford Brown. Tidying up the kitchen, one day, Brown peeled off some wallpaper and discovered a door leading to a pantry. Opening the door slightly, he shone a torch into the space beyond. There, to his horror, he saw the body of a woman, seated and hunched forward, clad only in bra, stockings and suspenders. He immediately called the police and when they arrived, they discovered another two women's bodies. They were the bodies of three prostitutes that Christie had lured back to the house and killed while he lived there – Kathleen Maloney, Rita Nelson and Hectorina MacLennan. Searching the remainder of the flat, they found the remains of Ethel Christie under the floorboards of the living room.

Christie had strangled her on 14 December 1952. She had been in poor health and Christie claimed later that he had merely put her out of her misery.

In the garden, another two women's bodies were discovered – Austrian prostitute, Ruth Fuerst and a workmate of Christie's whose catarrh he had promised he could cure with a special type of inhaler. Bringing her to the flat, he made her breathe in a conction he had put in a jar. However, he had connected the jar to the gas supply. As she unknowingly breathed in the gas and weakened, he strangled her and as she died, had intercourse with her.

Christie's impotence, it seemed, only dissipated when he had complete control over the woman with whom he was having sex. Of his first victim, he later said, 'I remember as I gazed down at the still form of my first victim, experiencing a strange, peaceful thrill.' It was a 'thrill' he would experience six times.

After wandering around London for several weeks, as the entire Metropolitan police force searched for him, Christie was finally arrested on Putney Bridge and confessed to the murders. He additionally admitted that he had killed Beryl Evans, but he never confessed to killing her baby, Geraldine. Nonetheless, many thought it highly unlikely that two stranglers could live in the same house.

On 15 July 1953, John Reginald Christie was

hanged on the same gallows as Timothy Evans.

Debate about the execution of Evans raged on for years until in 1966 the Brabin Report concluded that Christie had killed Geraldine Evans and persuaded Timothy Evans not to go to the police. Home Secretary, Roy Jenkins awarded Evans a posthumous pardon in the case of Geraldine Evans. However, he has still not been declared innocent of the murder of his wife, for which he was not tried.

JOHN GEORGE HAIGH

THE ACID-BATH MURDERER

Was he really insane or was his bloodlust – the drinking of a glass of each of his victims' blood – merely a story made up in order to make them think he was mad and allow him to get away with murder?

The court did not believe he was mad and he went to the gallows on 10 August 1949, sentenced to death for the murders of six people, although he, himself, claimed to have killed nine. Mostly, he killed for personal gain, making money from selling his victims' possessions or houses, but one doctor described him as suffering from 'the most rare and terrible paranoia of all the "egocentric" paranoias – the "ambitious" or "mystical' paranoia, through which he saw himself as omnipotent and even guided by an outside force, possibly divine'. In this condition, he was uninterested in sex, the sexual urge being sublimated into self-worship. He believed himself to be untouchable.

In fact, John Haigh was absolutely certain that the law could not touch him for the murders he committed for the simple reason that the bodies no longer existed. He had dissolved them in baths of acid.

When Haigh was assessed medically, his upbringing came under a great deal of scrutiny and it undoubtedly had a great bearing on the man and the killer that he would become. He was born in 1909 and spent almost the first twenty-four years of his life in Outwood in Yorkshire. His parents were members of the strict religious sect, the Plymouth Brethren, and Haigh was, therefore, not allowed to participate in sport or entertainment when he was young and he was certainly not allowed to have any friends. So strict was his father in his beliefs that he built a ten feet-high fence around the garden to shield the family from the outside world. Like another murderer, John Reginald Christie, he developed a hatred for dirt.

John Haigh Sr had a bluish mark on his forehead that he described to his son as the Devil's brand, telling him that he had been given it because he had sinned and that if John Jr sinned, he would be similarly marked. He told him that his mother remained unmarked because she was an angel and Haigh had something of a mother-fixation as a result. Throughout his childhood, however, he lived in terror of sinning and receiving the Devil's brand, staying awake at night, praying that the mark would not appear on his face. Eventually, he realised that it was all a con to make him behave.

He was a solitary child but had a great love of music, joining the choir at Wakefield Cathedral. He began to move away from his parents' religion but claims to have meditated on the bleeding Christ he saw in portraits at the cathedral and that his longing for blood began there.

In 1934, aged twenty-five, he married a woman he had only met a few months previously, but the marriage ended after just four months as he was arrested for fraud and sent to prison. Released from prison, he went into business, but when his partner died in an accident, he decided that his future lay in the south. He moved to London.

He found work as a secretary/chauffeur for an amusement park owned by William McSwan, rapidly becoming a close friend, meeting McSwan's parents and sharing an interest in fast cars and flashy clothes with him. A year later, however, he moved on but it would not be the last the McSwans would see of him.

He set up a fake solicitor's business and began to defraud people by creating phoney estates to be liquidated and company shares to be sold that he did not own. He was soon found out, however, and went to prison for four years. On his release, he went back in again for twenty-one months for theft. He vowed never to go back to prison and decided that the best way to make substantial sums of money instead of the piddling sums of which he had so far managed to defraud people, was to fleece rich old women. A method was developing in his head and he did some experiments while working in the prison's tin shop. He worked with sulphuric acid to test its powers for dissolving things, trying it out successfully on mice and finding that they dissolved in thirty minutes.

Released again from prison, Haigh worked as an accountant and looked like marrying again, to Barbara Stephens, daughter of the owner of the company he was working for. Of course, he was still married to his first wife, but that was irrelevant.

Haigh always presented a car crash in which he was involved in 1944 as a turning point in his murderous career. He suffered a head injury and blood from it went into his mouth. He wrote later that it took him back to dreams he had about blood when he was a child. He wrote about 'a forest of crucifixes' that became trees with blood dripping from their branches. A man was going to each tree and catching the blood which he then gave to Haigh to drink. That year, he killed for the first time.

His victim would be his old friend, William McSwan, whom he bumped into again. Later writing that he had needed blood, Haigh hit McSwan on the head with a length of pipe at his workroom at 79 Gloucester Street on 9 September 1944. He then cut the unconscious man's throat. Putting a cup against the wound, he filled it with blood and drank it.

But how to dispose of the body? He remembered that in his workroom he had a quantity of sulphuric acid. He obtained a forty-gallon oil-drum and squeezed McSwan's body into it. He then poured the acid into it until the body was fully covered. He locked the room for the night and went home.

When he opened the drum a couple of days later, all that remained of his victim was a black, evil-smelling sludge that he disposed of down a drain, scooping out the congealed lumps that lay at the bottom, and then washing out the drum.

There was no body and, consequently, he reasoned, he could not be tried for murder.

He now began the process of getting his hands on McSwan's money and possessions. He first persuaded the dead man's parents that their son had run away to Scotland to avoid military service, faking postcards from William to them. Meanwhile, he also improved his method of killing, fashioning a mask to prevent his being affected by the acid fumes and a pump to get the acid into the drum more efficiently.

Two months later, he killed William McSwan's

parents, using the same length of pipe, drinking their blood and stuffing them into drums filled with acid. He told their landlady that they had gone to America and had their mail redirected to his address, including letters containing Mr. McSwan's pension. He then sold their properties, using forged documentation. He made £6,000 from their murders and did it all so well that they were never reported missing and their deaths only became apparent when he confessed in 1949.

It was now 1945 and he was living in the Onslow Court Hotel in Kensington, an establishment much favoured by wealthy widows, just the type of prey that Haigh was looking for. In the meantime, he later claimed, he killed a young man by the name of Max but no one by that name was ever reported missing and it is not known if this claim was a self-aggrandising attempt by Haigh.

He had developed a serious gambling habit and by the end of 1947 had spent just about all the McSwan money. It was time to kill again.

He read an advert in the newspaper offering a house for sale. It had been placed by a well-off couple, fifty-two-year-old Dr Archibald Henderson and his forty-one-year-old wife Rose. He could not afford it, but befriended the couple anyway, playing piano for them and spending time in their company. Around this time, he began renting premises in Crawley from a company called Hustlea Products, moving his work materials there from Gloucester Street.

On 12 February 1948, he shot Dr Henderson in the head with his own gun, stolen by Haigh. Leaving the dead man in his storeroom in Crawley, he returned to Rose Henderson and told her that her husband had been taken ill. When she went into the storeroom, he shot her, too. He then claims he drank their blood before dissolving them in acid.

He was becoming careless, however, or perhaps he just felt invincible. Amongst the filthy sludge he dumped in the yard was Dr Henderson's foot, still intact.

He paid the couple's hotel bill next day and took possession of their dog. He also took possession of a property they owned and sold it. He sold his girl-friend some of Rose Henderson's clothes and one of her handbags was purchased by a Mrs Olive Durand-Deacon, a wealthy widow who lived at the Onslow Court. He wrote to Mrs Henderson's brother, Arnold Burlin, and told him that the couple had emigrated to South Africa. Burlin had been tempted to report them missing, but Haigh concocted a story that the doctor had performed an illegal abortion and could be in trouble.

He claimed later that he next killed a girl called Mary from Eastbourne, but as with Max, his earlier claim, no evidence has ever been found that she ever existed.

He was tired of his car, a Lagonda, and reported it stolen. He had actually crashed it over a cliff. When an unidentified body was found a month later in the vicinity of the place where he had crashed it, no link with the car was made, even after his later confession. He bought a new Avis.

He had soon gambled away most of the money he had earned from the murder of the Hendersons and in the first few months of 1949, began a search for another victim.

Mrs Durand-Deacon, to whom he had sold Rose Henderson's handbag, had approached him with a business idea involving false fingernails. To discuss the matter further, he invited her to Crawley where, as usual, he put a bullet in her head and bathed her in acid. Haigh told people that she had failed to arrive for the appointment. But one of her friends at the Onslow Court Hotel reported her disappearance to the police and a photograph and description of her was issued. Haigh was questioned, and when detectives learned of his unpaid bills at the hotel, they became suspicious. When they checked criminal records, they discovered that he had been in prison several times for fraud, forgery, obtaining money by false pretences, and theft. He was questioned again and it was noticed that he wore gloves at all times and was a compulsive hand-washer, due to his lifelong hatred for dirt. They checked the Crawley premises where, he told them, he performed what was known as 'conversion work' – an industrial practice in which industrial materials were broken down in acid. They found all of his equipment and, crucially, a briefcase bearing the initials 'J.G.H.' There were documents relating to Dr Henderson as well as the McSwans. They also found a .38 Enfield revolver that had been fired recently and a dry-cleaning receipt for a Persian lamb coat that had belonged to Mrs Durand-Deacon. They learned that Haigh had recently pawned items of the missing woman's jewellery in Horsham.

As they searched the yard outside his workshop, they were puzzled by the sludge he had poured there. A doctor involved in the search noticed something about the size of a grape amongst it. It was a human gallstone. They found three more, as well as part of a human foot, eighteen pieces of human bone, dentures, the plastic handle of a red bag and a lipstick container.

Haigh was arrested but remained chillingly calm throughout. He was convinced he would be sent to Broadmoor, the hospital for the criminally insane – especially when he laid it on thick about the drinking of his victims' blood – and would then be released in a few years. He told them everything, confessing in full to the murders he had committed and gilding the lily with a few others he probably did not commit. By his account, he killed nine people – the police charged him with killing six.

Haigh underwent a number of tests to decide whether or not he was insane but to his great disappointment, he was found to be fit to stand trial and, on 18 July 1949, he stood in the dock.

There was little doubt about the verdict and it took the jury only fifteen minutes to find him guilty of murder. On 6 August, he was executed at Wandsworth prison after donating his clothes to Madame Tussauds and allowing them to make a death mask of his face. He also gave them instructions that the wax model's trousers should always be immaculately creased, the hair neatly parted and its shirt-cuffs showing just below the sleeve of his jacket. Given his fear of dirt, it has to be hoped that he also ordered them to dust it frequently.

DENNIS NILSEN

In the police station, Dennis Nilsen calmly explained to the investigating officers, 'The victim is the dirty platter after the feast and the washing up is an ordinary clinical task.' He had performed that 'ordinary clinical task' no fewer than fifteen times, disposing of the bodies of the young men he had had brought home and from whom he could not bear to be parted.

It had all begun on 30 December 1978. He had befriended a young man at a local pub and taken him home with him to his flat at 195 Melrose Avenue in north London. Stephen Dean Holmes, it would later emerge, was only fourteen years old at the time and was on his way home from a concert when he met Nilsen. The two continued to drink at the flat and then climbed into bed together.

When Nilsen awoke towards dawn, he realised with an overwhelming sense of sadness that Holmes would be leaving when he woke up. Nilsen had spent Christmas entirely on his own and did not relish the thought of a solitary New Year. He picked up his tie from the piles of clothing they had thrown on the floor the night before and climbed on top of the boy, encircling his neck with the tie, pulling it tight. Holmes woke up immediately and they fell from the bed onto the floor as he struggled for his life. Nilsen pulled tighter and gradually, the life flowed out of Holmes and he went limp. He was only unconscious, however, and Nilsen went to the kitchen and filled a plastic bucket with water. He brought it back in and, placing Holmes on some chairs, dangled his head into the bucket, drowning him. Holmes did not struggle and within a few minutes, he was dead.

Nilsen was unnerved at having killed someone – especially someone whose name he could barely remember. He drank some coffee and thought about what to do. He carried the corpse into the bathroom where he washed its hair. He then returned it to the bedroom and put it to bed.

He later told how he thought that Holmes's dead body was rather beautiful but, of course, he realised that he had to get rid of it somehow. He went out to buy an electric knife and a large cooking pot, but when he got back home, he could not bring himself to slice up his new friend. Instead, he dressed him in clean underwear and clothes, like a doll. He thought about having sex with the body, but was unable to.

Then he laid it on the floor and went to bed for a while.

Later, when he got up again, he had some dinner and watched television, the body lying all the while on the floor. Suddenly, he had a brainwave. He prised loose some floorboards and tried to shove the body into the space beneath them. Unfortunately, rigor mortis had set in by this time and he could not manage it. He stood Holmes against the wall and decided to wait until the stiffness had worn off. Next day, he finally succeeded in squeezing him under the floorboards before nailing them back down.

A week passed and he wanted to have a look at the body again. He lifted the carpet and prised up the floorboards again. He was dismayed to see that the corpse was a bit dirty and so he took it out of the space and gave it a bath, before washing himself in the same water. All of this had aroused him and he masturbated over the body before inserting it in its grave under the floorboards again.

Remarkably, the body of Stephen Holmes would remain under those floorboards for more than seven months before Nilsen took it out into his garden and burned it, throwing pieces of rubber into the flames to disguise the stench of burning flesh.

A year later, a young Chinese student, Andrew Ho, escaped from Nilsen as they played bondage games in the flat. He actually went to the police and accused Nilsen of trying to strangle him, but the police decided not to charge him.

His second victim was Kenneth Ockendon, a Canadian whom Nilsen met at a pub, on 3 December 1979. Nilsen liked him a lot and was devastated to learn that his new friend was flying home to Canada the following day. As Ockendon listened to some music through headphones, Nilsen sneaked up on him and strangled him with their chord. He listened to some music with the body lying on the floor beside him and then dragged him into the bathroom to clean him up. He put him in his bed and climbed in beside him, remaining there for the night, stroking and caressing him. In the morning, he stuffed him into a cupboard and went to work.

The following day, he took the body out and photographed it in various positions before taking it to bed with him and having sex with it. Ockendon was then put under the floorboards but when Nilsen felt lonely, he would get the body out and sit beside it watching television. Nilsen would then clean the body again, dress it and put it back to bed under the floor, wishing him a gentle 'goodnight'.

Five months later, in May 1980, he strangled Martyn Duffey, a sixteen-year-old homeless boy. Duffey had to be drowned before Nilsen took a bath with his body. He kissed him all over and then masturbated while seated on his stomach. It was then two weeks in the cupboard for him before he went under the floor.

Nilsen next killed a twenty-six-year-old Scottish male prostitute, Billy Sutherland, strangling him, it later emerged, with his bare hands. Nilsen did not remember killing Sutherland. He seemed to enter a trance of some kind when he was killing and his memories of many of his acts when he was in this state were wiped.

Many of his victims were itinerants or homeless and they were, consequently, never identified. The names of the next seven young men Nilsen killed have never been known. The first, his fifth murder, was again a male prostitute of oriental – possibly Thai – origin. His sixth was a young Irish labourer and the seventh was what he described as a 'hippy type' whom he encountered sleeping in a doorway in London's Charing Cross area. Number eight remained under his floorboards for a year and numbers nine and ten were young Scottish men, picked up in the pubs of Soho. Number eleven was a young skinhead who had a tattoo around his neck – a dotted line saying 'Cut Here'.

On 10 November, 1980, he picked up a Scottish barman who woke up back at the flat with Nilsen trying to strangle him. Douglas Stewart fought him off and ran out of the building. He went to the police but they refused to take action, putting it down to a homosexual domestic argument.

Martyn Barlow was next. Twenty-four-years-old with learning difficulties, he loitered outside Nilsen's building and then complained of weakness from epilepsy. Nilsen called an ambulance and had him taken to hospital. On his release, on 18 September 1981, he returned to Nilsen to thank him and the two had a meal and drank together in the flat. When Barlow fell asleep, Nilsen strangled him. This time it was not because he did not want him to leave. He simply found him a bit of a nuisance. He squeezed his corpse into a cabinet under the sink in the kitchen.

Of course, the question of hygiene was becoming pressing and the neighbours began to complain about the smell in the building. Nilsen told them it was because the building was old. Meanwhile, he sprayed his flat twice a day to kill off the countless flies that were hatching in the putrefying flesh.

He got rid of the bodies by stripping to his underwear and cutting them up with a kitchen knife on the stone kitchen floor. He would often put the head in the large pot he had bought and boil the flesh off it. He knew how to butcher, having learned during a stint in the army as a chef. He would put pieces of bodies in the garden shed and disposed of internal organs in plastic bags between the double fencing in the garden. The rest he would burn in the garden.

He moved to a new flat at 23 Cranley Gardens in the Muswell Hill area of north London, having tidied up the old flat, remembering at the last moment that he had left Martyn Barlow's hands and arms beside a bush in the garden. The new place had no garden and was an attic flat. He believed he would be able to bring an end to his murderous spree if he could not dispose of the bodies. He was wrong.

He met John Howlett in a pub and they went back to his flat to carry on drinking. For once Nilsen wanted him to leave, but 'John the Guardsman' climbed into Nilsen's bed and refused to go. Nilsen took a length of upholstery strap and strangled Howlett with it. It was a tough one as Howlett was a fairly strong man. He hit him on the head, and the fight was over. Howlett would still not die, however, and he had to drown him before putting him out of sight in a closet.

He decided to dispose of the body by cutting it into small chunks and flushing it down the toilet. He then boiled some of the flesh and Howlett's head, hands and feet, disposing of the bones in the rubbish.

Soon, he killed another man in the attic flat. He does not remember strangling Archibald Graham Allan. He just noticed him sitting there with a piece of the omelette he had been eating protruding from his mouth. He left him in the bath for three days before dissecting him.

Last of all, he killed twenty-year-old drug addict, Steven Sinclair, after meeting him in Leicester Square. He strangled him with some thick string and on removing some bandages from his victim's arms afterwards, realised that he had recently tried to slit his wrists. He gave the dead man a bath and put him to bed. He then placed mirrors by the bed, undressed and lay down beside Sinclair's body, becoming excited by looking at them in the mirror. He disposed of Sinclair in the same way that as the others at Cranley Gardens.

In February 1983 it all began to unravel when one of the five tenants of the house experienced difficulty in getting his toilet to flush. In fact, none of the toilets in the house were working properly and a plumber was called. He was unable to fix the problem, however, and a specialist was summoned. Nilsen began to worry that the toilets must be sticking because of what he had been flushing down his. He swiftly disposed of what he could from his flat. He stuffed what remained of Sinclair's body into plastic bags and locked it in a cupboard.

Two days later, someone arrived to investigate the blockage. He clambered down a manhole at the side of the house and immediately noticed a strong smell. He was certain it was the smell of something dead. There was sludge in the sewer which he discovered was coming from numerous pieces of rotting flesh. Its source was a pipe from the house. He phoned in to his bosses and told the tenants, Nilsen amongst them, that he would have to notify the police. To their horror, he showed them the piles of flesh he had dragged out of the sewer.

Incredibly, that night Nilsen tried to get rid of the pile, dumping them over the fence, but he was spotted by a watchful neighbour. Next day, he is reported to have said to his colleagues at work, 'If I'm not in tomorrow, I'll either be dead or in jail.'

When he went home, three officers were waiting for him. A search of the flat very quickly uncovered Steven Sinclair's body parts, amongst others. Nilsen accompanied them to the police station and began to talk, providing them with a full confession of what he had been up to for the previous four years.

Dennis Nilsen's trial began on 24 October 1983 and on 3 November he was found guilty of six murders and two attempted murders. He was sentenced to life imprisonment with a minimum term of twenty-five years, but it is unlikely he will ever be released. Still, prison has its advantages – at least he will never be lonely again.

PETER SUTCLIFFE

THE YORKSHIRE RIPPER

For almost six years, he dealt death and terror to the women of the north of England, attacking twenty women, thirteen of whom he brutally murdered. The area was in the grip of hysteria and the biggest police force ever to be involved in a manhunt in the United Kingdom struggled to deal with the countless pieces of information.

They caught him on Saturday 3 January 1981, more by luck than judgement, as he sat in his car talking to a prostitute. She was lucky because in his pockets were the tools of his grisly trade – a ball-peen hammer and a knife – and the moment she stepped out of the car, he would have used the hammer to smash her skull and the knife to mutilate her body, as he had done with the others. As it was, however, two policemen who happened to be passing in a patrol car, stopped to investigate the brown Rover parked on the driveway of the British Iron and Steel Producers Association.

Peter Sutcliffe had seemed an unlikely Yorkshire Ripper suspect. He had always been quiet, and in his work as a lorry-driver had a reputation for being slightly different to the others. A quietly-spoken man, he never talked about women the way the other drivers did, never used bad language and seemed to be in an idyllic marriage to his wife Sonia.

He had been born in Bingley in 1946 to John and Kathleen Sutcliffe but instead of being the action man that his sports-mad father wanted, he turned out to be a loner, a bit of a 'mummy's boy' who was bullied at school, until he became interested in body-building. Nonetheless, he was never any good at school and left aged fifteen, working in a number of jobs during the next couple of years.

When he was twenty, he finally – much to the relief of his father – found a girlfriend, Sonia Szurma, daughter of Czech immigrants. They married in 1974 and to her family and others he seemed to be a nice, hard-working young man who thought the world of his wife.

Under that loving and caring surface, however, there were less desirable traits. He was a habitué of prostitutes, as his brother-in-law would discover when they went out drinking together. A friend, Trevor Birdsall, who would later report his suspicions about Sutcliffe to the police, spent countless evenings cruising the red-light districts of Yorkshire with him.

Not long after his marriage, Sutcliffe gained an HGV licence. He and Sonia also learned that after many miscarriages, she would never be able to have children. They were both devastated.

Around this time, he attacked a woman, the first of two attacks he would make before he finally killed. She lived in Keighly but had fallen out with her boyfriend. As she banged angrily on the door of her boyfriend's house, Sutcliffe leapt out from the shadows and dealt her a crushing blow to the head with a hammer. As she lay on the ground, he hit her twice more and lifted her skirt. Pulling down her underwear, he slashed her across the stomach with a knife. A neighbour, hearing the noise, came out to ask what the commotion was. Sutcliffe calmly told him it was nothing and that he should go back indoors. With that, he left the scene, his victim surviving the attack. But investigating officers were bemused. No money had been taken and the attack did not appear to be of a sexual nature.

A month later, on Friday 15 August, Sutcliffe was out carousing with Trevor Birdsall in the pubs of Halifax when he caught sight of forty-six-year-old Olive Smelt. She was out drinking with friends while her husband stayed at home looking after the kids. She and her friends were given a lift home by some men they knew and Olive was dropped close to her house.

Meanwhile, Sutcliffe had left Birdsall alone in his beloved white Ford Corsair, saying he would be back in a minute. As Olive walked down an alleyway, she heard a voice behind her saying, 'Weather's letting us down, isn't it?' before feeling a shattering blow on the back of her head. He struck her once more as she hit the ground and lashed out with the knife, slashing her in the lower back. A car suddenly approached, however, and he was unable to finish the task. He returned to Birdsall waiting in the Corsair as if nothing had happened.

Again the police were puzzled by the incident but they critically failed to link it to the earlier attack. It would be a full three years before they realised that the same man had been responsible for them.

Two months later, he killed for the first time.

The body of twenty-year-old mother-of-four Wilma McCann was found by a Leeds milkman in the early hours of 30 October, lying on her back on a dark recreation ground just a hundred yards from the front door of her council house. The previous night she had left her children to go drinking in Leeds and had drunk heavily before making her way home. Several people had seen her, including a lorry driver who stopped to offer her a lift, but she was incoherent and he thought better of it. She was then seen at 1.30 am being picked up and was never seen alive again.

She had been struck twice on the back of the head and then stabbed frenziedly fifteen times in the neck, chest and abdomen. There was semen on her trousers and on her underpants, but she had not been raped. Her purse was missing, however, and the police conveniently used this as the motive for her killing. A large force consisting of 150 officers was thrown at the task of interviewing 7,000 householders and checking every detail with which they were presented. It was to no avail, however. They were no closer to finding their man.

Emily Jackson was not a full-time prostitute. She lived with her husband and three children in a respectable Leeds suburb but money troubles had forced her on to the street. She left her husband in the lounge of the Gaiety Pub on 20 January 1976, stepping outside in search of business. When she failed to return to the pub at closing time, her husband went home, expecting her to follow later.

She never returned. Her body was found next morning a short distance from the Gaiety, on her back with her legs spread apart. Her tights and pants were still in place, but her bra had been lifted, exposing her breasts. She had been dealt two sickening blows to the head with the hammer and then stabbed 51 times with a Philips screwdriver that had been sharpened for the purpose. They had their first clue, however – the print of a size 7 Dunlop Warwick Wellington boot was imprinted on her thigh where he had stamped on her in his rage.

The same man that had killed Wilma McCann had killed Emily Jackson. Police now knew they had a serial killer on their hands.

Sutcliffe had been working as a delivery driver for a tyre company, but his lateness in the mornings resulted in him being sacked. He now spent several months looking for a job. In the meantime, his evenings were often busy.

Marcella Claxton, a twenty-year-old prostitute was attacked on 9 May. Sutcliffe picked her up and drove her to a large open space where he offered her £5 to have sex with him. She told him she had to urinate first and as she did so, he hit her twice from behind with the hammer. As she lay on the ground drifting in and out of consciousness, she opened her eyes to see him masturbating in front of her. He put a £5 note in her hand and warned her not to call the police before climbing back into his car.

She staggered and crawled to a nearby phone box and dialled 999, but as she waited, bleeding and crumpled on the floor of the kiosk, she saw him pass in his white car several times, as if he was looking for her in order to finish her off. She survived and was able to provide a description of her attacker.

The Yorkshire Ripper, as he was now being called by the newspapers, was the main topic of conversation amongst the prostitutes of the Chapeltown area of Leeds. The newspapers compared him to Jack the Ripper, the killer who had stalked the streets of London's East End, killing prostitutes, almost ninety years previously. However, there was a prevailing feeling that no one really cared because his victims were prostitutes. The girls working the area were terrified, however, and many moved away to other cities.

Sutcliffe finally found work as a lorry driver in October 1976 and it seemed to stop him killing for a while. On 5 February 1977, however, his old urges re-surfaced. Irene Richardson's skull was fractured by three blows to the head. She was also stabbed in the neck, throat and stomach, the knife wounds so savage that her intestines spilled out. This time, they found tyre tracks but were dismayed to learn that these could belong to any one of around 100,000 vehicles.

On 23 April, Patricia Atkinson went to the Carlisle pub for a drink with friends. The next day she was found dead on the bed in her flat from where she operated as a prostitute. She had received four hammer blows before being stabbed six times with a chisel in her abdomen and in her back. The print of the sole of a size 7 Dunlop Warwick Wellington boot was found on a bed-sheet.

Life changed for the Sutcliffes around this time. Sonia was training to be a teacher and would hopefully find a job in the autumn term. They also bought a house in Bradford for £15,000. The night after they had first gone to have a look at the house, Sutcliffe travelled to Chapeltown again.

Jayne MacDonald was sixteen years old and was walking home when she was attacked and dragged into a playground by Sutcliffe. When she was found, on the morning of Sunday 26 June, her breasts were exposed. She had been stabbed repeatedly in the chest and once in the back, after being felled by three blows to the back of her head. She was not a prostitute and suddenly the public seemed to awaken to the danger in their midst. The investigating team was inundated with information and a huge number of interviews and house-to-house calls were carried out.

On the night of 9 July, Sutcliffe drove into Bradford. In the early hours of Sunday morning, he stopped at a taxi queue and offered a lift to Maureen Long who had been drinking and dancing in the bars and clubs of the city. He drove her to Bowling Back Lane where he killed her with the customary blow to the back of the head before stabbing her as she lay on the ground. He was disturbed in his savage work, however, and she survived although it would be many weeks before she left hospital.

Another 12,500 statements were taken and 10,000 cars were checked. Information that the car was a white Ford Corsair was exciting until they discovered that it was the vehicle of choice for thousands of taxi drivers in the area.

It became irrelevant, however, when Sutcliffe sold the white Corsair and replaced it with a red one. Sonia, meanwhile, had been given her first teaching post.

On 1 October, Jean Jordan climbed into his new car in Manchester's rough Moss Side area. She had agreed to have sex with him in a quiet piece of parkland for £5. She slipped the £5 note into a hidden pocket in her handbag but once she had climbed out of the car, he hit her no fewer than thirteen times in a frenzy of rage. In his new house the next day, however, he began to worry about the £5 note he had left behind. It had been brand-new, he remembered and could, consequently, be easily traced back to him.

He had concealed her body well and eight days later it had still not been found. Therefore, when he had to drive some visitors home on the night of 9 October following a party, he decided to return to the scene of her murder to retrieve the note. Having dropped off his friends, he drove back across the Pennines and found her body where he had left it. He was unable to locate the handbag, however. He became furious and ripping her clothes from her body, began stabbing her viciously. In his fury, he attempted to decapitate her, but did not have the proper tools. Her hideously mutilated body was found the next day.

The handbag and the hidden £5 note were found five days later. Sutcliffe had been correct – the serial number of the note provided a massive clue and its provenance was soon found as part of a batch that had been distributed to firms that employed around 8,000 men in the Bradford and Shipley area. They were all interviewed, including Sutcliffe, but there were no new developments as a result.

Sutcliffe botched an attempt to kill a prostitute, Marilyn Moore, in mid-December and then killed Yvonne Pearson on 21 January 1978, although her body would not be discovered until March. Prostitute Helen Rytka was murdered on 31 January – this time he had sex with her as she lay on the ground bleeding from a blow to the head before stabbing her through the heart and lungs.

On 16 May 1978, Vera Millward had gone out to buy some cigarettes and pick up some painkillers when Sutcliffe jumped her on the grounds of Manchester Royal Infirmary. She was hit on the head three times before being viciously slashed and stabbed in the eye. Her screams were heard, but such noises were not unusual in that area at that time of night and no one reported them. Tyre tracks found nearby matched those found at other murder scenes.

Eleven months passed before the next incident, but during that time his beloved mother had died. Sutcliffe had been very close to her, but had been devastated to discover that she had had an affair with a neighbour, a policeman. One night his father had arranged to be with Peter and Sonia at a hotel to meet his wife, but she arrived believing she was meeting her lover. John Sutcliffe humiliated her by forcing her to show them the nightdress she had brought with her for her tryst. It was a humiliating incident that made a big impact on Sutcliffe.

Just when the police began to believe it was all over, Sutcliffe killed Josephine Whitaker, a building society clerk as she walked home late at night from her grandparents' house in April 1979. He stopped her in a stretch of open grassland, asked her the time and then swung his hammer into her head. He stabbed her twenty-five times in her breasts, stomach, thighs and even her vagina.

Amongst the thousands of letters that were being sent to investigating officers and newspapers were several that the officers thought might be genuine. They had been posted in Sunderland and the suggestion that the killer might be a Geordie was reinforced by a cassette tape that they received. For some time, the Geordie connection became something of a red herring, drawing officers away from the real killer who was, of course, closer to home.

He killed again on 1 September 1979. It was a student this time – Barbara Leach whom he had first spotted in a pub, the Mannville Arms, in Bradford. He followed her as she walked home, killing her with one blow as he leapt out of the shadows. He stabbed her, as usual, and covered her with an old piece of carpet.

The police campaign took on new life. £1 million was spent on newspaper and billboard ads. They still focused on a man with a Geordie accent, however.

By now, along with the other employees of his company, Sutcliffe had actually been interviewed a number of times. His workmates had even started calling him the Ripper because the police had spoken to him so often. But he had alibis provided by Sonia for all the nights on which the murders had taken place. He was never a real suspect.

His next victim was a forty-seven-year-old civil servant, leaving work late one night. This time, however, she did not fall to the ground after he had struck her with his hammer and he was forced to strangle her to stop her screaming. Police carelessly ruled her out of the Ripper investigation because of the method of her death.

His next two victims, on 24 September and 5 November survived but on 17 November, he killed Jacqueline Hill, a student at Leeds University, who died from a single blow to the head. Ironically, she had moved into a university residence because of her family's fears for her safety in view of the Ripper attacks.

Sutcliffe was sentenced to life imprisonment with no opportunity for parole for thirty years. Although found sane at his trial, he has since been diagnosed as schizophrenic and was sent in March 1984 to Broadmoor Hospital under Section 47 of the Mental Health Act. There was speculation in February 2009 that his doctors no longer believed him to be a danger to the public, but Prime Minister, Gordon Brown, said in a press conference that it was unlikely that he would ever be relesed.

PATRICK MACKAY

It is astonishing how many people who grow up to become killers have been brought up in an abusive and violent environment. It is almost as if they learn from their abuser and later begin to do to others exactly what has been done to them. Patrick Mackay is just such a man, born in 1952 to a father who was an aggressive and violent drunk. Harry Mackay, a veteran of World War II, was an unsuccessful accountant who came home every night to his wife, the worse for wear, and accused her of things she had not done. A severe beating would follow. In time, he would vent his anger on his son, Patrick.

Alcoholism and a faulty heart killed Harry Mackay when Patrick was ten but the boy found it difficult to come to terms with the loss of his father. He had not been allowed to see his body or go to the funeral and began to believe that his father was still alive, although it was probably more of a hope born of the desolation he felt, having wished his father dead many times over the years.

His mother suffered a nervous breakdown around this time and was hospitalised for four months. With his father gone and his mother in hospital, he felt abandoned. His personality changed and he had his first brush with the law, accused of stealing from a neighbour's house. He became a bully at school and was subject to tantrums and fits of extreme anger. He was a loner, a liar and a troublemaker, an outsider with no friends and was often dirty and neglected. He was also cruel, reportedly setting the family tortoise on fire on one occasion. He was also said to have pinned birds to the road in order to watch cars drive over them. Like his father, alcohol made him violent and he began drinking at an early age. He mugged people on the street and burgled old people's flats and houses. Once, he set fire to a Catholic church.

His father had told him many gruesome stories about the war, describing colleagues being blown up and shot and Patrick developed an unhealthy interest in death, spending a lot of time dissecting the bodies of dead birds and animals.

It became obvious that there was something seriously wrong with him and his mother had him sent to various homes for boys with problems, but she eventually brought him home again, against the advice of the psychiatrists who had been observing him. Bizarrely, she re-located the family to Guyana in

South America but before too long they were back living in London. There then followed a spell in Gravesend, Patrick failing to hold down a job, possibly as a result of his persistent bullying.

He was unravelling dangerously, however, and a probation officer warned of dire consequences if he was not removed from the family home. His prediction was proved to be correct when Patrick tried to strangle his mother and commit suicide. His response to questions from investigating officers was that he lived with his father and saw snakes. However, following an examination to judge whether he was mentally ill, he was released. Shortly after, he tried to kill a young boy, but was restrained.

Incarcerated in the first of a series of psychiatric facilities, he was diagnosed by one doctor as 'a cold psychopathic killer'. It was 1968 and he was sent to Moss Side Hospital in Liverpool, one of the few institutions in Britain that had the required security to keep a man like Patrick Mackay out of harm's way. He underwent numerous tests and examinations which were fairly inconclusive apart from the opinion of one psychiatrist who thought he had inherited a genetic defect from his father that made him likely to be psychopathic. His troubled relationship with his mother did not help and it was no coincidence, they felt, that many of his violent fits occurred around her.

He suffered from Intermittent Explosive Disorder, they suggested, a condition characterised by explosions of uncontrollable anger. He was, they concluded, very disturbed.

He was also very immature and would take a doll to bed with him every night that had to be kissed. His behaviour was extreme and one doctor was convinced he could be a murderer of women. He was a psychopath but without the mania that sometimes accompanies the condition. An independent tribunal examining him found nothing wrong with him. He was released several times in spite of the fears about his violent tendencies. He was also becoming obsessed with the Nazis.

Mackay idolised Adolf Hitler, even fashioning a Nazi uniform for himself and purchasing a pair of stormtrooper boots. He began to have delusions that he was powerful and that one day he would change the world. Like other serial killers, such as Moors Murderer, Ian Brady, he believed that he was superior to others people.

In 1972, they released Mackay from Moss Side. He was twenty years old and about to unleash his own form of hell.

He tried to make a living, but found it impossible to hold down a job. Eventually, he moved in with some people he knew in London, starting to drink heavily and consume large quantities of drugs, not the best thing for someone with his particular history. As usual, however, he proved difficult to live with because of his mood swings and aggression. He did not want to live with his mother because she was constantly nagging him about paying his way and other family members soon showed him the door after one more temper tantrum.

Meanwhile, his interest in the Nazis persisted and a photograph of Hitler's right-hand man, Heinrich Himmler, sat proudly by his bedside.

One day, as he walked in some woods near to his mother's home in Kent, he found a Carmelite convent that housed eight nuns who looked after elderly patients. Next door to the convent lived sixty-four-year-old priest, Father Anthony Crean. Father Crean bumped into Mackay that day and offered to buy him a drink in the local pub. He thought that Mackay looked like he needed a friend. The two men became friends – as much as Patrick Mackay could have a friend, that is – and began meeting for a drink in the pub regularly. Mackay could not resist his impulses, however, and broke into the priest's house, stealing a cheque for £30. Mackay was arrested but Father Crean was reluctant to press charges. The police proceeded with the case anyway and Mackay was ordered to repay the money. He never did, however, and had even altered the amount on the cheque to 'eighty' instead of 'thirty'. Mackay went back to London and left the priest seriously out of pocket.

He continued to drift from job to job and was convicted of petty crime, spending some time in jail. His behaviour was still violent and some commentators speculate that by this time, late 1973, he had possibly killed five people. Later, he admitted to drowning a homeless person in the Thames but he is suspected of other killings.

In February 1974 he tried to kill himself and was picked up by the police. After being examined by a psychiatrist and deemed not to be mentally ill, he was observed on a ward for a while before being released on 14 February. He headed for the home of eighty-four-year-old Isabella Griffiths whom he had helped to carry her groceries back to her home in Chelsea not long before. She told him she did not require any help that day, and he became angry, bursting into the house anyway and strangling her in a rage. He then proceeded to take his anger out on her with a twelve-inch kitchen knife, mutilating her body before having something to eat and listening to the radio in her living room.

He later claimed that he now thought about killing himself with the knife but decided against it. He arranged Isabella's body, closing her eyes and covering her. He put dishes in the sink along with her shoes and turned on the taps. He left the house having stolen only a cigarette lighter, tossing the knife he had used to kill her into some bushes.

It was two weeks before she was found but the police found no clues and the case remained unsolved.

Mackay became the lodger of a social worker who was ordered to take him in. He would discuss endlessly the violent fantasies he had and suggested that he might be possessed. Eventually, to the man's great relief, he moved on. He was now living rough, abandoned by his family who wanted nothing to do with him. He robbed the social worker's house and went to prison for four months. By the time he was released, he was angrier than ever and determined to take revenge on the society that had let him down so badly.

He began by mugging women and then formed a plan to rob well-off elderly women. He had enjoyed killing Isabella Griffith. It gave him a sense of power and he wanted to experience that feeling again.

On 10 March 1975, he knocked on the door of eighty-nine-year-old Adele Price, strangling her after she opened it. The euphoric feeling it gave him stayed with him for several days, he later admitted. After killing her, he took a nap on her sofa but was wakened by the sound of someone trying to get into the house. It was Mrs Price's granddaughter. She went off to phone her grandmother from a phone in the hall and Mackay ran out past her. However, there were other flats in the building and she thought he had come from one of them.

Once again, it was a motiveless crime that left police stumped.

Again Mackay tried to end it all and was locked up in a psychiatric hospital. On his release, some friends taunted him about his friendship with Father Crean, jokingly suggesting that it had been a homosexual relationship. It put the priest back into Mackay's mind and he set off for Kent to find him. He had decided that the only way to stop this kind of scurrilous talk about him was to kill Father Crean.

He travelled from London with two knives, first visiting his mother and telling her to cook a chicken he had brought with him. Then he strolled over to the convent. He said later that he found Father Crean's front door ajar and he walked in and called out his name. Seeing him, and being afraid, Crean attempted to get out but was stopped by Mackay. There was a struggle and Mackay became angry. He punched the priest in the face but Father Crean broke free, running towards the bathroom, presumably to lock himself in. But Mackay caught him before he got there, pushing him backwards into the bath while beating him with his fists. He took out one of the knives and stabbed him in the neck and the side of the head. He then found an axe which he swung at his head. 'It was something in me that just exploded,' he later said.

The blows of the axe rained down on the priest, now stretched out in the bathtub. Mackay watched as his skull was split open and then he put the plug in and turned on the taps. It took an hour for the priest to die, at one point touching his exposed brain with his fingers, an action that Mackay later claimed to find very erotic.

He left Father Crean's house and went back to his mother's house to eat the chicken she had cooked for him but the body was discovered later that night, and it did not take the police long to work out who had killed him. Mackay was arrested and confessed to the murder within thirty minutes.

Initially, he confessed to three murders but in prison he began to boast of others and was questioned again. This time, he admitted to eleven murders committed during a two-year period. He had stabbed a woman on a train, bludgeoned three elderly people in their homes and stabbed a woman and her grandson. A man had been thrown in the river and another man had been beaten to death as he closed his shop for the night.

Medical assessment confirmed what others had found. Mackay was a psychopath who felt no remorse for his crimes. He was judged sane, as he knew exactly what he was doing, and stood trial for three murders on 21 November 1975, pleading guilty with diminished responsibility.

Patrick Mackay was sentenced to life imprisonment.

PART FOUR

20TH CENTURY AMERICAN PSYCHOPATHIC KILLERS

BABY FACE NELSON

John Dillinger was sitting in the passenger seat as Baby Face Nelson, drove across St. Paul to collect their associate, Homer Van Meter, from his hotel. Nelson, never what you would describe as the most patient of men, went through a red light and scraped the bumper of an oncoming vehicle. The two cars stopped and the driver of the other one got out and approached Baby Face's car, berating him for his bad driving. Baby Face calmly pulled out his .45 pistol from under his jacket and shot the man between the eyes. When Dillinger protested, saying, 'You didn't have to do that!' Baby Face replied, shrugging his shoulders, 'Hell, why not?' He pushed the corpse away from the car, jumped in and drove off.

Of all the ruthless killers that the Depression era spawned in America, there were few as cold-blooded as Lester Gillis, aka Baby Face Nelson. Baby Face – a name he loathed – quite simply loved to kill. Other gangsters of the time such as Clyde Barrow, Pretty Boy Floyd and John Dillinger, would kill to get out of a tight spot or to evade capture; Nelson killed for fun, because he liked it. Even his close associates were scared of him.

Born in Chicago's down-at-heel southwest side in December 1908, Nelson was a small man with the face of a spoilt brat. Five feet four inches in height, his parents were poor immigrant Scots who had moved south from Nova Scotia and had never adapted to the harsh realities of city life. Their son Lester had no trouble, however, in fitting in and making his way through the hustle and bustle. His father worked as a packer in an ice house on Canal Street while his mother, a devout Christian, tutored French. The parents were always working while their sons wandered the streets, learning how to be tough guys.

He had to be tough because his diminutive size made him easy meat for the neighbourhood bullies. Before long, however, he had learned to fight back and what he lacked in height he made up for in sheer vindictiveness. People began to avoid him and the switchblade he had learned to use.

He gradually began to become involved in petty crime, mugging drunks, robbing stores and stealing cars. He became familiar with the local police station and the local police began to look out for the sandy-haired boy in the alleys near his house. He was sure to be doing something wrong because that was the way he lived.

He left school early and began hanging around with a gang, the Halsted Street Boys. In 1922, aged fourteen, after being arrested for car theft, he was sent to a boys' home for two years. Released in 1924, he returned to the streets but after only five months of freedom, he was locked up again after breaking into a department store.

In 1926 he was out again, working for the gangster who ruled Chicago, Al Capone. Capone was coining it from Prohibition. The Volstead Act had banned alcohol production and sale in the United States but it had become no more than a license to print money for the mobsters of the time. They manufactured their own booze or imported it from Canada and other places and sold it in speakeasies.

Capone was a New York gangster who had come to Chicago in 1919 and through corruption of police officers, politicians and city officials, had created a crime empire that floated on a sea of illicit alcohol. He creamed money off the unions and ran brothels and protection rackets.

This world, where violence was never far away – there was always someone who resisted or failed to pay on time – was tailor-made for Baby Face Nelson. Capone had delegated to his top man, Jack McGurn, the task of creating an army of 'convincers', men who would be paid good money to enforce Capone's rule.

Nelson signed up. But he proved too bloodthirsty even for these bloodthirsty men. Too many 'clients' were ending up dead as a result of his methods which usually involved a pocket knife, a .32 calibre revolver, a Thompson machine gun or a baseball bat. He was upsetting too many people, especially as some of the union men he 'disciplined' were well-connected, either with politicians or the local Mafia. Capone began to get nervous, telling McGurn to let Baby Face Nelson go his own way.

Nelson opted for a new career – armed robbery. He stole a car and robbed a number of Chicago jewellery shops. It was a lot of risk for not a lot of money especially as the most he got away with was a measly $2,000. Then, he hit paydirt towards the end of 1930 with a $5,000 heist from a successful jeweller in Wheaton, Illinois. As Wall Street was collapsing, Lester Gillis was doing alright. He even had a girlfriend, eighteen-year-old Helen Wawzynak who he planned on marrying.

It all went wrong in January 1931 when he was arrested in the course of a robbery. He was sentenced to one year to life and went to Joliet penitentiary. He was also charged with the robbery at Wheaton and when that came to court, his lawyers reckoned, he would be looking at twenty-five years inside, at least.

He was married now and Helen visited often but

he was not inside for very long. On 17 February 1932 he was taken to a pre-trial hearing at the Wheaton Civic Building, handcuffed to a plain-clothes detective. On the way back to Joliet he pretended to be ill and was freed from his handcuffs to use the toilet. He immediately launched himself on the detective, sending him sprawling. Nelson sped out of the carriage and jumped onto the station platform before running down an embankment and onto the running board of a waiting car which sped away.

From Chicago, he travelled with Helen to Reno, Nevada, working there for a while in a succession of odd jobs. From Reno, he moved on to California, one step ahead of the cops who followed his footsteps to Reno, but arrived too late.

In California he came under the protection of Sicilian gangland boss, Joe Parente who employed him as a jack of all trades. He was a bodyguard, barman and sometimes a parking valet, a lowly job that he hated. Nonetheless, he kept his nose clean, got on with the job and gained the respect of Parente who promoted him to bootlegger.

It was at this time that Lester Gillis changed his name to Baby Face Nelson, or rather, George Nelson, a name borrowed from a boxer of the time. It was Parente who added the epithet 'Baby face', the nickname that Nelson loathed but which stuck with him.

His job was now to get local speakeasies to sell Parente's illegal alcohol. With numerous villains ploughing the same furrow, it took a special skill to force a bar-owner to change allegiance. Baby Face Nelson possessed that skill in spades and if not-so-gentle persuasion did not work, there was always the machine gun or the pipe bomb to fall back on. He gained a reputation as a man that was crossed at your peril, a man for whom ruthless violence was an easy option.

Around this time, Nelson met John Paul Chase, another of Parente's men. Chase would become Baby Face's right-hand man – he worshipped the pint-size terror. The two of them planned and schemed, linking up with another couple of Parente's men: Tommy Carroll, a former boxer and Eddie Green, a bank marker or 'jug maker'. A jug maker was a man who scouted banks to find out which was most suitable for robbery. Green was one of the best. They were both highly experienced bank robbers who had hit numerous banks across the Midwest states.

Tired of Parente and his bootlegging work, Nelson, Helen and Chase left Chicago and drove to the Midwest, stopping at Long Beach in Indiana, a favourite place for bad guys in search of easy work. Nelson sought out Homer Van Meter, John Dillinger's top man, asking to enlist in Dillinger's gang. Van

Meter gave him short shrift, however, despite Baby Face's glowing CV. Not long after, however, he bumped into Green and Carroll again and they decided to get together to rob banks.

They hit lots of small town banks in Wisconsin, Iowa and Nebraska, stealing piles of cash. They would run in, spray the ceiling with bullets, overcome the guards, gather the customers and tellers into a corner, get the cash drawers and the vault open and roar off in their getaway car. If anyone tried to stop them, Baby Face would do what he did best with his machine gun. Chase would drive the car and Helen would sometimes be hiding in the back seat.

He loved the publicity he garnered. It became his gang in newspapers that had somehow found his nickname. Baby Face Nelson became famous. The only thing that really annoyed him was when one of his robberies was credited to another gangster – to pretty Boy Floyd or Dillinger.

He lived in the Hotel St. Francis in San Francisco, hanging out in its speakeasy with stars and celebrities such as Clark Gable, Jack Benny, Harry Houdini and Charlie Chaplin. He was having a ball and it got even better when Homer Van Meter invited him, at last, to join the Dillinger gang. Van Meter and John Hamilton were the only members of the gang still at large. The others, including Dillinger, himself, were locked up, but they were planning on getting Dillinger out of Crown Point Jail in Indiana soon.

A couple of weeks after Van Meter's approach, Dillinger did, indeed, break out, being introduced to Baby Face Nelson in St. Paul. Their partnership got off to a bad start, however, Nelson trying to lay down the law to Dillinger. 'Before we go any further,' he snarled, 'I want you all to know I don't take no orders; I walk into a bank, open fire, kill anything that moves, I grab the money and am outta there! If you don't like it, find yourself another patsy!' Apparently, Van Meter, sick of this aggressive little man, went for his gun at this point, as did Baby Face. They both had to be restrained.

Their first job was to rob the Security National Bank at Sioux Falls. When they entered the premises, however, announcing their intentions, someone set off the alarm. Nelson went ballistic, screaming at the assembled customers and tellers, threatening to kill them all. Dillinger reminded him that he was the lookout and ordered him over to the window. Outside he saw a police car arrive. Climbing onto a desk, he opened fire through the plate glass window and a police officer just getting out of the car, fell to the ground, badly wounded. Nelson was excited and Dillinger began to wonder what he had got himself into. He had always avoided shooting policemen, realising the trouble it brought down on you.

Eight days later, they hit a bank in Mason City, Iowa. This time Dillinger kept Nelson outside, in the getaway car. The robbery did not go well. The bank manager locked himself in his office with the keys to the vault and there was a guard in a steel cage taking pot-shots at them and dropping teargas canisters on them. A police officer in a building across the road shot Dillinger in the arm and they only just escaped, surrounded by hostages, one of whom Baby Face would have shot for swearing at him if Dillinger had not nudged the hand in which he was holding his gun.

The authorities were clamping down on them, however. J. Edgar Hoover headed up a department dedicated to taking gangsters such as Dillinger, Floyd and Nelson out of circulation. They almost got Dillinger in St. Paul but he escaped after a gun battle. Baby Face and Helen, meanwhile, hid out in a rented cabin in the wooded area of Iron County, Wisconsin. The others disappeared for a while, but Eddie Green died in a gunfight in St. Paul in April after agents located him at his girlfriend's apartment.

Dillinger was now Public Enemy Number one with a reward of $20,000 on his head. This was much to Baby Face's annoyance. He was only Public Enemy Number Two with a reward of only $10,000 on his head.

When they got together again to plan their next move, in April 1934 at a lodge in northern Wisconsin, they came under the scrutiny of the local police, curious as to why a group of smooth, suited city slickers would be spending time there in the off-season. They passed their suspicions to the FBI and they had soon worked out that the men at the lodge were the Dillinger gang.

On the evening of 22 April, a convoy of vehicles rolled towards the lodge with their lights extinguished. It began badly when three innocent men, emerging from the lodge, were shot, one fatally. Hearing the gunshots, Dillinger, Van Meter, Carroll and Hamilton fled into the woods behind the lodge. Nelson had been asleep with Helen in a cabin outside the main building. Characteristically, he emerged from the building, gun in each hand blazing. He then slipped into the cover provided by the forest. The agents followed. Dillinger, Hamilton, Van Meter and Carroll escaped in stolen cars. Nelson found himself in a clearing on the edge of which were small fishing cabins. There was a car in which the keys had fortunately been left in the ignition. As he climbed in, however, ready to make his escape, another car drove into the clearing. He hunched down, realising immediately that the three men in the car were FBI agents looking for him. He jumped out, pointed his guns at the three men and opened fire, emptying his weapons into them. One died instantly and the others were seriously wounded. He pulled them from the vehicle and sped off into the night.

He finally made it to Public Enemy Number One a short while later when Dillinger was killed by a gang of agents as he left a cinema in Chicago. He had been hiding out at an Indian reservation near lake Flambeaux in Wisconsin but returned to Chicago where he was reunited with Helen. It was his intention to put together a new gang and to that end he met up with Chase. However, Eddie Green was dead and Tommy Carroll had been gunned down by police officers in Waterloo, Iowa. The authorities were beginning to win the war against crime. John Hamilton was killed, as was Homer Van Meter, dying in a hail of bullets in St. Paul. Baby Face moved back to the west coast.

It was proving difficult to find recruits for his new gang. He was just too hot and certainly too dangerous to become involved with, most criminals thought. They were right. The police were looking for him round the clock. All main and connecting roads were being watched. They eventually found him on Highway 14 on 27 September 1934. Agents William Ryan and Thomas McDade followed his car but were forced to stop when bullets were fired into their radiator. A second federal car, containing agents Herman Hollis and Samuel Cowley, took up the chase. Baby Face's car was damaged by FBI bullets. He crashed it into a ditch where he and Chase clambered out of the car and took up position with their machine guns.

Suddenly, however, Baby Face stood up and started walking up the road, carrying his machine gun. When Chase asked him what he was doing, he replied that he had had enough – he was angry and was going to kill the agents. Gunfire erupted but Nelson kept walking, bullets ripping through his body. He continued firing and Hollis fell to the ground dead. Then Cowley also slumped to the ground, dying.

Baby Face Nelson had been hit by seventeen bullets. He crawled to the agents' car but was not able to lift himself into it. Chase and Helen picked him up and laid him on the car's back seat before driving him to a priest so that he could at least have the last rites said over him. He died at eight o'clock that night, having lost his temper one time too many.

ED GEIN

On 17 November 1957, following a robbery at the hardware store in Plainfield, Wisconsin, in which she worked, Bernice Worden had disappeared. Police discovered that the last customer in the store had been Ed Gein, a local man who lived alone in a ramshackle, dilapidated old farmhouse in a desolate location on the outskirts of the small town of Plainfield, Wisconsin. They travelled out to the gloomy farm to interview Gein. What they found when they arrived would shock and horrify the nation.

The first thing they noticed was the stench. Decomposing rubbish and rotten junk covered every space and work-surface and littered the floor to the extent that it was difficult to walk. The local sheriff, Arthur Schley was making his way gingerly through the room with a torch when he felt something brush against him, something hanging from the ceiling beams. He shone his torch upwards into the dark to see a large carcass, hanging upside down, decapitated, the ribcage sliced open and the insides gutted, just like you would a deer, something common to this area where hunting was a popular activity. But this was no deer, the policeman quickly realised to his horror. It was the body of the missing woman, Bernice Worden, who had been shot dead at close range with a .22 calibre rifle. That was not all they found in this charnel house, however.

In Gein's small bedroom the bed had a bizarre decoration on each of the four corner posts — human skulls; skin had been used to make a lampshade and to upholster the seats of chairs; sliced off women's breasts were being used as cup holders; human skullcaps were being used as soup bowls; a human heart lay in a saucepan on the cooker; the pull of a window shade was a pair of human lips. There was a mammary vest made of woman's skin; a belt made from human nipples; socks made from human flesh and a box of human vulvas that Gein later admitted to wearing. Finally, they found a suit made entirely of human skin.

Thirty-nine-year-old Edward Theodore Gein had taken the death of his mother, Augusta, in 1945 pretty badly. His late father, George, was a violent alcoholic who rarely worked and whom his mother and the two boys essentially ignored. Divorce was not an option for Augusta due to her strict religious convictions – she was a strict Lutheran who read Ed and his brother passages from the Old Testament every afternoon to keep them on the straight and narrow.

Augusta had run a successful small family grocery store that allowed the family to live comfortably, despite her husband's inadequacies, before buying a remote farm located just outside the small town of Plainfield. She moved there to remove any undue outside influences from her precious sons. She lectured them on the evils of the opposite sex – women were wicked, no more than prostitutes and to be avoided at all costs. The only reason for sex, she told them, was for reproduction. But there was little chance of Ed being led astray. He had always been a strange boy, laughing randomly at his own private jokes and being bullied for his slightly effeminate manner and for a minor growth that he had over one eye. He was a loner – he had to be, as Augusta would not permit him to make friends – leaving home only to attend the local school. The rest of his time was spent working on the farm.

She was a hard woman to please and often berated them for their shortcomings, fearing they would end up like their no-good father. Nonetheless, when George died in 1940, they tried to help out by taking odd jobs and the people of Plainfield considered them to be reliable and trustworthy. Interestingly, while both boys were employed as handymen, young Eddie

Gein liked nothing better than to baby-sit for neighbours. He seemed to get on better with younger kids than those his own age.

Ed's brother, Henry, however, was less fond of the life that his mother was trying to mould for the two boys. He thought Ed's relationship with his mother was unhealthy and began to be critical of her in front Ed. But Ed thought his mother was the embodiment of all that was good and was deeply shocked to hear Henry talk like this. It may have led to Henry's death.

In May 1944, the two boys were fighting a forest fire that was threatening the farm. They had separated in order to fight the fire from two different directions. According to Ed, he lost sight of his brother and as night approached, there was still no sign of him. Ed informed the police and when they arrived at the farm led them straight to his brother's body. A couple of things did not seem right. For a start, he was lying on a piece of ground that had not been burned. He also had bruises to his head. Foul play was at no point suspected – the police officers just did not believe that Ed was capable of murder, let alone the murder of his brother. The cause of death was later recorded by the coroner as asphyxiation.

It was two years later that Augusta suffered a series of strokes and died, leaving thirty-nine-year-old Ed on his own at the farm for the first time in his life. He boarded up his mother's rooms — the upstairs rooms, downstairs parlour and living room — keeping them as a shrine to her memory. He took up residence in the kitchen and a small room off it, that became his bedroom. Here, he spent his time reading about Nazi atrocities, south sea cannibals and, eerily, anatomy. His neighbours, for some of whom he did odd jobs, spread nasty rumours about him. Some young boys who visited the farm, saw shrunken heads, but their parents dismissed the story as childish fantasy. Nonetheless, he was known as 'Weird Ed'.

His favourite hobby, however, was visiting the local cemetery. There, he would dig up the graves of recently buried middle-aged women who looked like his mother. He would drag the bodies home, skin them and tan the skin from which he would make the macabre objects that littered his rooms.

Following Augusta's death, Ed had decided that he wanted to have a sex change. It was for this reason that he wore the suit made of women's skin, so that he could pretend to be his mother rather than have to go through with the operation a sex change necessitated.

They estimated that Ed had carved up fifteen bodies at the farmhouse.

Coincidentally, Wisconsin Police had noticed an increase in the 1940s and 1950s in the number of people who had disappeared. An eight-year-old girl, Georgia Weckler had vanished on her way home from school in 1947. A huge search of a ten square mile area was launched involving hundreds of locals. However, no evidence was found apart from a set of tyre tracks made by a Ford. She was never seen alive again. In 1952, two hunters had stopped for a drink in Plainfield — no sign of Victor Travis and Ray Burgess or their car was found after they left the bar in spite of a huge search. In 1953, fifteen-year-old Evelyn Hartley, was babysitting in the town of La Crosse when she disappeared. Her father had phoned to check that she was alright but receiving no reply, went to the house where she was. When there was no answer to his knocking at the door, he looked through the window. All he could see was her shoes and her glasses on the floor along with some bloodstains. There had obviously been a struggle and the police found bloodstains on the grass outside the house. Again a massive search was launched but not a trace of the girl was found apart from some items of clothing with blood on them near to a highway. Then, in the winter of 1954, Plainfield tavern-keeper, Mary Hogan disappeared from her bar — again a trail of blood was left behind in the car park. There was also an empty bullet cartridge on the floor of the tavern.

It seemed that Ed Gein had killed them all and maybe more.

The gruesome discoveries at the farm had a devastating effect on the men who found them. One officer, Art Schley had been so upset that during his interrogation of Gein, he banged the killer's head and face against the wall, rendering his initial confession inadmissible. Schley became a tragic figure, so mortified by Gein's crimes and his fear of having to testify, that he died before the case came to court, aged only forty-three.

Schley's frustration was understandable because for the first day, while exhaustive searches were being made of his farm and the surrounding area, Gein said nothing. After twenty-four hours, however, he opened up, explaining in graphic detail how he had killed Bernice Worden and how he had plundered many of the body parts in his house from the local cemetery. Bernice Worden, he claimed was the only person he had killed. The others had been already dead.

The eeriest thing about his confession was the lack of remorse or emotion he displayed, the true sign of the psychopath. In actual fact, he had no conception of the crimes he had committed. It was thought that he was almost certainly insane and that he should plead not guilty on the grounds of insanity. They had done tests and psychiatrists had interviewed him.

They concluded that he was both schizophrenic and a 'sexual psychopath'. The reason, they added was the unhealthy relationship that he had enjoyed with his mother. She had given him unnatural and conflicting feelings about women, both loving and hating them. This conflict eventually manifested itself as a psychosis.

The remains of ten women were discovered on the farm and the difficult and controversial decision was taken to exhume the bodies of the women at the cemetery whose graves he had said he had plundered. All the coffins showed signs of having been tampered with and parts had undoubtedly been stolen from them.

Gein was found to be mentally incompetent and unfit to be tried for first degree murder and was committed to the Central State Hospital in Waupun, Wisconsin. Ten years later, however, he was deemed competent to stand trial for the murder of Bernice Worden and was, finally, found guilty of first-degree murder. However, he was judged to have been insane at the time of the crime and was later found not guilty by reason of insanity. They sent him back to hospital where he happily spent the remainder of his life. On 26 July 1984, he lost a long battle with cancer and died. They laid him to rest in his favourite place – next his mother in Plainfield cemetery. He was also tantalisingly close to the graves he had plundered all those years previously.

After he was convicted, Ed Gein's farm went up in flames, probably as a result of arson – the towns-people were tired of the ghoulish curiosity of morbid out-of-towners. Plainfield fire department took the call and attended the fire, but it was too late. Perhaps they failed to deal with the incident with a great deal of urgency, given who the fire chief was. His name was Frank Worden and he was the son of Bernice Worden, one of Weird Ed's unfortunate victims.

HARVEY GLATMAN

Harvey had been different from birth. He was slow and never had any friends. He behaved oddly from an early age. His mother, Ophelia, first discovered there was something not quite right with her son was when he was just four years old. She walked into his room to find that he had tied a length of string around his penis, put the other end in a drawer and had then leaned back against the tugging string. The parents dismissed this as a bit of childish experimentation, but it was a lot more than that and, later, rope would replace string and become his means of conquest.

At school, Harvey was called names on account of his large ears and buck teeth. But, above all, he was afraid of girls and never joined in activities and games after school. He would rather go home and play his own game which involved his beloved rope. He would tie it round his neck, throw it over a pipe or rafter and pull on it while masturbating. He had discovered auto-erotic asphyxiation at an extraordinarily early age. When he was eleven, his parents found out about the game and took him to a doctor who just put it down to growing pains.

He did well at school, but girls were still an alien life form; he stammered and blushed whenever any came near him. Moreover, his confidence was not helped by a very bad case of acne. So, to get his thrills, he started to break into houses. But, unlike other everyday burglars, he did not do it for gain; he broke into houses simply for the excitement.

His breaking and entering soon graduated into something different. He would follow a woman home from the centre of Denver, break into her house, force her into her bedroom and tie her with the rope he carried everywhere with him. He would also gag her with a piece of cloth. He had stolen a .25 pistol during one of his burglaries and it came in handy. The woman was at his mercy and he was free to touch her as he pleased. He would unbutton clothes and fondle their bodies as he pleased, doing the same to himself. He never fully undressed them or raped them. However, it made him feel like a real man and not the loser he really was.

In May 1945, however, when he was seventeen, he was finally caught breaking into a house and the police discovered the rope and the gun on him. He confessed to some of the burglaries he had committed, but was careful to leave out the ones that had involved the women. Seeming not to have learned his lesson, although perhaps not able to control his desires even if he had, while awaiting trial, he abducted a woman called Norene Laurel, tied her up and drove her to Sunshine Canyon. He performed his usual acts and then let her go. At the police station, she recognised his face in an album of mugshots and he was arrested again, this time without bail. He was sentenced to a year in Colorado State Prison but was paroled after eight months.

Ophelia, Harvey's mother wanted him to make a fresh start and set him up in a flat in Yonkers. He got a job as a TV repairman, a trade he had learned in prison and she returned to Denver. Harvey, meanwhile, was on the lookout for excitement. He bought a toy gun – possession of a real one would mean a long prison-stretch if he was caught with it – and he carried his pocket-knife and his trusty length of rope, made of the finest hemp.

At midnight on 17 August 1946, Thomas Staro and Doris Thorn were accosted by a man with a gun. They were marched into a grove of trees and the man tied Staro's legs together and made him lie down. The man with the gun began to touch Thorn's breasts. However, unknown to Glatman, Staro had worked himself free of his ropes and was tiptoeing up behind him. There was a struggle and Glatman slashed

Staro's shoulder with the knife before running away into the night.

He fled to Albany where he rented a flat and prepared for his next attack. It came on the night of 22 August. He pushed off-duty nurse, Florence Hayden into a yard where he bound her wrists together. As he did this, however, she screamed and Glatman fled. The next evening, he tried it on with two women walking together, but lost his nerve, eventually just taking their purses.

The Albany Police Department was, by this time, becoming interested in this man who targeted women. The descriptions given by the women all matched; so they knew the crimes were being perpetrated by the same man.

Within two days, he was arrested and he confessed. In spite of the pleas of his mother who all this time had believed him to be leading a quiet life in Yonkers, he was sentenced to five to ten years in prison; he was in the big league now. At Elmira, where he spent the first two years of his sentence, he was diagnosed as a 'psychopathic personality – schizophrenic type'. He was then moved to maximum security at Sing Sing. As is reported to often be the case with sociopaths like Glatman, he played the system well and got time off for good behaviour, being released after serving only two years and eight months. There were conditions though; he had to return to the care of his mother, get a job and be under court supervision for four and a half years.

He behaved himself and in 1956, he was free of all restrictions. He moved to Los Angeles and went crazy.

Harvey had enjoyed photography in his art classes at high school and now he took it up again, but with a more sinister purpose. He intended to use it to photograph girls from the modelling studios that had sprung up everywhere in LA. Girls who had arrived in Hollywood dreaming of being stars like Marilyn Monroe offered themselves to be snapped clothed, semi-clothed, or naked, according to how much they were paid.

He worked as a TV repairman again and rented a small apartment on Melrose Avenue, saving enough to buy a used 1951 Dodge Cornet and some expensive photography equipment. He invented a name, Johnny Glenn, for his photographer identity and spent months hanging around the modelling studios, taking thousands of photographs.

But, it was not quite enough for Harvey.

Judith Ann Dull was a nineteen-year-old divorcee working to fund a child custody battle she was waging with her ex-husband. Glatman called her on the morning of 1 August 1957, and asked if she would be interested in posing for a true crime magazine layout. She was wary, but agreed to pose for him at her own apartment at two o'clock that afternoon. He asked her to wear a tight skirt and sweater.

Arriving at her apartment, he told her the light was not good enough and suggested they go to his studio. Once there, he explained that the pictures were to illustrate a story about bondage and she would have to be tied up. Innocently, she allowed him to tie her wrists and ankles, at which point he pulled a .32 Browning automatic pistol from his pocket. He undid the ties on her wrists and ordered the now terrified Judith to strip off, slowly. He photographed her all the while, barking out instructions as to how he wanted her to pose.

He then raped her several times and forced her to sit beside him while he watched television. He said he would take her home afterwards.

Of course, he had no intention of taking her home. When he told her he would drop her on the outskirts of town, she presumed that was to allow him to make his escape. They got in the car and he drove a hundred miles out of town before stopping the car. He made as if to untie her and for a moment she must have thought it was going to be alright, but quickly he put the rope round her neck, pushed her down onto her knees and ran the other loop of rope around her ankles. Pulling up on the rope, her neck snapped and she was dead. He finished the evening off by using his flash attachment to take photos of the dead girl, arranging her body in a variety of poses.

He stuck the photos all over his bedroom walls.

It was seven months before he killed again.

He met twenty-four-year-old Shirley Ann Bridgeford, a divorced mother of two children, through the Patty Sullivan Lonely Hearts Club. 'George Williams' promised to take her square dancing on 7 March 1958. Williams – in reality Harvey Glatman – picked her up at her home where, to his surprise and concern, a houseful of people greeted him. He suggested to her that rather than go dancing, they go for a drive in the country and get some dinner somewhere en route. She agreed and they stopped in Oceanside.

After dinner they drove on. Somewhere near Anza State Park he stopped the car and pulled his gun out, ordering Shirley to undress. He raped her and then took photographs of her. He then waited until the sun came up to take pictures of her in daylight before garotting her. As with Judith Dull, he then photographed the corpse in different poses.

Four months later, it was the turn of Ruth Mercado, her body photographed and dumped near to Shirley Bridgeford's remains.

In the summer of 1958, Glatman went to the Diane Studio, one of the better agencies on Sunset

Boulevard. It was arranged for him to work with Lorraine Virgil, a woman who had signed on with the agency only the previous week. He was to pick her up at eight that evening

But the owner, of the studio, Diane, was suspicious of the man with the big ears, unkempt hair and smelly body odour. She phoned Lorraine and told her to be careful.

As soon as Lorraine got into his car and he started heading in the wrong direction alarm bells began to ring in her head. When she questioned him, he told her someone had already booked the studio and they were actually going to his own private studio.

As they sped down the freeway, she became even more anxious. Again she asked him where they were going. He said 'Annaheim'. However, she knew that they had already sped past the Annaheim turn-off. As she became more and more concerned, he began to shout at her to shut up. He swung the car dangerously into an exit ramp, crossing two lanes to get to it. Off the freeway, he stopped the car and asked her to put her arms out. He told her he was going to tie her up to keep her quiet and to emphasise his point, he pulled out his gun. Lorrraine reached for the door handle, trying to escape, but he grabbed her and they struggled. He tried desperately to wrap a coil of rope around her, but, unlike the other women, Lorraine fought back.

She grabbed the gun barrel and the gun went off, the bullet burning her thigh as it skimmed past. Suddenly, Glatman released his hold on her and she wrenched open the car door and fell out. He climbed out behind her, trying to haul her back into the car, but just as he grabbed her sweater, the pair were bathed in a pool of light. It came from the headlights of a patrol car.

She stumbled towards them, still holding the gun and fell at their feet. Glatman, meanwhile cowered by his car, sobbing and whimpering that it was not his fault.

When Glatman's mother left the prison after visiting her son, she said to the assembled press: 'He is not a vicious man – he is sick.' And that was his only hope of escaping the gas chamber; to prove that he was not of sane mind. Harvey did not want to be examined, though; he wanted to die. However, he was persuaded to undergo psychiatric tests. There was no point. The report said: 'he shows no evidence of a psychosis. He knows right from wrong, the nature and quality of his acts and he can keep from doing wrong if he so desires.'

Harvey pleaded guilty and on 15 December 1958, he was sentenced to die in the gas chamber.

On 18 September 1959, he entered San Quentin's

notorious 'green room'. The chamber door was locked shut at a minute past ten. He was strapped in by two minutes past ten. The cyanide pellets were released a minute later and by twelve minutes past ten, Harvey Glatman was dead.

He might have enjoyed it a bit more if he had been hung on the end of a rope of the finest quality hemp.

ALBERT DESALVO

THE BOSTON STRANGLER

For a few years in the 1960s, the city of Boston was gripped by panic. A spate of gruesome murders had forced women indoors, cowering behind double-locked doors and jumping at the slightest sound. The dead women were all single women, thirteen of them being killed between 14 June 1962 and 4 January 1964. The police believed the murders – six of them elderly victims and the remainder younger women – to be the work of one killer, the monster the media dubbed the Phantom Fiend, or, more famously, the Boston Strangler.

There was a sexual motive to each killing and a number of the victims were strangled with articles of their own clothing, sometimes tied at the neck in a macabre large bow.

The case has become one of the most famous in American criminal history with debate raging even now as to whether there was one killer or a number of them committing copycat murders. One commentator even speculates that there were seven or eight murderers operating in the Boston area at the time. The main question is, however, was Albert DeSalvo, the man who ultimately confessed to the killings, the Boston Strangler? Or was he just a small-time criminal and sex attacker who wanted the infamy and the money that a confession would bring, even when he was locked up for life on other convictions?

DeSalvo was a twenty-nine-year-old construction worker who had been arrested frequently for burglary. Born in Chelsea, Massachusetts in 1931, he was regularly beaten as a child by his abusive father. His criminal career started early and he was a frequent visitor to the police station on assault and other petty criminal charges. In 1948, he enlisted in the US Army, meeting his wife, Imgard during a posting to Germany. He received an honourable discharge from the forces in 1956.

Meanwhile, his first child was born, a girl who was unfortunately physically handicapped. At this time, his wife became concerned that if the couple were to have another child, it, too, would be handicapped. She refrained from having sex with DeSalvo which created problems for a man with an abnormally high sex drive.

A year before leaving the army, he had been arrested for molesting a young girl but the case never came to court. Nothing much changed after he left the army and he was arrested several times for breaking and entering. Nonetheless, he always had a job, working for a rubber company and then in a shipyard. As the new decade dawned, he was working in construction maintenance.

Everyone characterised him as a hard-working, devoted family man but there was another side to Albert DeSalvo which would pretty soon catch up with him.

In the early 1960s there had been a series of bizarre sexual offences in the Cambridge, Massachusetts area. A man in his late twenties would knock on an apartment door and if it was opened by a young, attractive woman, he would introduce himself as an employee of a modelling agency that was on the lookout for prospective models. He would claim that the woman's name had been passed to the agency and that, if she was interested, she could earn $40 an hour. He reassured them about the type of work, that it was all above board and would involve no nudity. All he needed to do, he said, was take their measurements. If they were up for it, he would take out a tape measure and take down their vital statistics. Someone from the agency would call them if they were suitable, he would say before taking his leave of them. In March 1961, DeSalvo was arrested as he tried to break into a house. He confessed to being the character that had become known as the 'Measuring Man' but was treated fairly leniently by the court, receiving an eighteen-month prison sentence. He was released in April 1962. Two months later the Boston Strangler killed his first victim.

Anna Slesers was an attractive fifty-five-year-old divorcee who had arrived from Latvia ten years earlier. Her son Juris found her on the evening of 14 June 1962 lying on the bathroom floor with the cord of her bathrobe tied tightly around her neck in an elaborate bow. Her bathrobe was open, her legs spread grotesquely wide apart and she had been sexually assaulted with an unknown object. The apartment looked as if it had been ransacked, the contents of her purse scattered on the floor and other items spread around the place. Although it looked like a robbery scene, detectives were puzzled to find a gold watch and Anna's jewellery intact.

Sixteen days later, sixty-eight-year-old Nina Nichols was found murdered in her apartment in Boston's Brighton area. Again, the apartment gave the appearance of having been burgled, but valuable items had been left untouched. Again her legs were spread and her housecoat and slip were pulled up to her waist. She had been sexually assaulted and the killer once again left his signature – two nylon stockings around her neck tied in a large bow. She was estimated to have died at around five in the afternoon but the Strangler was having a busy day. Between eight and ten that night, he struck again in the Boston suburb of Lynn.

Helen Blake, a sixty-five-year-old divorcee, had also been strangled with a nylon and her brassiere had then been fashioned into a bow on top of them around her neck. She was lying face down on her bed and had been sexually assaulted, like the others, with an object. This time the killer had taken a couple of diamond rings from her fingers and seemed to have tried unsuccessfully to break into a metal strongbox.

Naturally, the female inhabitants of Boston were terrified. The Police Commissioner warned women in the area to lock all their doors and windows and to be very wary of strangers. Police leave was cancelled and every detective on the force was ordered to work solely on the Strangler case. It made little difference. On 19 August, he struck again.

Seventy-five-year-old widow, Ida Irga, was strangled in the city's West End. As in the other cases, there was no sign of forced entry. In spite of all the warnings, she had let the man into her apartment. Once again, her legs were spread widely apart, this time balanced on individual chairs, exposing her private parts. She had been strangled with a white pillowcase before being sexually assaulted.

A day later, sixty-seven-year-old Jane Sullivan was found ten days after she had been murdered. She was on her knees in her bath, her feet up over the back of it and her head beneath the taps. She had been strangled with her nylons before being sexually assaulted with a broom-handle. This time he had not even bothered to ransack the apartment.

For three months there were no attacks but the police enquiries continued. Then, on 5 December, Sophie Clark became the only African-American Strangler victim. At twenty-one, she was a good deal younger than his other victims, but much of what police found matched the other killings, apart from the fact that semen was found on a rug near the body.

A neighbour told police that earlier that day a man had knocked at her door saying that he had been sent to repair her bathroom ceiling. When she let him in he started making comments about her figure. She became concerned as his manner changed completely. When she told him that her husband was asleep in the next room, he left, saying he had the wrong apartment. She described him as between twenty-five and thirty years old, of average height and with honey-coloured hair. He was wearing a dark jacket and green trousers. When they checked, they found that the building supervisor had not sent anyone to fix her ceiling. It had undoubtedly been the Strangler.

On 31 December, the boss of an engineering firm became concerned at the non-appearance at work of his secretary, Patricia Bisquette. He climbed through the apartment window with the help of the building's janitor and found her in bed with the covers up to her chin. When the cover was pulled down, they found nylons and a blouse tied around her neck.

In early March 1963, they found sixty-eight-year-old Mary Brown who had been beaten, strangled and raped. Then on 8 May, twenty-three-year-old Beverley Samans failed to turn up for choir practice. She was found with her legs wide apart on a sofa bed, her hands tied behind her and nylons encircling her neck in the customary bow. Unusually, however, the cause of death in this case were four stab wounds to her neck. The killer had stabbed her twenty-two times in all, eighteen of them in circles around her left breast. In this instance, the bow was tied around her neck purely as a signature.

The pressure on the authorities to find the Strangler was intense and, desperate, they turned to unorthodox methods such as clairvoyants and seers. Using these methods, a couple of suspects were uncovered but there was not enough evidence to link them with the murders.

The summer of 1963 passed without incident, but on 8 September Evelyn Corbin, a fifty-eight-year-old divorcee was found strangled by her nylon stockings with semen in her mouth. On 25 November, Joann Graff was discovered in her apartment in Lawrence. She had been raped and killed and wore a bow fashioned from stockings around her neck. Earlier that day, a woman and her husband heard someone sneaking around the corridors of the building. When they opened the door, they saw a man knocking on the door of the apartment opposite. When the man had asked if Joann Graff lived there, they told him she lived on the floor below. He went downstairs and they heard the door of the apartment below opening and closing. When they telephoned Joann ten minutes later, there was no reply.

The last victim was murdered on 4 January 1964. Two young women came home to find their roommate, Mary Sullivan strangled. As with the others, she wore the customary bow. This time, however, the Strangler had left a greetings card at her feet. It wished them 'A Happy New Year'. She had semen in her mouth and had been sexually assaulted with a broom-handle.

In November 1964, Albert DeSalvo was arrested for the October assault on a woman who woke to find him in her bedroom. He had put a knife to her throat and tied her feet and arms to the bedposts, in a spread-eagle fashion. He kissed and fondled her before apologising and leaving the apartment. She recognised him in an identity parade but he was also recognised by the police force in Connecticut who had been searching for a sexual attacker known as the Green Man from the green trousers he wore when he carried out his attacks. The Green Man was a prolific assailant, having assaulted four women in one day. DeSalvo admitted to assaulting 300 women and breaking into around 400 apartments.

There was no doubt that DeSalvo was going to prison for the rest of his natural life. He made sure of that when he confessed to being the Boston Strangler. In fact, he opened up the possibility of being condemned to death, although the death sentence had not been carried out in Boston for seventeen years. He displayed a remarkable knowledge of the crime scenes and of the murders themselves, but it has been speculated that all of this information could have been gleaned from the newspapers of the day. Furthermore, people have claimed, DeSalvo possessed a remarkably photographic memory.

Another theory put forward was that DeSalvo had learned about the details of the killings from the real Boston Strangler. A man called George Nassar was also an inmate of Bridgewater State Hospital where DeSalvo was being held. Nassar was actually recognised by several witnesses as being the Strangler.

DeSalvo, it has been suggested, confessed to being the Strangler because he had nothing to lose. He was going to be in prison for the rest of his days, anyway. Confessing could actually prove lucrative, with book and movie deals to be made. It was one way of providing for his family while he was inside.

The problem for the authorities was that his confession was inadmissible as evidence. At his trial for the Green Man attacks, his lawyer, F. Lee Bailey, attempted to prove that DeSalvo was not mentally competent to stand trial, using the thirteen murders to prove this. Witnesses described how he would break in or con his way into their apartments. Then, threatening with a knife or a toy gun, he would tie the woman up and strip her, fondle her breasts and demand fellatio or cunnilingus. He did not rape his victims, however. Expert witnesses testified to DeSalvo's paranoid schizophrenia but after only four hours deliberation, the jury found him guilty on all counts in the Green Man case. He was sentenced to life.

Albert DeSalvo was stabbed to death at Walpole State Prison in November 1973. Some say he was killed because he was about to reveal the real identity of the Boston Stranger. Others have said he was killed because of a prison drugs deal gone wrong. He was never charged with the gruesome murders committed by the Boston Strangler. No one was.

JOHN WAYNE GACY

The smell coming from the house was terrible, a rancid stench that neighbours commented on. His second wife, Carole thought there was a dead rat under the floorboards and exhorted Gacy to do something about it. He said it was a build-up of moisture in the crawl space under the new two-bedroom 1950s ranch-style house at 8213 West Summerdale Avenue in the Chicago suburb of Norwood Park. It was a tidy, family-friendly neighbourhood and the smell did not seem to put off the neighbours or his friends when John Gacy threw one of his parties. There he would be, the centre of attention, often dressed in his clown outfit, acting out the role of Pogo the Clown, a costume he wore to entertain children in local hospitals

Pogo the Clown appeared at other, more sinister times, however. David Cram met him one night. He worked for Gacy's contracting business and Gacy had given him the job of enlarging the crawl space under the house. While Cram was carrying out the work,

Gacy let him live in the house. One night Cram came into the house to find Gacy drunk and dressed in his clown outfit. Cram sat down and had a few drinks with his boss before Gacy tricked him into putting on a pair of handcuffs. Gacy suddenly changed, beginning to growl at Cram and spinning him round. 'I'm going to rape you!' he snarled. Cram somehow managed to knock Gacy to the ground, grabbed the key to the handcuffs and locked himself in his room. Few of Gacy's victims were so lucky and most of them lay in the ground under the house, slowly decomposing.

John Wayne Gacy was born on St. Patrick's Day, 1942, the second of the three children that Marion and John Gacy Sr. would have, and the only boy. His childhood was fairly normal apart from the fact that John Sr. was an abusive alcoholic who was violent towards his wife and to John Jr., who he beat with a belt and called a 'sissy'. The boy, meanwhile, did his best to win his father's affection, but it was a lost cause.

Aged eleven, Gacy Jr. had an accident when he was hit on the head by a swing. It caused a blood clot that was not discovered until he was sixteen. In the meantime, he had been suffering from blackouts and headaches. He was put on a course of medication that dissolved the clot. Then at seventeen, he began having heart trouble, although throughout his life it was never discovered exactly what was wrong with his heart.

Gacy failed to graduate from school, dropping out and travelling to Las Vegas where he worked as a janitor in a funeral parlour. It was a tough time for him. He was desperate to find a proper job and earn a decent wage but without a high school diploma, he was eventually forced to return to Chicago where he enrolled at a business college. He exhibited skill at selling and found a job as a management trainee with a shoe company. Before long he was managing a shoe shop in Springfield, Illinois.

Around this time, he became involved in community organisations such as the Chi Roh Club where he became membership chairman, the Catholic Inter-Club Council of which he was a board member, the Federal Civil Defence for Illinois and the Jaycees to which he devoted most of his time, becoming the vice-president and being voted 'Man of the Year'. He worked so hard for these organisations that at one stage he was hospitalised suffering from nervous exhaustion.

In September 1964 he settled down, marrying Marlynn Myers, whose parents owned a number of Kentucky Fried Chicken franchises in Waterloo, Iowa. Marlynn's father offered him a job at one of the restaurants and Gacy and his new wife moved to Iowa.

He worked hard, as ever, also throwing himself once again into volunteer work for the Jaycees.

Meanwhile, Marlynn gave birth to a son followed by a daughter.

It was all going so well. A lovely house in a good suburb, a good job, two nice kids. But soon the wheels began to come off. Rumours began to spread about John Gacy's sexual predilections. He always seemed to be surrounded by young boys, both in his charity work and at his restaurant and whispers suggested that he had made passes at more than one of them. In spring 1968 he was indicted by a Black hawk County grand jury. They alleged that he had committed sodomy with a teenager, Mark Miller. The boy explained to the court how Gacy had tricked him into being tied up when he was visiting him before violently raping him. Gacy, in his defence, claimed that Miller had actually engaged in sex with him willingly to earn money. He also suggested that he had been set up by Jaycee members opposed to a bid that he had been making for the presidency of the local branch of the organisation.

Gacy made a big mistake about four months later when he hired another boy, Dwight Andersson to beat Miller up. Miller fought back, however, when cornered by Anderssson and escaped to call the police. When they picked up Andersson, he told them that he had been hired by Gacy. He was brought in for psychiatric evaluation to see if he was fit to stand trial. They found him to be mentally competent, but that he was an antisocial personality. Gacy pleaded guilty to the sodomy charge and, aged twenty-six, was sent to prison for ten years, Marlynn divorcing him shortly after.

In prison, he stayed out of trouble, gaining parole just eighteen months into his sentence. On 18 June 1970, he was back on the outside and heading back to Chicago.

His father had died by now, leaving Gacy depressed that he had never properly reconciled with him or said goodbye. He moved in with his mother at West Summersdale Avenue, living in one half of the building while his mother and sisters owned the other half.

He seemed to be putting his life back together again after prison, but was unable to fight the urges that consumed him. He was charged with disorderly conduct, having picked up a young boy at a bus station and forced him to perform sexual acts on him. He was lucky, however. When the victim failed to show up on the day the trial started, the charges were dropped.

He married Carole Hoff on 1 June 1972 and she and her two young daughters moved into his half of the West Summersdale Avenue house. She knew about his past but was convinced that he had learned his lesson and was a changed man.

In 1974 he started a company, Painting, Decorating and Maintenance Incorporated, or PDM. It was noticeable that he hired only young men, but that was to keep the costs low. He did not have to pay teenagers as much as he would older men. However, some, especially his wife, Carole, were not fooled. Their marriage had started to come apart at the seams. Their sex life was practically non-existent and his moods were unpredictable. When she began to find magazines filled with photographs of naked young men she confronted him only to be informed that he preferred boys to women. In March 1976 they were divorced.

Gacy now launched a political career, hoping to one day run for public office. He was nominated for the street lighting commission, becoming secretary treasurer in 1975. Once again, however, the whispering started.

One story came from the previous year. In 1974, Gacy had volunteered his teenage workers to clean up the Democratic headquarters. He made a pass at one of the boys, sixteen-year-old Tony Antonucci, puling his old trick of handcuffing the boy. Antonucci managed to slip out of the cuffs, however, and he threw Gacy to the floor, handcuffing him. When Gacy promised he would not try anything again, Anonucci set him free.

Seventeen-year-old Johnny Butkovich worked for Gacy to fund his interest in cars. He drove a 1968 Dodge into which he put most of his time and money. When Gacy refused to pay him for two weeks, Johnny visited him on 17 July 1975 with a couple of friends. During an argument, Butkovich threatened to expose to the authorities the fact that Gacy was not paying tax on his workers' earnings. Nonetheless, Gacy still refused to pay the boy. They left and he dropped his two friends off at their house. He was never seen again.

But he was not the first of Gacy's victims. On 18 January, he had killed eighteen-year-old Timothy McCoy, whose body would not be identified until June 2007. After Butkovich, he murdered eighteen-year-old Darrell Sampson in April and then a month later it was the turn of Sam Stapleton, the youngest of his victims, at just fourteen years of age. Another seventeen-year-old, Michael Bonnin, disappeared in June 1976, while en route to meet his stepfather's brother at a railway station, followed a few days later by Billy Carroll. Billy had always been in trouble, sent to a juvenile home for stealing a purse aged nine and being caught in the possession of a gun at the age of eleven. By the time he was sixteen, he was making good money from pimping young boys to adult men. On June 13 he left home and was never seen again.

Gacy carried on killing through the summer and autumn – seventeen-year-old Rick Johnson in August and Kenneth Parker, a sixteen-year-old and fourteen-year-old Michael Marino in October. On 12 December, seventeen-year-old Gregory Godzik dropped his girlfriend off at her house. The next day police found his beloved 1966 Pontiac, but there was no trace of Gregory. He had worked at PDM for Gacy.

In January, nineteen-year-old John Szyc drove off in his 1971 Plymouth Satellite and was never seen again. However, a short while later, a youth was intercepted while driving the car. He told the police that the car was owned by a man in whose house he was living. They visited Gacy who explained very plausibly that Szyc had sold the car to him before he vanished. If the detectives had been a little more diligent in their investigation, they would have discovered that not only had the car been signed over to Gacy eighteen days after Szyc had disappeared but that the signature was false. They might also have learned that although Szyc had not worked for PDM, he had been a friend of Johnny Butkovich and Gregory Godzyk and was acquainted with Gacy.

Between January 1977 and December 1978, another thirteen boys and young men would die at Gacy's hands. In December 1978, fifteen-year-old Robert Piest disappeared from outside the pharmacy where he worked. His mother had come to pick him up but was told that he had gone to see a contractor about a job. He never returned from the meeting.

Lieutenant Joseph Kozenczak, leading the investigation, found out that the contractor with whom Robert had an appointment was John Wayne Gacy. He went to Gacy's house to invite him to the police station for questioning. Gacy, however, claimed that there had just been a death in his family and said he had some phone calls to make. He turned up at the station a few hours later but claimed to know nothing. However, Kozenczak ran a check on him and found out that he had gone to prison for sodomy. He obtained a search warrant and visited Gacy's house once again.

They uncovered a treasure trove of incriminating evidence such as Swedish pornographic films, the drugs amyl nitrate and Valium, a pair of handcuffs, a gun, clothing that was too small for Gacy, police badges and beneath the insulating material in the loft, an eighteen inch dildo. In one of Gacy's vehicles they discovered strands of hair that matched Robert Piest's.

Gacy was brought in but had to be released as the police as yet did not have enough evidence to hold him. However, he was put under round-the-clock surveillance. Eventually, they arrested him on charges of possessing marijuana that they had found in the house.

At last, however, thay found compelling evidence linking Gacy to one of the boys who had disappeared. A ring found at the house belonged to John Szyc. They also learned that three boys who had gone missing had all worked for PDM. Detectives returned to the house to resume their search. Under the house, amidst the stench of death, they found human remains.

On 22 December 1978, John Wayne Gacy confessed to killing at least thirty people, most of whom he told them were buried in the crawl space. He added, however, that he had run out of space and had thrown a number of his victims off a bridge into the Des Plaines River.

Victims were found with socks or underwear lodged in their throats. Gacy explained that he would slowly garrot his victims with a plank of wood as he had sex with their bound bodies. The socks and underwear were to stop their screams from being heard. By 28 December, twenty-seven bodies had been dug up from beneath the house, plus one in the river. They then took pickaxes to the patio and found more.

The trial began on 6 February 1980 in the Cook County Criminal Court in Chicago. Gacy's lawyers tried to make the jury believe that the murders were irrational and impulsive, that Gacy was insane and not in control of his actions. The case fell apart in the face of more than sixty prosecution witnesses who testified otherwise. The jury decided that John Wayne Gacy had raped and tortured his unfortunate victims in a premeditated and planned manner. They found him guilty and he was sentenced to death.

On 10 May 1994, he was executed by lethal injection at Stateville Correctional Center in Crescent Hill, Illinois. His last meal was a dozen deep fried shrimps, a bucket of original recipe chicken, French fries and a pound of fresh strawberries.

As execution parties took place outside the prison, with John Wayne Gacy t-shirts and other merchandise on sale, Gacy died without remorse. His last words to a correctional officer were, 'Kiss my ass.'

GARY M. HEIDNIK

She had fallen out with her boyfriend and stormed out of the house. But now what? It was rainy and cold and she really wished she had a ride. As she stared down the street into the rain, a silver and white Cadillac Coupe de Ville rolled slowly past her, splashing through the puddles at the side of the road. It stopped and the window rolled down. As she leaned in, the man in the driver's seat asked her if she needed a lift. She thought for an instant, taking in his neatly trimmed beard and blue eyes. His watch looked expensive and the car was to die for. At the same time, however, his clothes looked cheap and dirty. The rain was not easing off and she decided he was probably alright, just a guy doing a good deed, maybe a little lonely.

He drove her to a McDonalds and bought some coffee and then suggested they drive to his house.

The next morning, Josefina Rivera awoke to the full horror of her situation. She lay on a dirty mattress in the centre of a small room. Metal clamps circling her ankles. The previous night, as he had been showing her round the house, he had jumped her from behind and started to choke her. Then he had pushed her into this room and chained her up. The last she remembered was him going to sleep, his head on her lap.

His name was Gary Heidnik and he lived at 3520 North Marshall Street in North Philadelphia. This was not the first time he had done this.

He had been as failure at school and in 1961 joined the army, serving as a medic. However, his mental instability resulted in an honorable discharge after fourteen months. 'Schizoid personality disorder' was how they described his condition. A few years later, his mother committed suicide.

Heidnik's first brush with the law, in 1976, resulted from a rent dispute with a tenant of a house he owned. He fired a gun at the man, grazing his face with the bullet. Then, in 1978, he kept his girlfriend's cognitively disabled sister prisoner in a storage cupboard in the basement of his house. He had taken her out of the hospital in which she lived and, when she was eventually discovered, they found she had been raped and odorised. He was arrested, charged with kidnapping, rape, unlawful restraint, false imprisonment, involuntary deviant sexual intercourse and interfering with the custody of a committed person, receiving a custodial sentence of three to seven years. The sentence was overturned on appeal, however, and he spent three years in mental institutions, instead of prison. He came out in 1983.

He met a woman named Betty through a matrimonial service and after writing to each other for two years, they married. It was a bad marriage, however. She came home one night to find him in bed with three other women, with whom he forced her to have sex. He raped and beat her and after three months she left him. She was pregnant, however, giving birth to his son after she left him. He would never see the boy.

She went to the police and Heidnik was arrested yet again, on charges of assault, indecent assault, spousal rape and involuntary deviant sexual intercourse. He was lucky, however. Betty failed to show at the preliminary hearing and the charges were dropped.

In 1986, Heidnik hatched a plan to kidnap ten women who would have his babies. Josefina Rivera was the first. He picked her up on 26 November and took her home in his silver and white Cadillac Coup de Ville. She was impressed by his expensive jewellery and watch and by the 1971 Rolls Royce parked in his driveway. But she was puzzled by the seedy, dilapidated nature of the house, the cheap, dirty clothes he wore and the strange key he used to open his door. He told her he had fashioned it so that a part of the key remained in the lock. No one else could get in without that key.

Now, the following morning, she took in the room she found herself in. In the middle of the floor, a pit had been excavated. Heidnik returned and began to make this hole wider and deeper. To her increasing horror, he told her of his plan.

He had always wanted a large family and had already fathered four children by four different women, but no longer had contact with them. Now, he told her, he was going to kidnap ten women and get them all pregnant, so that he could have his family. He then raped her for the first of many times.

Later that morning she began to scream, hoping to alert neighbours or passers-by, but Heidnik came back and used a stick to viciously beat her. He then shoved her into the pit, covering it with wood and weighing it down.

Not long after, Heidnik removed the wood above her prison and helped her out of the pit. There was now another woman in the room and Heidnik introduced her as Sandy Lindsay. He had befriended her at the Elwyn Institute, a local hospital for the mentally and physically handicapped. She had already had an abortion when she had become pregnant with Heidnik's baby. When he had found out, he had been enraged and offered her $1,000 to have his baby. She refused and he kidnapped her.

Sandy's family began looking for her and he wrote

a note to her mother, posting it in New York and explaining that she was going away for a while.

Josefina and Sandy remained in the room together for weeks, being fed only now and then and being raped on a regular basis. They were beaten when they screamed for help and were punished by a visit to the pit whenever they breached one of his rules. He would also suspend them for hours at a time by one arm.

Meanwhile, Sandy's mother told the police that she thought her daughter was being held against her will by a man she knew as Gary and gave them Heidnik's address. When an officer went to the house, he got no reply and the case was dropped.

In late December, Heidnik brought another victim into the room, nineteen-year-old Lisa. He was just under a third of the way to his ten slaves. Twenty-three-year-old Deborah Dudley arrived shortly after. She was feisty, often fought back and was savagely beaten.

Heidnik now began to use the girls against each other, appointing one to be in charge when he went out and to report any infractions to him on his return. She would then be ordered to beat the others. If no one was reported to have misbehaved, he would beat them all anyway.

Their food depended on his changeable moods. Eventually, he reduced them to a diet of tinned dog food, beating them until they ate it.

A fifth girl arrived in the middle of January – Jacqueline, a petite eighteen-year-old. She was so small, in fact, that the shackles would not fit and he had to improvise with handcuffs. It was Josefina's birthday that day, and he surprised them with a meal of Chinese food. Josefina was rapidly turning into his favourite. He also thought – wrongly as it turned out – that she and Sandy were pregnant by him.

In early February, Sandy grew sick and after a week, she died. He dragged her upstairs and before too long the surviving girls were horrified to hear the sound of a power saw. They could only imagine what he was doing and when one of his dogs came into the room carrying a long, meaty bone, their worst imaginings were confirmed. Heidnik had ground up Sandy's flesh and began serving it to the girls mixed with dog food. He cooked other parts of the body and kept some in his fridge. When the house began to smell very badly as a result of the rotting flesh, the neighbours complained. Heidnik, smooth as ever, told the police officer who called round, that he had merely overcooked a roast dinner.

He became increasingly paranoid that the girls were plotting against him. Therefore, to put an end to this, he hung them from a beam, took a screwdriver and gouged inside their ears in an attempt to deafen them. The pain was intense and their screams were muffled by gags he had stuffed in their mouths. He left his favourite, Josefina, alone.

One day, when Deborah had been causing her usual share of trouble, he unchained her and took her upstairs. When she returned, she was uncharacteristically cowed. He had lifted the lid on a pot on his stove, she told the others, and inside was the head of Sandy Lindsay looking up at her. He showed her Sandy's ribcage cooking in the oven and opened the fridge to show her an arm and other parts of her body. He warned her that this is what would happen to her if she persisted in causing trouble.

He introduced new punishments, electrocuting the girls with bare wires, all except Josefina who now slept in his bed and spent time alone with him. One day, he ordered her to fill the pit with water and he threw the girls in. He then touched Deborah with the exposed wire and she writhed in agony before collapsing into the water. She was dead. He wrapped her body up and put it in his freezer.

As the weeks passed, he began to soften slightly towards the girls, letting them watch television and giving them mattresses, blankets and pillows. He also began to let Josefina accompany him on trips out of the house, on one of which they disposed of Deborah's body. On another, they found a slave to replace Deborah, a woman called Agnes. Josefina, however, was merely waiting for her chance. On 24 March, four months after she had been captured, she persuaded him to let her visit her family, on condition that she would bring back another woman. Naturally, as soon as her boyfriend opened the door to the apartment they shared, she blurted out her story. He found it hard to believe and so did the police when they arrived. When she showed them the manacle marks on her ankles, they began to believe her.

They arrested Heidnik at a petrol station and then went to 3520 North Marshall Street where they discovered the full horror of what he had done. The girls were chained to a beam and clad in nothing more than flimsy blouses and socks. They found Agnes cowering in the pit. In the kitchen they found an industrial food processor, recently used, and an oven dish containing a human rib. When an officer opened the fridge door, he was confronted by a human forearm lying on one of the shelves.

Incredibly, when he was first arrested, Heidnik was initially released, having claimed that the women had already been at his house when he moved in. This legal tactic has since become known as the 'Heidnik Defence' and has been used in countless cases around the world. Serial killer Jeffrey Dahmer used it, claiming that the body parts and vat of hydrochloric acid he used to dissolve the bodies of his victims were already in his apartment when he moved in. Heidnik turned out to be a wealthy man, with $550,000 in an investment account, registered in the name of the United Church of the Ministers of God, in an effort to avoid paying tax. But it proved little help to him when he was put on trial. In fact, it hindered him at one point. His smart investments served as proof, it was suggested, that he was perfectly sane. During the trial, he persistently denied the abuse of his victims, claiming, for instance, that Sandy Lindsay had been killed by the other captives because she was a lesbian.

He was found guilty on two counts of first degree murder, five of rape, six of kidnapping, four of aggravated assault and one of involuntary deviate sexual intercourse. He was sentenced to death and, as he had done throughout the trial, showed not an iota of emotion as the sentence was read out, claiming at one point that he wanted to be executed because the execution of an innocent man would help the case against the use of the death penalty in America.

Eleven years later, on 6 July 1999, at 10.29 pm, he was executed by legal injection. No one came forward to claim his body.

JEFFREY DAHMER

The night of 22 July 1991 was an oppressively hot one in Milwaukee, Wisconsin's largest city. Sweat dripped from the two police officers as they sat in their patrol car around the area near Marquette University at around midnight. Suddenly, they spied a short black man wearing what looked like a pair of handcuffs. The cuffs suggested he might have escaped from police arrest, and they apprehended him. When questioned, however, Tracy Edwards started to tell them about a 'weird dude' who had invited him up to his apartment, put the handcuffs on him and threatened him with a knife.

It sounded to the officers like a lovers' tiff, but they decided to investigate just the same and knocked on the door of apartment 213 in the Oxford Apartments at 924 North 25th Street. The door was opened by a well-groomed, good-looking thirty-one-year-old man with blond hair.

The blond man seemed very calm and rational and his apartment looked reasonably tidy. However, a strange smell pervaded the place. Without any fuss, he said he would go and get the key to the handcuffs which was in the bedroom. Edwards warned the officers that the knife he had been threatened with was also in there. So one of the officers went to check, but, on his way, saw that there were photographs lying around showing dismembered bodies and skulls in a refrigerator. He shouted back to his colleague to cuff the blond man and arrest him. The blond struggled and screamed as the other cop tried to put the cuffs on him, but the officer quickly managed to subdue him.

The first officer at this point decided to have a look in the fridge and when he opened the door, he froze in horror. A pair of eyes stared out at him from a disembodied head. 'There's a fucking head in the refrigerator,' he screamed.

The freezer contained a further three heads, wrapped tidily in plastic bags. In the closet in the bedroom he found a stockpot containing decomposed hands and a penis. On the shelf above were two skulls. There were male genitalia, preserved in formaldehyde and a range of chemicals – ethyl alcohol, chloroform and more formaldehyde.

There were also photographs in a filing cabinet, taken as the victims died as well as afterwards. A man's head was shown in one, lying in the sink;

another depicted a victim, cut neatly open from neck to groin; others showed victims still alive, in erotic and bondage poses.

Jeffrey Dahmer was born in Milwaukee in May 1960, to Joyce and Lionel Dahmer. The family later moved to Iowa, where Lionel was working on his Ph.D at Iowa State University and then on to Akron, Ohio.

At first, Jeffrey was an ordinary, happy little boy. At the age of six, however, he had surgery for a double hernia and his father believes he was never the same again. 'he seemed smaller, somehow more vulnerable . . . he grew more inward, sitting quietly for long periods, hardly stirring, his face oddly motionless,' he later wrote. And it did not get better as Jeffrey grew older and became tense and extremely shy. At his trial it was revealed that, as a child, he would collect dead animals and strip the flesh from them, on one occasion mounting a dog's head on a stake.

In his late teenage years, as others began to carve out notions of what they were going to do with their lives, Jeffrey seemed completely unmotivated. Instead of thinking about girls and a future career, he was locked into a gruesome fantasy world that featured death and dismemberment. By now he was drinking a lot and was considered a loner and alcoholic by classmates.

When Jeffrey was almost eighteen, his parents got

divorced, Lionel remarrying a few months later. It was around this time that Dahmer committed his first murder, killing Steven Hicks, an eighteen-year-old hitch-hiker. He invited Hicks back to his house, and killed him by hitting him over the head with a barbell because he 'didn't want him to leave'. He cut up his body and buried it in the woods behind his house.

Jeffrey enrolled for Ohio State University in 1978, but his drinking got in the way of his studies and he dropped out after just one semester. His father had now had enough of this strangely morose and mono-syllabic son of his and gave him a stark choice, either he got a job or joined the army. There was no way he was getting a job. So, Lionel drove him to the army recruiting office in January 1979.

Again, however, Dahmer's drinking made life impossible and, after being stationed in Germany for a couple of years, he was discharged early for drunken-ness. He moved in with his grandmother back in Milwaukee and got a job.

A string of offences followed – drunkenness, disorderly conduct and then indecent exposure and, in 1989, child molesting; he was reported to have masturbated in front of two boys. He persuaded the judge that he had, in fact, just been urinating and was put on probation for a year.

His father wrote later that his son had become 'a

liar, an alcoholic, a thief, an exhibitionist, a molester of children. I could not imagine how he had become such a ruined soul...There was something missing in Jeff... We call it a 'conscience' ... that had either died or had never been alive in the first place.'

Dahmer had, by this time, already killed his second victim, Steven Toumi, in a hotel room in September that year. He had picked him up in a gay bar and the two went to a hotel to drink and have sex. When he woke up next morning, Dahmer found Tuomi dead. He stuffed his body into a large suitcase, took it to the basement of his grandmother's house, had sex with it and masturbated over it before dismembering it and disposing of it in the rubbish.

His third victim was fourteen-year-old Native American, Jamie Doxtator and the fourth was Richard Guerro in March 1988.

His grandmother began to object to the noise and partying in Dahmer's room in the basement and so he moved into his own apartment in September, 1988. The next day he picked up thirteen-year-old Laotian boy called Sinthasomphone, who agreed to pose for photographs for $50. By grim coincidence, he was the older brother of a boy Dahmer would kill in 1991.

But he did not kill Sinthasomphone and, when the boy returned home, his parents realised he had been drugged. The cops picked Dahmer up on charges of sexual exploitation of a child and second-degree sexual assault. He pleaded guilty, claiming he thought the boy was older.

However, even as he awaited sentencing, he struck again, killing Anthony Sears, a handsome black model. Dahmer boiled the skull to remove the skin and painted it grey. He still had it when he was arrested.

In court, Dahmer put on the kind of manipulative performance only a psychopath can and he escaped the prison sentence being demanded by the prosecution, receiving five years' probation. He was also ordered to spend a year in the House of Correction under 'work release', which meant he went to work during the day and returned to jail at night. In spite of a letter from Dahmer's father, pleading with the judge not to release him without treatment, he was released after just ten months and went to live with his grandmother, before moving into his rooms in the Oxford apartments in May 1990.

Exactly a year later, a naked fourteen-year-old Laotian, Konerak Sinthasomphone, was found wandering on the streets of the Milwaukee neighbourhood in which Dahmer's flat was located. He talked to a couple of women, but was largely incoherent, having already been drugged by Dahmer. The police were called and took the boy back to Dahmer's flat to investigate. Dahmer told them, however, that

Konerak was his nineteen-year-old boyfriend and that they had had a drunken argument. The police handed the boy over to Dahmer, noting a strange smell in the apartment. Dahmer killed Konerak a few hours later.

From September 1987 to July 1991, Jeffrey Dahmer killed sixteen men, the majority of them black. Their ages ranged from fourteen to thirty-one and they all lived high-risk lifestyles.

The killing process was always the same. He picked his victim up at a gay bar, lured him back to the basement to pose for photographs, usually in return for payment, and then he would offer him a drugged drink, strangle him, masturbate on the body or even have sex with it. He would then cut the corpse up and get rid of it. He would take photographs throughout and would also sometimes boil the skull, to remove the flesh and then paint it grey to look like plastic, keeping it and other body parts as mementos. He began experimenting with various chemical methods and acids to dispose of the flesh and bones which would be poured down a drain or flushed away in the toilet. He often preserved the genitals in formaldehyde.

He told police that he also ate some of the flesh of his victims, claiming that by doing so, they would come alive in him again. He experimented with seasoning and meat tenderisers. Eating human meat gave him an erection, he said, and his fridge contained strips of human flesh.

Before they died, he sometimes tried to perform a kind of lobotomy on his victims. After drugging them, he would drill a hole in their skulls and inject muriatic acid into their brains. He was trying to create a functioning zombie-like creature that he could exercise ultimate control over and control, after all, was really what it was all about. Needless to say, most died during this procedure, but one, apparently, survived for a few days.

On 29 January 1992, the jury was selected for Dahmer's trial. He was indicted on seventeen charges of murder, later reduced to fifteen, to which he pled guilty, against the advice of his legal team, but claiming insanity. His counsel had to pursue the argument that only a person who was insane could have committed Dahmer's crimes. The prosecution, on the other hand, had to prove that he was legally insane, an evil psychopath who murdered his victims in cold blood and with malice aforethought.

Security in the courthouse was unlike that for any trial in Milwaukee's history. A sniffer dog was brought in to search for bombs and everyone entering the courtroom was searched and checked with a metal detector. A barrier, eight feet high, made of steel and bullet-proof glass was erected around the place where

Dahmer would sit, to protect him from the public.

The jury deliberated for five hours before deciding that Jeffrey Dahmer should go to prison and not hospital. He was found sane and guilty on all fifteen charges.

On the day of his sentencing, he read out a statement, an apology of a kind. 'Your Honour, it is now over. This has never been a case of trying to get free. I didn't ever want freedom. Frankly, I wanted death for myself. This was a case to tell the world that I did what I did, but not for reasons of hate. I hated no one. I knew I was sick or evil or both. Now I believe I was sick. The doctors have told me about my sickness, and now I have some peace. I know how much harm I have caused . . . Thank God there will be no more harm that I can do. I believe that only the Lord Jesus Christ can save me from my sins...I ask for no consideration.'

He got none. He was given fifteen life sentences, a total of 957 years in prison.

They sent him to the Columbia Correctional Institute in Portage, Wisconsin where, for his own safety, he was kept apart from the general prison population. The segregation was not entirely successful, however, as he was attacked by a razor-wielding Cuban one day while leaving the prison chapel. His wounds, however, were superficial.

On the whole, though, he was a model prisoner,

becoming a born-again Christian, and gradually persuading the prison authorities to allow him more contact with other inmates. This proved costly for him.

One day, he was paired with two other dangerous inmates on a work detail. One was Jesse Anderson, a white man who had murdered his wife and blamed it on a black man. The other was Christopher Scarver, a black schitzophrenic doing time for first-degree murder who suffered from delusions that he was God. It was a volatile combination, Scarver being partnered with one man, Dahmer, who had killed so many black men and another, Anderson, who had tried to blame a black man for a murder he had committed.

On the morning of 28 November 1994, the guard left the three men to get on with their work. He came back twenty minutes later to find Dahmer and Anderson lying in pools of blood. Dahmer's skull had been smashed in with a broom handle and he was pronounced dead at eleven minutes past nine in an ambulance on the way to hospital.

TED BUNDY

On 7 June 1977, Ted Bundy, vicious serial killer of young women, was visiting the library at the Pitkin County courthouse in Aspen during a recess in his trial for the murder of Caryn Campbell in January 1975. Bundy had trained as a lawyer and was doing some research. In a brief unguarded moment, he took advantage of an open window, even though it was a couple of floors up, and jumped, slightly injuring his ankle in the process. He was not wearing handcuffs or leg-irons and so was able to blend in with the shopping crowds in the ski resort of Aspen in Colorado. He walked towards Aspen Mountain, climbing to the top, but lost his way and missed two trails that would have led him to his destination, the town of Crested Butte. On a trail on the mountain, he met one of the search party, but the smooth-talking Bundy easily talked his way out of the difficult situation and carried on his way.

The authorities had immediately set up road blocks at all the town's main exits, but Ted was no fool. He knew that to try to leave town would result in certain capture. His main chance lay in staying where he was for the time being. Bloodhounds were brought in to sniff him out and a massive search team of 150 people began combing the town.

He lived off food he found in holiday cabins and camper vans for a few days but realised that he needed a car to make good his escape. He knew it would be alright because he believed himself to be invincible, better than everyone else and certainly better than the people who were scouring Aspen for him. On 13 June, having been on the run for six days, he stole a Cadillac but his erratic driving at a checkpoint alerted two deputies to him. He was recognised and re-arrested.

However, he was determined to get away and six months later he did, with murderous consequences.

He was being held in a jail at Glenwood Springs, Colorado where he had managed to accumulate $500 and had acquired a hacksaw blade that he later claimed had been given to him by another inmate. Using the blade, he sawed through the fixings for a small metal plate in the ceiling. Over a period of time, he had been dieting, trying to lose enough weight to be able to squeeze through the narrow opening in the ceiling. He had to be very careful and on one occasion, had come close to discovery when an inmate informed the prison authorities that he had heard someone moving around above him, but the matter was not investigated.

He knew he had to make his move soon when he was told that the trial, due to start on 9 January 1978, was to be held in Colorado Springs. Consequently, he would be moved to another prison for the duration. On 3 January, he bundled up books and files under his blanket to make it look as if he was sleeping in his bed, put on the warmest clothes he could find, removed the metal plate from the ceiling and squeezed up through the hole into the roof-space. He crawled to a spot directly above the linen closet of an apartment occupied by one of the jailers, dropped down into the apartment and strolled out of the prison.

It was bitterly cold and snowing, but he had soon stolen a car, an MG. The MG broke down in a blizzard in the mountains but with the snowstorm raging around him he succeeded in getting a lift from a passing car into the town of Vail. From Vail he took a bus to Denver and then booked a ticket on the 8.55 am flight to Chicago. Meanwhile, back at the prison, they did not discover his absence until noon that day, some seventeen hours after he had walked out the door. He had a good start on them.

From Chicago, he took a train to Ann Arbor, Michigan, where he caught up on some sleep at the

YMCA and watched a football game on television in a bar. He then stole a car and drove to Tallahassee in Florida where he rented a room in a boarding house, calling himself Chris Hagen. It was 8 January 1978.

Bundy lived off petty theft for a while, shoplifting and purse-snatching. He also stole a student identity card in the name of Kenneth Misner, using it to obtain a birth certificate and social security card. He was set up.

By the time of his initial arrest back in 1975, Ted Bundy had killed more than twenty women, beginning in May 1973 when he had murdered a hitch-hiker. His method was almost always the same. He would pretend that he was incapacitated somehow, wearing a plaster cast on an arm or using crutches and would seek help to carry something, such as books, to his car. When they arrived at the vehicle, he would bludgeon them with a crowbar and bundle them into the car. On one occasion, eight different witnesses came forward to tell police about a man called Ted, his left arm in a sling, who had been approaching people looking for help unloading his sailing boat from the back of his car. One told how she went with him, but on arriving at the car found that there was no boat. Many of them were students and the remains of a number of them were never found. He sometimes decapitated his victims with a hacksaw and kept several of the heads in his room or apartment. Some victims were disposed of on Taylor Mountain in Utah and he confessed to visiting the bodies long after death, applying make-up, lying with them and having sex with them. This would continue until putrefaction had set in.

Once again, as he hid out in Tallahassee in January 1978, he felt the need to return to his old habits. Conveniently, his room was in a building close to Florida State University and much of his time was spent wandering around the campus, even going unnoticed to lectures.

On the night of 14 January, he broke into the Chi Omega sorority house where he took the lives of two sleeping women students – Lisa Levy and Margaret Bowman – bludgeoning and strangling them. Levy was also sexually assaulted. He also bludgeoned, but did not kill, two other students as they lay in bed. Within half-an-hour, he was running out of the door of the building. As he did so, another student, Nita Neary, who was returning from a party, caught sight of him running down the stairs. She had been surprised to discover the door to the building lying open and had heard commotion in the rooms above. Hearing footsteps approaching, she ducked back out of sight in a doorway. Bundy, a blue woollen cap pulled low over his eyes and holding a log with a piece of cloth wrapped around it, bolted down the stairs and out of the door.

Nita ran upstairs and rushed to the room of a friend, telling her of the strange man she had seen. The two girls then went to the housemother's room to report the incident, but en route were shocked by the sight of one of the girls Bundy had failed to kill, staggering along a corridor, blood dripping from her head. They then found the other survivor, again with serious head wounds.

When police arrived, they found the two dead girls. Lisa Levy had been battered about the head with the log the man had been carrying and had then been strangled. There were bite marks on her buttocks and on her nipples. Her attacker had also sexually assaulted her with a bottle of hairspray. The other dead girl had been beaten severely on the head and then strangled with a pair of tights but had not been sexually assaulted or bitten.

Bundy was not finished for the night, however. A few blocks away, he broke into a house, beating and seriously injuring another student, Cheryl Thomas. Police arriving from the Chi Omega house, only minutes away, found her sitting on her bed, blood pouring from head wounds and a mask at the foot of her bed. It would prove to be identical to a mask taken from Bundy's car when he had been arrested in August 1975.

There was little evidence – only some hair samples on the mask and the teeth marks on Lisa Levy's body. Forensic science was not as sophisticated as it is today and, anyway, Ted Bundy was completely unknown to the Florida police.

A few weeks later, he struck again. Twelve-year-old Kimberley Leach from Lake City was reported missing. Last seen getting into a car, her body was found in a state park at Suwannee County eight weeks later. A few days earlier, however, a fourteen-year-old girl had a narrow escape when she was approached by a man claiming to be from the Fire Department. Fortunately for her, her brother turned up and she climbed into his car and drove off. The brother was suspicious of the man's story and took down the registration of the van he was driving. The girl's father, a policeman, had the number checked, finding it belonged to a man called Randall Regan whose licence plates had recently been stolen. When he discovered that the vehicle had also been stolen, the officer took his children to the police station to show them mug-shots of various villains, amongst which was a picture of Ted Bundy. They recognised him instantly as the man who had approached the girl.

Bundy, meanwhile, was on the move again, heading for Pensacola in a stolen car, an orange Volkswagen Beetle. Officer David Lee spotted this striking-looking car at 10 pm on 15 February and when he ran a check on the car's registration, found it to be stolen. He set off in pursuit, his blue lights on.

Initially, Bundy fled, but then pulled into a petrol station where he stopped. Officer Lee ordered him out of the car, shouting at him to lie on the ground. As he tried to put the cuffs on Bundy, however, the killer spun round onto his back and began to struggle. He managed to push the policeman off, scrambled to his feet and ran away. Lee took aim and fired his gun at the fleeing figure. He missed, but Bundy staggered and fell to the ground, pretending to have been hit. Officer Lee approached him, but again Bundy got up and started fighting. This time, however, the policeman overcame him, managing to get the handcuffs on him. Bundy was soon in custody again and this time there would be no escape.

They linked him to the disappearance of Kimberley Leach through evidence found in the van he had used – there were fibres of material that originated from his clothes – her blood type was found on the van's carpet and Bundy's semen and blood type were found on her underwear. He was charged with her murder and shortly after, with the murders of the two Chi Omega girls.

His past began to emerge. He had been born at a home for unmarried mothers in Vermont and though the true identity of his father remains unknown, many have suspected over the years that his mother Louise's violent and abusive father, Samuel Cowell, was actually his father. Back then, however, Samuel and his wife, Eleanor, pretended that Bundy was in fact their child. For the first part of his life, therefore, he believed that his mother was his sister.

In 1951, now living in Tacoma with relatives, Louise met and married a man called Bundy and Ted was adopted by him, taking his surname. Bundy was a good pupil at his school but remained shy and introverted, later claiming that he did not understand social behaviour and found it impossible to make friends. He also became fascinated with images of sexual violence and had evolved into a petty crook, twice being arrested for theft.

At Seattle's University of Washington in 1967, he befriended a fellow student, Stephanie Brooks, but she ended the relationship following her graduation. Bundy is said to have changed around this time, becoming much more assertive and focused. He found work managing the Seattle office of Nelson Rockefeller's presidential campaign while he studied psychology at Washington University. He did well, graduating as an honours student. He also began a relationship with an unmarried mother, Elizabeth Kloepfer, that would continue for six years.

In 1973, he bumped into his former flame Stephanie Brooks again on a trip to California, re-kindling his relationship with her, while still continuing his involvement with Elizabeth Kloepfer. He was very solicitous towards her and they even planned to marry. Two weeks after proposing, however, he unceremoniously dumped her. It was his way of taking revenge on her for dumping him several years previously. Several weeks later, he launched his career as a serial killer and during his rampage, co-eds began disappearing at the rate of roughly one a month.

His eventual downfall occurred on 15 August 1975 after he failed to stop for a police officer. When his car was searched, officers discovered a ski mask, a crowbar, handcuffs, an ice-pick and other material thought at the time to be the tools of a burglar. His car was connected to a failed kidnapping he had perpetrated in November the previous year when he had persuaded Carol DaRonch at a shopping mall that he was a police officer and that someone had been seen trying to break into her car. She went with him back to the car where he asked her to accompany him to the police station. En route, he suddenly tried to put handcuffs on her but she fought him, only just stopping him from bringing the crowbar down on her head. She managed to escape from the car and he drove off, kidnapping and killing seventeen-year-old Debbie Kent at a nearby high school within an hour of leaving DaRonch. Combing the area of the school, however, detectives found a small key. It fitted DaRonch's handcuffs which, it transpired, were identical to the ones now found in Bundy's car.

At his trials for the murder of Kimberley Leach and the Chi Omega sorority girls, Bundy used his previous law school experience – he had studied law briefly at Washington University – but the evidence was overwhelming. He was sentenced to die in the electric chair.

On 24 January 1989, having exhausted the appeals process Theodore Robert Bundy was executed at the State Prison at Starke in Florida. His last words before 2,000 volts pulsed through his body were, 'I'd like you to give my love to my family and friends'.

ED KEMPER

THE CO-ED KILLER

Edmund Emil Kemper III had always been a little odd, but had been behaving increasingly strangely since the break-up of his parents' marriage. At the age of nine, he had buried the family cat alive in the back garden of his house in Burbank, California. He had then dug it up, decapitated it and mounted its head on a stick. He dreamt of murdering people and would cut up his sister's dolls and engage in strange sex games with them. His behaviour was not helped by his mother locking him in the basement at night for eight months, fearing that he would molest his sisters.

In 1963, aged fifteen, his mother was finding it impossible to control him and after he had run away from his father's house, he was sent to live with his father's parents on their remote Californian farm at North Fork, high in California's Sierra Mountains. Life there was very boring for Kemper. He was away from school and isolated from his normal life. One day there was an argument when his grandmother insisted that he stay home and do housework instead of going into the fields to work with his grandfather. He picked up a rifle to go outside and shoot something but when she told him not to shoot any birds he turned round and fired a bullet into her head before shooting her in the back. He heard his grandfather arrive and killed him with a single shot as he got out of his car. Kemper said to police interviewing him: 'I just wondered how it would feel to shoot Grandma.'

He was diagnosed as suffering from paranoid schizophrenia and detained in Atascadero State Mental Hospital for the criminally insane.

In 1969, aged twenty-one, standing six feet nine inches tall and weighing three hundred pounds, he was released into the care of his mother, Clarnell. The doctors considered Clarnell to be at the root of most of Kemper's problems and warned him not to go back to her, but he did. Needless to say, life with her was no better than it had been before. They argued violently and she would blame him because she could not get any dates. Indeed, she seemed to get on better with the students at the University of Santa Cruz where she worked as a secretary than she did with her own son. He eventually moved out, to Alameda near San Francisco, sharing a rented flat with a friend. Most of his time was spent cruising around the California highways, picking up young, female hitch-hikers.

Kemper held down a job at a Green Giant canning factory and, still a virgin, worked out his sex and violence fantasies with pornography and detective magazines. In 1971, he had a motorcycle accident for which he received fifteen thousand dollars in compensation. He was unable to work and now had time and money on his hands.

In spring 1972, Kemper after yet another tempestuous argument with his mother, he went out looking for a victim on whom he could vent his anger. He quickly picked up two hitch-hikers, Mary Anne Pesce and Anita Luchessa, eighteen-year-old students making their way back to Stanford University. He pulled a gun on them and informed them that he was going to rape them. Pulling off onto a side road, he made one girl climb into the boot of the car. He handcuffed the other one and then stabbed and strangled her. Opening the boot, he stabbed the other girl. He then drove the bodies back to the apartment where he decapitated them and cut off their hands.

Returning to his apartment that night, he removed the clothing from the bodies and had sex with them. The next day he buried the heads and bodies in different places in order to make it difficult for them to be identified if discovered. He got rid of the clothes in remote parts of the Santa Cruz mountains. One of the girls' heads was found the following August, but without the remainder of her body, it was impossible to prove how she had died.

In September he struck again. He picked up a fifteen-year-old Asian ballet student, Aiko Koo, and told her she was being kidnapped. When she became hysterical, he pulled his gun out and told her to be quiet. North of Santa Cruz, he smothered her until she lost consciousness and then strangled her and had sex with her dead body. He then visited his mother and chatted with her while the body lay in the car's boot. Returning to his apartment, he had intercourse again with the corpse and in the morning he cut it up and drove it out into the country where he buried the hands and the torso in different places again. This time, he kept the head in the boot and it was still there when he visited a psychiatrist.

Around this time, in November 1972, Kemper's records were sealed, meaning that they no longer existed as a blemish on his character. His mother had been fighting for this and he had been examined by two psychiatrists who agreed that he had made good progress. Little did they know what kind of progress he had really been making and it was not long before his murderous instinct forced him to strike again.

He picked up a girl one afternoon and killed her

with a single shot from the new gun he had purchased; with his records sealed he could now own a gun. He drove her back to his mother's house and hid her in the closet of his bedroom. The next morning, when his mother left for work, he dismembered the corpse, removing the bullet from the head, in case it was found. He tossed the parts off a cliff into the sea, some of them being found within days. He buried the head in the garden under his mother's window. 'She always wanted people to look up to her,' he later joked.

By now, of course, there was panic and security was heightened everywhere. Papers spoke of the Co-ed Killer and girls were warned to be careful, but he still managed to pick two up on the UCSC campus less than a month later. He had shot them even before he had driven off university property. The guards at the gate failed to spot the bodies slumped inside the car and he drove them to his mother's where he decapitated them in her driveway while she was in the house. It gave him a thrill to have her so close when he did it. He took the heads into his bedroom and masturbated over them. For a couple of days he drove around with the bodies in the car before disposing of them in the usual way, taking care to remove the bullets.

A few months later, he bought another gun, a .44,

but a sheriff noted the name on the record of the sale of the gun and decided to pay Kemper a visit. He asked Kemper for the pistol and said it would be retained by the authorities until a court decided whether it was lawful for him to own a gun. Kemper went to the boot of the car and took the pistol out, handing it to the officer who then left. But Kemper was shaken. He had come very close to being found out. The car, after all, had a bullet hole in it and had been awash with blood very recently. He realised that it was time for the endgame; he would kill his mother and then give himself up.

On 20 April, Kemper and his mother had their usual argument and, as usual, she humiliated him. At five, next morning, while she slept, he smashed her skull with a claw-hammer and slit her throat. He raped the corpse and cut her head off. He placed it on the mantle piece and used it as a dartboard. He then called Sally Hallett, a friend of his mother, and invited her to the house for a surprise dinner. When she arrived he clubbed her, strangled her and decapitated her. He then slept in his mother's bed before going out and driving for miles through a number of states. He stopped in Colorado, called the police and gave himself up. It was over.

Ed Kemper confessed to everything, waiving his right to an attorney. He told them that he had kept hair, teeth and skin of some victims as trophies. He also told them that he had sliced some flesh off two of his victims' legs, and cooked it in a macaroni casserole. When asked what punishment would fit the crimes he had committed, he replied: 'Death by torture.'

The trial was over very quickly. Psychiatrists testified that he had been sane when committing the murders and he was found guilty of eight counts of first degree murder and sentenced to life imprisonment. He has proved to be a quiet, well-behaved inmate.

RICHARD SPECK

It was unmistakably a man, but he had women's breasts and was wearing blue silk panties. He paraded around, took a bit of cocaine, had sex with another inmate of the prison and said: 'If they only knew how much fun I'm having, they'd turn me loose.'

The video tape had been sent anonymously to Chicago television news editor, Bill Kurtis, in 1996. It had been made in Stateville Prison in 1988 and depicted scenes of sex and drug use. At the centre of it was the bizarre spectacle of nurse-killer, Richard Speck, who had died in 1991 and whose breasts were the result of hormone treatments that had been smuggled into the jail. Speck joked when asked why he had killed eight nurses on the night of 14 July 1966. 'It just wasn't their night,' he says. Then asked how he has felt since then, he replies, coldly: 'Like I always feel. Had no feelings.'

Speck was born, the seventh of eight children, on 6 December 1941, in the small town of Kirkwood, Illinois. His parents, Benjamin and Mary, were religious people, but his father died when Richard was six years old and Mary, having moved the family to Fair Park, near Dallas, Texas, remarried. Her new husband, Carl Lindbergh, was the antithesis of Benjamin Speck. He drank, was abusive and was often gone from the family for long periods. He hated Richard and Richard hated him.

By the age of twelve, Richard Speck was already going off the rails. He was a poor student, eventually dropping out in ninth grade, and had discovered alcohol. In his defence, however, it has been suggested that the alcohol was used to counter the headaches from which he suffered. These were apparently a direct result of head injuries he suffered throughout childhood – aged five, he was injured while playing in a sandbox with a claw hammer; he twice fell out of trees and at fifteen, he ran into a steel girder, injuring his head yet again.

Aged nineteen, he had a tattoo done which would become significant in later life. It read: 'Born to Raise Hell' and that is just what he did. By his mid-twenties, a drug-dependent alcoholic, he had thirty-seven arrests to his name. Charges included public drunkenness, disorderly conduct and burglary.

At twenty he had married fifteen-year-old Shirley Malone and fathered a child, but the marriage ended in 1966. According to Malone, Speck often raped her at knifepoint, claiming that he needed sex four to five times each day. He spent a large part of their marriage in prison. He told people he wanted to kill his ex-wife, but he never got round to it and, heading back to Illinois, in a three month period, he seems to have vented his anger on other women.

The first to die was Mary Pierce, a divorcee who had rejected his advances. On 13 April, her naked body was found, strangled, in a shed behind the bar where she worked. A few days earlier, a sixty-five-year-old woman had been grabbed from behind and raped by a man with a southern drawl whose description matched that of Speck.

The cops were on to him and, tracing him to the Christy Hotel, they found jewellery and a radio belonging to the rape victim. Other items from burglaries he had carried out were also discovered. But Speck was gone.

He landed work on the iron ore barges of the Great Lakes, but was dismissed for repeated drunkenness on the job as well as his violent behaviour. On 2 July he was in the area of Indiana Harbor. Not far from there, that day, three young girls disappeared and their bodies were never found. All that remained were their clothes, left in their car.

On 13 July, Speck was drinking heavily in the Shipyard Inn in south Chicago. As ever, he was angry and depressed. He had tried to get work on a ship bound for New Orleans but had been unable to do so. Therefore, having consumed quantities of pills and booze, he decided that it was time to 'raise some hell.' He set off towards one of the nearby student dormitories of the South Chicago Community Hospital. In his possession was a hunting knife, a pocket-knife and a .22 caliber pistol.

For the past several weeks, Speck had been watching the women coming and going from the buildings, sunbathing in a nearby park and leaving the building to attend their classes. He knew their schedules well enough to know that, at that time of night, they would be home and in bed.

Twenty-three-year-old Cora Amurao, a nursing exchange student from the Philippines, opened the door at Jeffrey Manor, a two-storey townhouse occupied by student nurses. In front of her stood Speck, dressed in dark clothing, reeking of alcohol, high as a kite and brandishing the pistol and the knife. 'I'm not going to hurt you,' he told the terrified woman. 'I'm only going to tie you up. I need your money to go to New Orleans.'

He went into the house and got the five other nurses there at the time out of bed. All six were herded into one room where he tied them up and sat them in a circle on the floor. In the next hour another three arrived home from evenings out. They, too, were tied up and sat on the floor.

Twenty-year-old Pamela Wilkening was the first to die. He took her into another room and stabbed her in the chest before strangling her with a torn piece of bedsheet. Returning to the room, he selected twenty-year-old Mary Jordan and twenty-one-year-old Suzanne Farris. He took them into another bedroom and stabbed Jordan in the heart, neck and eye. Turning to Farris, he stabbed her eighteen times and then strangled her already dead body. He also raped her.

Nina Schmale, twenty-four years of age, was now taken to a room where he told her to lie on a bed. He cut her throat and strangled her. Valentine Pasion, twenty-three, was stabbed in the throat and Nerlita Gargullo was stabbed four times and then strangled. He washed his hands before returning to carry Patricia Matusek into the bathroom where he kicked her in the stomach and strangled her.

For the next twenty minutes he raped Gloria Davy upstairs and then took her down to the ground floor where he raped her anally with an unknown implement. Then he strangled her, before leaving the house, thinking everyone was dead.

Unknown to Speck, however, Cora Amurao, who had first opened the door to him, had slithered under one of the beds in the room and pressed herself up against the wall. She lay there, terrified, until 6 am to be certain that he had gone. Then she clambered out on to the balcony shouting: 'My friends are all dead! I'm the only one alive! Oh God, I'm the only one alive!'

When the police arrived on the scene, the house resembled a charnel house. The carpet squished underfoot from the amount of blood it had soaked up. Experienced policemen took one look and then ran outside to throw up. There was one strong clue, however, to the killer's identity. The neatness of the square knots used to tie the girls up suggested that he was, most likely, a seaman.

The cops went to work and within hours knew their killer was Richard Speck. Cora, although heavily sedated, had managed to give a description of the killer and a gas station attendant recalled that one of his managers had been talking about a guy of the same description who complained about missing a ship and losing out on a job just a couple of days before. A police sketch artist drew an uncanny likeness of Speck, which was taken to the Maritime Union Hall. Someone there remembered an angry seaman who had lost out on a double booking - two men had been sent for one job – and he was able to retrieve the crumpled assignment sheet from the wastebasket. The sheet gave the name of Richard Speck.

CHARLES VI

Charles VI (1368–1422) as king of France from 1380 and dubbed with the name 'the Foolish' and also 'Charles the Mad'. The French monarchy had its share of mad rulers and Charles VI was certainly one of them. Throughout his life he suffered from bouts of madness which, based on his symptoms, would today have been diagnosed as schizophrenia.

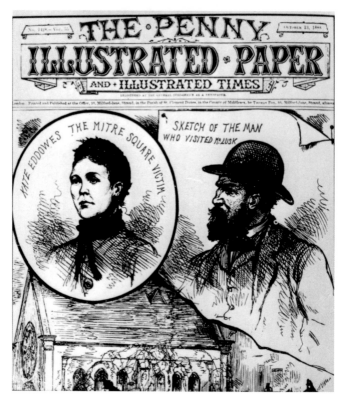

An extract from the 'Penny Illustrated News', 13 October 1888. This illustration is connected with the infamous Jack the Ripper murders and shows one of the London victims, Kate Eddowes, and a sketch of a man who was thought to be implicated in the case. The murders were never solved.

The run-down garden of Number 10, Rillington Place, London, in 1953 – the house where serial killer John Reginald Christie (inset) lived and buried the bodies of his victims.

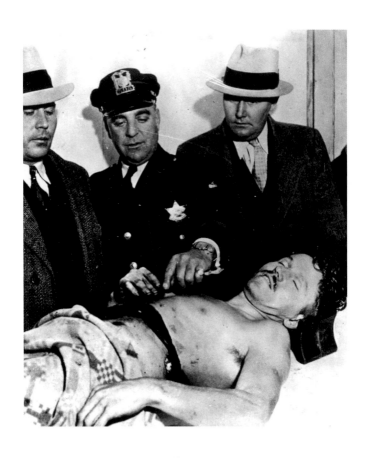

A picture of Lester M. Gillis aka George 'Baby Face' Nelson in 1934. He was a member of the infamous Dillinger gang and was regarded as the most psychotic outlaw of the 1930s. He can be seen here lying on an undertaker's slab following his assassination.

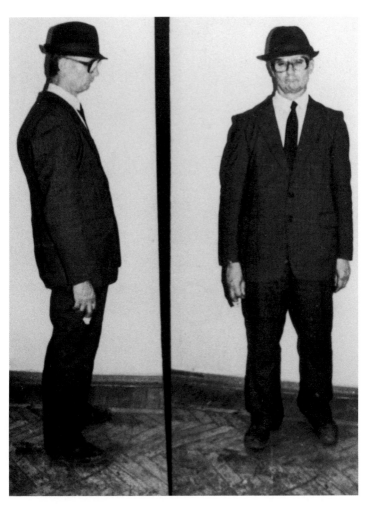

Two full-length portraits of Russian serial killer Andrei Chikatilo. Chikatilo, who was arrested in late 1990, was convicted and executed for the murders of more than fifty people over a twelve-year period.

When the graves were full and gravediggers could no longer keep up, the corpses were fed to crocodiles in the Nile. This was the evil dictatorship of General Idi Amin Dada, who ruled Uganda with an iron fist from 1971 until 1979. It is estimated that as many as 300,000 people died under his reign of terror.

French self-confessed serial killer Michel Fourniret arrives in a police car to attend his trial at the Charleville-Mezieres courthouse, northern France, on 20 May 2008. Fourniret, sixty-five, is being tried, with his wife Monique Olivier, for the rape and murder of six young women and teenage girls aged between twelve and twenty-one. This evil psychopath either strangled, stabbed or shot his victims.

The mass murderer Aileen Wuornos remains strangely intriguing even after her execution in 2002. She claimed that all her seven victims had attempted to rape her, but her aggressive nature inspired contempt in most people who had any dealings with her. Wuornos's sad, but compelling, story was turned into a Hollywood film entitled 'Monster' in 2004.

Speck was on the loose for the next few days, drinking and crashing in cheap hotels in Chicago. The police were always close on his tail and at one point he was interviewed by a couple of them in his room because he had a gun. They did not realise who he was, however. Eventually, he was staying in a hotel in Skid Row, the Starr. He had drunk a pint of cheap wine and, feeling suicidal, he smashed the bottle and dragged its jagged ends across his wrist and inner elbow, severing an artery. He then lay, bleeding on the bed in his tiny cubicle in the hotel, surrounded by newspapers carrying his picture. He called out for water and help, but was ignored.

Eventually, one of the down-and-outs Speck had been drinking with in the last few days recognised Speck's picture and, having returned to the hotel, discovered him lying on the bed. He called the police anonymously to tell them where he was, but no patrol car was dispatched.

Instead, Speck was taken to Cook County Hospital, the very same hospital in which the nurses' bodies lay. Leroy Smith, a first year resident examined Speck and thought there was something familiar about him. He washed the blood off his arm and there it was – the tattoo saying 'Born to Raise Hell'. He found a newspaper and confirmed that it was Speck from the photo. When Speck asked for water, Smith held him tight by the neck and asked him: 'Did you give water to the nurses?'

The trial began on 3 April 1967, in the Peoria County Courthouse, in Peoria, Illinois, three hours south of Chicago. Cora Amurao testified at the trial and a dramatic and defining moment came when she was asked if she could identify the killer of her fellow students. She rose from her seat in the witness box, walked across the courtroom to stand in front of Speck. She pointed at him, almost touching him, and said: 'This is the man'.

On 15 April 1967, after forty-nine minutes of deliberation, the jury found Richard Benjamin Speck guilty of all eight murders. The court was cleared and Judge Paschen sentenced Speck to death in the electric chair. He avoided it, however, when the Supreme Court declared capital punishment unconstitutional. Instead, Speck was sentenced to fifty to 100 years in prison for each count of murder – a total of 400 to 1,200 years.

In Stateville Prison, in Joliet, he was known as 'birdman' after the *Birdman of Alcatraz* due to the fact that he kept a pair of sparrows that had flown into his cell. He was often caught with drugs or distilled moonshine, however, and was far from a model prisoner. Punishment for such breaches never phased him. 'How am I going to get in trouble? I'm here for

1,200 years!' His time in prison, however, was cut short when he died from a massive heart attack on 5 December 1991.

No one claimed his body. He was cremated and his ashes were dispersed in an unknown location.

RICHARD RAMIREZ

THE NIGHT STALKER

Ricardo Leyva, aka Richard Ramirez, loved his cousin Mike. He was older and had even fought in Vietnam. He had killed people and tortured them. He had raped women. And he had the photographs to prove it. Killing made you feel good, Mike told him on one of the days when they would sit smoking pot and drinking beer. You have power over others, you feel like a god. Richard listened in awe, taking it all in.

Mike would take him hunting in the desert at night and would show him how to kill things. One day, however, Mike's wife nagged him one time too many about getting a job. He pulled a gun and shot her in the face, killing her. The teenage Ricardo was in the room and witnessed it. He was covered in the dead woman's blood. Mike was found to have killed her while temporarily insane and was sent to a secure hospital.

Not long after that, the epileptic Ramirez, youngest in a family of five, began to go off the rails, smoking marijuana to excess, the habit funded by theft and doing nothing with his young life. He had dropped out of school aged fourteen, embracing a diet of junk food that had rotted his teeth, giving him chronic halitosis that would be recalled with horror by many of his later victims. Ramirez would become one of the most horrific and frightening of serial killers, the devil-worshipping nightmare known as the 'Night Stalker', a bogey man who gave a serious boost to sales of alarm systems in a terrified California in the 1980s.

He had been born in El Paso in Texas in 1960. He was a quiet boy and his parents seemed decent enough. Behind closed doors, however, his father's temper would sometimes explode, resulting in a beating for one of the children. Ramirez was so afraid of his father that he would hide in a local cemetery, occasionally staying there all night. It is also possible that he was abused by a male teacher. He was not a popular boy, set apart somewhat by his epileptic seizures. He had to stop playing football as a result and coupled with his thin, girlish appearance, it forced him into being a loner. In 1978, he left it all behind when he moved to Los Angeles but life still proved difficult for him. In his first few years, he experienced several run-ins with the law, for possession of dope and car theft.

Somewhere along the road, he had become fascinated by Satanism. His father blamed his penchant for marijuana, but he loved satanic rock music, especially Australian heavy metal outfit AC/DC's song *Night Prowler* from the album Highway to Hell. The words to this song were like a prediction of what was to come.

Not much is known about his first few years in Los Angeles. He graduated from simple theft to breaking and entering homes to steal whatever valuables he could get his hands on. There is speculation that he might have lingered a little longer than necessary in some of the homes he burgled, perhaps even photographing the inhabitants as they slept.

The first time he killed was on 28 June 1984. Jennie Vincow lived in Glassel Park and he was able to get into her house through an open window. He slashed her throat so badly that she was almost decapitated. He also stabbed her frenziedly and sexually assaulted her before ransacking her apartment and stealing her valuables.

Eight months afterwards, he felt the urge to do it again. On 17 March 1985, twenty-year-old Angela Barrios came home from work to the condominium she shared with thirty-four-year-old Dayle Okazaki in Rosemead, a town north of LA. As she got out of her car in the garage, she sensed a figure behind her. It was a man dressed in black with a baseball cap pulled low over his face. In his hand was a gun and it was pointing at her. Suddenly, he fired the weapon and she fell to the ground, a pain in her right hand. The bullet had miraculously struck the car keys she was holding before ricocheting away. She pretended that she had been hit more seriously and he walked round her and through the door leading into the building from the garage. She waited a moment before springing to her feet and running out of the garage. But, to her horror, she bumped straight into her attacker, who was coming out of the condominium's front door. She staggered away from him back towards the garage, expecting at any moment to feel the heat of a bullet as he finished her off. Instead, however, she watched as he slowly put the gun into his belt at his waist and took off.

She was safe, but her housemate did not have such luck. He lay dead in a pool of blood on the kitchen floor, shot in the forehead.

Ramirez was not finished for that night, however. Nearby, a police officer came upon a car with its engine running. Inside was a thirty-year-old woman of Taiwanese origin who had been shot several times. Tsian-lian Yu died before the arrival of the ambulance he had summoned.

Three days later, he killed an eight-year-old girl in Eagle Rock. Age did not seem to matter for Ramirez. It was the killing he enjoyed.

A week later, he struck again, but this time it went according to the crazed plan he had devised in his twisted mind.

Sixty-four-year-old pizzeria-owner, Vincent Zazzara and his forty-four-year-old wife were discovered by their son Peter. Vincent had been killed instantly by a single shot to the temple, while Maxine lay on their bed, her eyes horrifically gouged out. She had been repeatedly stabbed and a T-shaped wound had been carved in her left breast. Thankfully, it seemed she had also died instantly from a bullet wound and the work with the knife had been carried out afterwards.

Six weeks later, he woke Harold and Jean Wu in their bedroom. He shot sixty-year-old Mr Wu in the head before beating sixty-three-year-old Mrs Wu, to force her to tell him where they kept their money. He tied her up and then searched the house before returning to the bedroom where he viciously raped her.

Mr Wu, meanwhile, had miraculously survived his bullet wound and crawled to a telephone, dialing 911. An ambulance and patrol car arrived shortly after, but he died in hospital. Mrs Wu was later able to give a description of the attacker.

It became clear to the police that this was the scenario preferred by this killer. He would first dispose of the male of the house before doing what he wanted with the woman.

On 29 May, he killed two elderly women in Monrovia. Malvia Keller was eighty-three and her invalid sister, Blanche, was eighty. They were bludgeoned to death with a hammer that had been wielded so viciously that its handle had split. Interestingly, a pentagram, a design often associated with Satan, was drawn in lipstick on Malvia's inner thigh. A second one had been drawn on the wall above Blanche's body.

On 30 May, Ruth Wilson was shocked awake by a bright light shining in her eyes. It was a flashlight held by a man who had broken into her Burbank home and was now holding a gun to her head. He ordered her to go to the bedroom of her twelve-year-old son where he held the gun to his head, handcuffed him and locked him in a cupboard. She gave him what valuables he had, hoping that he would then leave. Instead, he took her back to her bedroom where he raped and sodomised her. She later recalled the stench of his foul breath, the result of all that junk food years ago.

This time, he did not kill and the boy managed to escape from the cupboard to phone 911. Ruth described her attacker to police officers as a tall Hispanic with long dark hair.

Los Angeles was in a state of terror. Amongst other things, the killer was being called the 'Valley Intruder', but the name that stuck was the 'Night Stalker'.

On June 27, he raped a six-year-old girl in Arcadia and the following day the body of a thirty-two-year-old woman, Patty Higgins, was found in the same area. Her throat had been slit.

Five days later and the body of seventy-five-year-old Mary Louise Cannon was found, again with her throat slit and the house ransacked. It was back to Arcadia for 5 July where he pummelled sixteen-year-old Deirdre Palmer with a crowbar. A blunt object of some kind was also used to beat sixty-one-year-old Joyce Nelson to death on 7 July.

It was a busy few days for the Stalker. That same night, he woke sixty-three-year-old Linda Fortuna around 3.30 am. Pointing a gun at her, he ordered her into the bathroom while he searched the house for cash and valuables. He took her back into the bedroom where he tried and failed to rape and sodomise her, failing to maintain an erection. She was terrified that he would blame her and kill her, but he left instead.

A couple of weeks later, he shot and killed Maxson Kneiling and his wife Lela, butchering them both horrifically into the bargain. He struck twice that day. Having finished with the Kneilings, he moved on to the house of thirty-two-year-old Chitat Assawahem who he shot dead before raping his wife Sakima and forcing her to perform oral sex on him. He then horrifically sodomised their eight-year-old son and left with $30,000 of jewellery.

On 6 August, he was in Northbridge, where he shot a married couple, Mr and Mrs Petersen who both managed to survive. Two nights later, he had more success in Diamond Bar, California, fatally shooting Ahmed Zia in the head and raping and sodomising his twenty-eight-year-old wife, Suu Kyi Zia.

The intervals between killings were growing less, suggesting that his anger was increasing as was his need to satisfy his grim urges. He surprised police by killing next in San Francisco. Peter and Barbara Pan were found in their blood-soaked bed in a suburb of the city on 18 August. The method was the same – Mr. Pan had been shot and then the Stalker had worked out his gruesome fantasies on Mrs Pan. She survived but was seriously injured and would be an invalid for the remainder of her life. Another pentagram was drawn on the wall in lipstick along with the words 'Jack the Knife' taken from a song called The Ripper by British heavy metal band, Judas Priest. The bullets recovered from Mr Pan's body matched those used by the Night Stalker in Los Angeles.

Police checked their unsolved cases and discovered this was not the first time he had taken his horrific show on the road. The day after he had killed the

Keller sisters in Los Angeles, twenty-five-year-old Theodore Wildings had been shot dead in San Francisco and his girlfriend had been raped by his murderer.

Now it was time for the city of San Francisco to panic as its inhabitants realised that the Night Stalker, now responsible for fourteen murders and five rapes, seemed to be on the loose there as well.

A man who ran a boarding-house in San Francisco came forward to volunteer information about a young Hispanic man with halitosis and bad body odour who had stayed at his place several times in the past year and a half. When they went to the room he used, they found a pentagram on the bathroom door. It had been used by the Night Stalker and he had vacated it the day that the Pans were attacked.

Back in Los Angeles, he attacked a couple in Mission Viejo, fifty miles south of the city. He shot and seriously wounded the man before dragging his fiancée into the next room where he told her that he was the Night Stalker, the killer who had been getting so much coverage in the media. He then raped her twice but was furious that there was nothing of value in the house. He made her say over and over that she loved Satan before making her perform oral sex on him. He then stepped away from her, laughed at her and left.

She crawled to the window and watched as he drove off in an old orange Toyota. Coincidentally, a teenager who had earlier become suspicious when he saw the vehicle in the neighbourhood, had scribbled down its licence number. He called the police with it the next morning. The car which had been stolen from Chinatown, turned up in the Rampart area but the Night Stalker had no further use for it and police waited in vain for him to return to it. However, they found a fingerprint in it which matched up with one Ricardo 'Richard' Leyva Ramirez. They now knew who they were after.

Seven days later he was captured. Looking for another car to steal, he had climbed into fifty-six-year-old Faustino Pinon's beloved Mustang. The problem was that Faustino was under the car at the time working on it. As Ramirez turned the key, Faustino sprang out from under the vehicle and reached through the window, grabbing Ramirez by the throat. He tried to speed away but crashed the car into a fence. Faustino threw the car's door open and dragged Ramirez out, pushing him to the ground. Ramirez jumped up and took to his heels, trying to steal another car driven by twenty-eight-year-old Angelina Torres. Her husband Manuel heard her screams and came after Ramirez with a length of metal post. By now there was a posse after the Stalker and one of them recognised him, shouting the fact to the others. Eventually, after pursuing him for a block, Manuel caught up with him, striking him a heavy blow on the head with the fence post. Ramirez collapsed to the ground where he was restrained. The Night Stalker had been taken and two cities breathed sighs of relief.

His trial was a circus, the case taking four years to come to court with the defence team throwing in as many delaying tactics as they could. Meanwhile, the Night Stalker played to the gallery where a bevy of female fans watched his every move, reminding some of the trial of Charles Manson and his 'Family' a number of years previously. He dressed in black and wore sunglasses, shouting 'Hail to Satan!' on occasion and displaying to the court a pentagram that had been tattooed on his palm.

The verdict was inevitable, however, and he was found guilty unanimously on each of forty-three charges. Nineteen of them had 'special circumstances' that made him eligible for the death penalty. He received, therefore, nineteen death sentences.

'Dying doesn't scare me,' he said. 'I'll be in hell, with Satan.' He has been on death row at San Quentin ever since.

In an astonishing postscript, Richard Ramirez was married in prison in October 1996 to a forty-one-year-old freelance magazine editor, Doreen Lioy. The bride wore a white wedding dress with long lace sleeves while the groom was clad in a freshly starched set of prison clothes with the shirt-tail hanging out. The bride described herself as a virgin, the essential accessory for the self-respecting Satan worshipper.

PART FIVE

20TH CENTURY EUROPEAN PSYCHOPATHIC KILLERS

BELA KISS

The call to the local police station was innocent enough. It was July 1916 and a landlord had been clearing out one of his properties, his tenant having gone off to fight in the First World War and not returned, letting the lease lapse. No one knew what had happened to him – he might be a prisoner of war or even dead. The landlord had found half a dozen large steel drums at the house and thought they might contain gasoline which would be useful, given that it was in short supply. The police had in fact investigated the drums before the war when local people thought that they might contain illicit alcohol. When their owner was questioned about them, he had said that with the inevitability of war in the very near future, he had merely been stocking up on gasoline.

The owner of the steel drums, Bela Kiss, had arrived in the small Hungarian town of Cinkota, not far from Budapest, in 1900, moving into a house at 9 Kossuth Street. A good-looking and cultured man, he earned his living as a tinsmith and soon became the town's most eligible bachelor. He had a steady stream of female companions over the years, women who seemed to come and stay with him for a few days before leaving again. By the time he was called up for the army in 1914, however, he was thirty-seven years old and still unmarried.

The landlord had become concerned about the steel drums after puncturing one. A dreadful smell emanated from inside and the chemist who had a shop next door told him that the smell was very similar to that of human decomposition.

Dr Charles Nagy, head of the detection branch of the Budapest Police, travelled out to Cinkota with another couple of detectives. There he met the landlord and Mrs Jakubec, who had been employed by Bela Kiss as a housekeeper. She was furious that these men were present on her employer's property. Nagy, however, paid her no attention, ordering the opening of one of the drums. Inside they discovered a woman's body, wrapped in a sack, with the rope that had been used to strangle her still around her neck. The drum was also filled with wood alcohol. In all there were seven drums, each containing the body of a woman. Each of them had been strangled and although they had been in the drums for a while, the wood alcohol had preserved them sufficiently for them to be identified. They then searched the house and garden where they were horrified to find another seventeen bodies buried. Twenty-four women had been strangled and hidden on Bela Kiss's property.

Dr Nagy immediately contacted the army, launching a huge manhunt. Word of the grim discovery spread rapidly through Cinkota and before long the Budapest newspapers were screaming about the 'Monster of Cinkota'. It was not going to be easy to locate Kiss, however. Thousands of Hungarian soldiers had been taken prisoner and the army was in a state of chaos, scattered and disorganised. Furthermore, there would be many men with the name Bela Kiss. It was not an uncommon name.

In the search of the house, Nagy noticed that there was one door that remained locked. Mrs Jakubec described it as Bela Kiss's secret room, telling him indignantly that he had ordered that no one be allowed to enter it. Against her wishes, Nagy forced her to open it and inside he found walls lined with books – mostly about poisons and methods of strangulation. There was a desk in the drawer of which he found an album of photographs of around a hundred women. There were also bundles of correspondence, filed in seventy-four packets. It seemed that Bela Kiss had placed adverts in the Budapest newspapers, looking for a wife and these were the replies he had received. In all, Nagy estimated, he had received about 174 proposals of marriage, seventy-four of which he had accepted. He corresponded regularly with many of the women with some of the letters dating back as far as 1903.

Marriage, however, was not Kiss's objective. It soon became clear that he had swindled many of these women out of their savings, sometimes taking everything they had.

Mrs Jakubec admitted that many women came to the house on Kossuth Street, but she had no idea what became of them. She did not live there and when the women were gone next time she visited, she just presumed they had gone back home again. Nagy was suspicious that she might somehow have been involved, especially when he discovered Kiss's will leaving a substantial sum to the housekeeper.

Dr Nagy began to work out Bela Kiss's method. It transpired that he would place his advert in the matrimonial columns of newspapers, always asking for information about a respondent's financial status. When he received a reply from a likely woman, he would pay her a visit, lavishing money and attention on her. He always made sure to enquire about her family. He was interested only in women who would not be missed if they disappeared. The women sent him substantial sums of money, sometimes their life savings but if they began to question what he was up to or threatened to go to the police, he simply murdered them.

Katherine Varga was typical of Bela Kiss's unfortunate victims. She had been a good-looking woman who owned a dressmaking business. She made contact with Kiss, met him, agreed to marry him, sold her business and moved to Cinkota to be with him. She had no close family and was not missed when he eliminated her.

Two women came forward, Mrs Stephen Toth and her daughter-in-law. In 1906 Mrs Toth's daughter had gone to Budapest to work and she introduced her mother to Bela Kiss during a visit. Kiss promised Mrs Toth that if she gave him money, he would marry Margaret. She gave him the money but the marriage never took place. Mrs Toth travelled to Cinkota to confront Kiss about his broken promise and to ask for her money back. Kiss, charming as ever, explained to her that he had only wanted to delay the marriage – but that it was all academic now as Margaret had become angry with him and moved to America. Mrs Toth even received a letter written by Margaret claiming that she could not bear the pain of rejection and was leaving to find a new love in the United States. The letter had, of course been written under duress before Kiss had strangled the unfortunate girl and put her into one of his drums.

In October 1916, Nagy received information from a Serbian hospital that a soldier called Bela Kiss had died of typhoid the previous year. Then, confusingly, he heard from the hospital that Kiss was not dead. He was alive and a patient there. Nagy hotfooted it to the hospital but when he arrived in the ward in which Kiss was said to be recuperating, there was a dead man in his bed and it was not his quarry. He had heard of the approach of the policeman, had placed the body of another man in his bed and fled.

In the years to come, sightings of the Monster of Cinkota flooded in from every part of the world. In 1920, a member of the French Foreign Legion reported that he believed that a fellow legionnaire was Bela Kiss. The man, known as Hoffman, an alias that Kiss was known to use, boasted about his skill at garrotting, a skill that Kiss had put to use in Cinkota, of course. Police rushed to the barracks, but Hoffman had disappeared.

A Hungarian soldier told the authorities that Bela Kiss had been imprisoned in Romania for burglary. Someone else claimed to have seen him strolling along a Budapest street in 1919.

He was spotted in New York by a detective named Henry Oswald who was nicknamed 'Camera Eye' because of the particular skill he possessed for remembering faces. He claims to have seen Kiss, now in his late sixties, emerging from the Times Square subway station in 1932 but lost him in the crowds of people thronging the square. Many became convinced that the killer had fled to the United States. Some had him working as a janitor in an apartment building but once again when police officers turned up to investigate, the subject of their enquiries had vanished into thin air and that was where he stayed.

HENRI LANDRU

The legend of Bluebeard is one that is present in many cultures – the man who marries numerous women and then kills them. In late 19th century France, a modern-day Bluebeard emerged, Henri Landru, a fraudster who ensnared eleven women and killed them, selling their possessions and cashing in their savings.

He was born in Paris in 1869, the son of a fireman at a local ironworks. He studied at the School of Mechanical Engineering before enlisting in the army where he achieved the rank of sergeant.

In 1893, he married a cousin with whom he already had a daughter and in 1894 he left the army and returned to civilian life. He was then convicted of fraud, being sent to prison for the first of seven times, reportedly attempting to commit suicide during his incarceration.

By the beginning of World War I he and his first wife had separated although they remained married. This, however, did not prevent Landru from embarking on a series of liaisons with generally vulnerable women which resulted in their disappearances and his own personal enrichment. Although not a handsome man, he seemed capable of sweeping women off their feet with his intelligence, quick wit and silver tongue. And while he was killing and robbing his female victims, he continued to defraud recently discharged soldiers of their pensions with a variety of scams and cons.

He usually found his victims through an advert placed in a newspaper. The first of these appeared in 1914 and read, 'Widower with two children, aged forty-three, with comfortable income, serious and moving in good society, desires to meet widow with a view to matrimony.' Thirty-nine-year-old Madame Cluchet, who had a sixteen-year-old son, André, answered his ad. He introduced himself to her as Monsieur Diard and she saw an opportunity to escape her life of drudgery working in a lingerie shop in Paris.

Their relationship was not without its problems and on one occasion when they had fallen out, she arrived at his house in the company of some members of her family to try to sort things out. 'Diard' was not home, but they went into the house anyway and had a look round. Her brother-in-law opened a chest that he found to contain numerous letters from women to Diard. He tried to persuade her sister-in-law that this was proof that her paramour was a fraud, but she would not listen. She chose Diard over her family, becoming estranged from them and moving to a villa outside Paris. She and her son were never seen again after January 1915 and around this time Landru deposited 5,000 francs – undoubtedly taken from Madame Cluchet – in his bank account.

Madame Laborde-Line was the widow of an Argentinian hotelier. She had informed friends that she was going to re-marry. Her fiancé was a Brazilian engineer. Then she announced that the wedding was taking too long to organise and that she was moving in with him anyway. She was never seen again after arriving at Landru's villa at Vernouillet and Landru was seen at her house collecting her furniture, some of which he kept and the remainder of which went into storage.

It was a busy time for Landru. Just a month later Madame Marie Guillin, a fifty-one-year-old widow, answered an advert and travelled to Vernouillet to meet him. She moved out of her apartment shortly after, putting her furniture into storage, and moved to Vernouillet. Two days later, a furniture removal van moved her furniture to Landru's garage at Nouilly. On this occasion, he was calling himself Georges Petit and claiming to be her brother-in-law. She had become paralyzed, he told people, and had asked him to take care of her affairs. He sold her bonds and used forged documents to get his hands on the 12,000 francs in her account at the Banque de France.

In December 1916, he moved to a new villa in the northern French village of Gambais. The first thing he did was to have a huge cast-iron oven installed and order a large quantity of coal. Then, using the name Dupont, he became acquainted with a widow nine years older than him, Madame Heon. Nine months later he was arranging the sale of her furniture. She had not been seen since December, but her friends had received postcards from her through Dupont.

Another advertisement brought him Madame Collomb. She thought she was meeting a Monsieur Cluchet. This one did not work out, however, and they separated for a year. Meeting again, she persuaded him to meet her family who took an instant dislike to the man in her life. She moved in with him but after Christmas the family lost contact with her. She had vanished.

In 1917, he disposed of a nineteen-year-old servant girl, Andrée Babelay, but it is unclear why. She had no money and had disappeared en route to her mother's house. He found her crying on a Metro platform and she told him she had had a row with her mother and was about to lose her job. He took her back to his room in Rue de Mauberge and a couple of months later she told her mother that she was getting married. She travelled out to Gambais at the end of March and the stove was lit. She was never seen again.

Soon he was courting a Celestine Buisson, a wealthy widow. They had been writing to each other for two years before she finally met him. Using the name of Fremyet, he manipulated her affairs in such a way that she became estranged from her family in a similar way to his first victim, Madame Cluchet. She moved to be with him at Gambais, abandoning her son, who went to live with an aunt. After April 1917 Madame Buisson was never seen again and his bank account had been augmented by 1,000 francs.

Louise Leopoldine Jaume disappeared in September 1917 and around this time neighbours began to complain about the thick, smelly smoke that often emerged from his chimney. He had met her through a matrimonial agency and benefited to the tune of almost 2,000 francs from her disappearance.

Ann Marie Pascal moved in with him, calling him 'Forest'. Before long, he was selling her furniture and even had help from Madame Pascal's son to do so.

In spring 1918, it was the turn of Marie Therese Marchadier who had been a performer on the stage, known as 'La Belle Mythese'. Now retired, she was running a small guesthouse at 330 Rue St. Jacques which she wanted to sell for 7,000 francs. The two having become friends, he proposed to her in January 1919. They moved out to Gambais where he persuaded her to sell her possessions. She sold her furniture in Paris for 2,000 francs and returned to Landru in Gambais where he had placed a large order for coal. She vanished as did her two dogs.

Meanwhile, he maintained a pretence that his victims were still alive, sending postcards and letters to family members and associates. In the case of Madame Jaume, he presented himself as her lawyer, claimed she was divorcing her husband and closed her bank accounts, withdrawing the money for his own use, of course.

When Madame Buisson's son died two years after his mother had gone off with Landru, the Buisson family wanted to contact her to inform her of his death. Recalling that she had said she was running off to Gambais with a Monsieur Guillet, her sister, Madamoiselle Lacoste, wrote to the mayor of the village asking for help in finding either Madame Buisson or Monsieur Guillet. The mayor, of course, had never heard of them, but suggested that she make contact with the family of a Madame Collomb who had disappeared in similar circumstances. Madame Collomb had, of course, met Landru shortly before her vanishing trick early in 1917.

Suspicions were aroused and the police paid a visit

to Landru's estate, Villa Ermitage. He had fled, however, leaving behind a series of aliases – Messieurs Diard, Dupont and Fremiet.

Madamoiselle Lacoste was a determined lady, however. She had actually met her sister's boyfriend and thought she would recognise him if she were to see him again. She began looking for him in the streets of Paris, close to where he used to live. Finally, in 1919 she saw him coming out of a dry goods shop with twenty-seven-year-old Fernande Segret. She followed them, but lost them in the crowds thronging the streets. Returning to the shop where she had seen him, she learned that his name was Guillet and that he lived on the Rue de Rochechouart. She informed the police who went immediately to his apartment and arrested him. When they picked him up, they noticed that he tried to keep possession of a black notebook. It was not surprising that he did not want to part with it. It was filled with notes on all his victims.

They searched the grounds of the Villa Ermitage and the house, but found only the bones of some dogsand in the ashes in the oven some bone splinters turned up, but they did find clothing and legal papers belonging to his victims.

His trial, which begun two and a half years later on 7 November 1921 at the Court of Versailles, was one of the most sensational in the history of French criminal law. Landru, who had been determinedly uncooperative with police in their investigations, maintained his innocence throughout. The women, he claimed, had merely been business clients of his and that anyway, as not one body had been found, how could he possibly be tried for murder? His neighbours gave an indication of what had happened to his victims, however, describing in court the acrid black smoke that used to swirl out of his chimney at regular intervals.

One neighbour said that he had seen Landru throw something into a pond near his house while another claimed that he had been fishing in the pond and had caught something that resembled putrid human flesh on the end of his line.

Meanwhile, Landru repeatedly refused to answer questions, claiming that it was no one's business what he knew about the women's disappearances. He also believed that because he had been judged sane, he would be acquitted. 'I have nothing to say,' he would say over and over during days of questioning in front of the jury.

The jury reacted badly to his evasions and the sarcasm with which he greeted some questions, taking only two hours to reach their verdict that he was guilty of the murder of eleven women. He was sentenced to death by guillotine.

In February 1922, he made his farewells to his legal

team and presented them with a drawing he had done while awaiting the date of his execution. He knelt down and the blade fell on the head of one of the coldest-hearted mass murderers in France's history. He never admitted to his crimes, did not explain how he had carried them out and expressed not a scintilla of remorse for the weak and vulnerable women whose lives he had taken.

Forty years later, the daughter of one of Landru's defence lawyers, was examining the picture that Landru had given her father all those years before and that had been hanging on the wall of his office ever since. She spotted some words scribbled on its frame. They read, 'I did it. I burned their bodies in the kitchen stove.' Finally, Henri Landru had confessed.

PETER KÜRTEN

As they led him to the guillotine that had been constructed in the yard of the Klingelputz prison, Peter Kürten turned to the prison psychiatrist who was accompanying him to the place of execution and asked him whether, after his head was chopped off, would he still be able to hear, at least for a moment, the sound of his own blood gushing from his neck? 'That would be a pleasure to end all pleasures,' he added.

A few weeks previously, the crowded courtroom had waited with baited breath. A special, shoulder-high cage had been constructed to prevent his escape and on tables behind it lay the grisly evidence of his awful crimes – skulls, body parts, knives, ropes, scissors and a hammer. At last he appeared, the 'Vampire of Dusseldorf', as he had come to be known. The gasp round the chamber was one almost of disbelief. He was not the monster they had been expecting. Rather, he was just an ordinary man, immaculately dressed in a good suit, with neatly parted hair and the air of a successful businessman. He spoke not in the growl they had anticipated before they saw him, but in a quiet, calm, un-emotional voice, recanting his confession and entering a plea of not guilty.

Peter Kürten exhibited all the characteristics of the true pathological personality. He was self-centred and narcissistic, a sadist intent only on satisfying his own needs at the expense of all else, including human life. Above all, he felt no remorse for anything. He killed for his own pleasure, which was mostly sexual and said that he had suffered so much in his life that it had expunged all feelings for others. Asked by the judge at his trial whether he had a conscience, he coldly replied, 'I have none, Never have I felt any misgiving in my soul; never did I think to myself that what I did was bad, even though human society condemns it. My blood and the blood of my victims will be on the heads of my torturers. There must be a Higher Being who gave in the first place the first vital spark to life. That Higher Being would deem my actions good since I revenged injustice. The punishments I have suffered have destroyed all my feelings as a human being. That was why I had no pity for my victims.' He described to the court the thoughts he had about devising methods of killing thousands of people in accidents. 'I derived the sort of pleasure from these visions that other people would get from thinking about a naked woman.'

It is fairly easy to see where it all started. Kürten's childhood was spent at the mercy of a drunk and abusive father who would rape his wife in front of his thirteen children, of whom Peter was the oldest, and he also committed incest with his daughters. He would, in fact, be sent to prison for committing incest with his thirteen-year-old daughter. Unfortunately, the young Kürten was soon abusing his sisters in imitation of his father.

Bereft of love and friendship Kürten was flattered by the bond he formed with a dogcatcher who lived in the same building as the Kürtens. This man taught him to masturbate and instructed him in the best ways to torture dogs.

Around this time, Kürten claimed, he committed his first murder when he drowned a school-friend with whom he was playing on a raft on the River Rhine. When another friend dived in to try to rescue the drowning boy, Kürten pushed him under the raft until he drowned. Their deaths were treated as accidents.

His killings were inextricably linked to his sexual urges and his perversions knew no bounds. He committed acts of bestiality on sheep and goats in stables close to where he lived, learning that the experience was made all the more intense if he stabbed the creature during the act.

The first of the twenty-seven prison sentences he received in his life was for stealing. Over the next few years, he would receive short sentences for the theft of clothing or food. Released from prison in 1899, at the age of sixteen, he moved in with a masochistic prostitute twice his age. He was able to practise his base urges on her and had finally graduated to human beings from animals.

Kürten's incarcerations infuriated him. He believed it wrong that someone as young as him should be locked up but it had its benefits. He arrived at a position in prison where he could achieve orgasm by imagining brutal sex acts. Intentionally breaking prison rules got him sent to solitary confinement where he could be alone with such thoughts and refine them in his sick head.

Not long after his release from one of his periods of confinement, he tried to kill for the first time. He attacked a girl in the Grafenberger Woods while he was having sexual intercourse with her. He left her for dead, but her body was never found and she was never reported missing which means that she probably survived and was too ashamed to report the incident to the authorities.

The more he was sent to prison, the greater became his sense of injustice. He began to consider his increasingly sadistic attacks to be acts of revenge on society.

His first murder took place on 25 May 1913, when he was twenty years old. He had been breaking into bars and inns where the owner lived in a flat above the premises. He knew they would be busy downstairs, leaving him free to pillage whatever he could from their accommodation. This particular night, he targeted an inn in Cologne owned by Peter Klein.

He broke in and made his way to the first floor of the building but was frustrated to discover nothing of any particular value in any of the rooms he entered. Opening one door, to a bedroom, he discovered a little girl, Christine Klein, aged about ten, in bed asleep. Something clicked in Kürten and instead of quietly closing the door and creeping away, he went over to the bed, grabbed the child by the neck and quickly strangled her as she struggled in his arms. He then inserted a finger into her genitals before taking out the pocket knife he always carried and slitting her throat. In his later confession, he described enthusiastically how the blood spurted from the gaping wound 'in an arch, right over my hand. The whole thing lasted about three minutes.'

Suspicion for the murder fell on Peter Klein's brother, Otto, who had unsuccessfully tried to persuade his brother to loan him some money the previous evening. In a violent rage at being denied the money, he had threatened to do something that Peter 'would remember all his life', as he had put it. The police could come up with no other reason for the murder to have been carried out and Otto was charged with the murder although he was later acquitted due to lack of evidence.

Meanwhile, the people of Dusseldorf were subjected to a series of axe and strangulation attacks.

They came to an abrupt stop during the war years, however, as Kürten was sent to prison after deserting the army. Released in 1921, he resolved to start a new life. He moved to Altenburg, found a job in a factory and married a prostitute. He became active in trade unionism, actually settling down to a normal life.

In 1925, however, he moved back to a city centre apartment in Dusseldorf where for the next four years he carried out arson attacks and petty crime as well as a rising tide of horrific attacks. People were dispatched with knives or scissors and on one occasion he intensified his experience by sucking blood out of a young girl's head.

The year 1929, however, was when his bloodlust really came to the surface, taking on a ferocity even he had never known. Between February and November of that year, there was an unparalleled spate of sex crimes, hammer and knife attacks and strangulation. The victims were indiscriminate – men, women and children. The authorities now knew that there was a maniac on the loose and the city was terrified. Elderly people and children stayed home and some even moved out of town until the perpetrator was caught. The newspaper headlines screamed that a vampire was stalking the streets of the city.

It began in early February 1929, when he attacked a woman, grabbing her by the lapels and stabbing her repeatedly. She had received twenty-four stab-wounds by the time he ran off. Kürten later told how he liked to return to the scenes of his crimes. He revisited the scene of this particular crime later that evening as well as several other times. 'In doing so,' he said, 'I sometimes had an orgasm.'

The body of Rosa Ohliger was discovered under a hedge on 9 February, stabbed thirteen times. He had stabbed her in the vagina and semen stains were found on her underwear. He had attempted to burn the body by pouring petrol over it and setting it on fire. He would later describe how he achieved orgasm as the flames caught hold.

He killed a middle-aged mechanic five days later, stabbing him twenty times in a frenzied knife attack. Again, he returned to the scene, entering into conversation with a detective working there.

The police thought they had their killer when they arrested a man named Strausberg who suffered from learning difficulties. He had assaulted two women using a noose and detectives involved in the Vampire case were convinced he must have committed the February crimes. They were, therefore, overjoyed when he confessed to everything they threw at him, almost bringing the investigation to a halt.

They were shocked back into action on 21 August, however, when, with their supposed killer in custody, their maniac went on a knifing binge, stabbing three people in separate attacks. As they walked on a country lane, a man passed and bid them 'Good evening'. The man, of course, was Kürten, and, as he passed, he lunged at them, stabbing them in the ribs and in the back.

On 23 August, like hundreds of others, Kürten attended the annual fair at Flehe. Two girls, sisters aged five and fourteen, had left the fair to walk home through some allotments. As they walked, a man emerged from some trees, following closely behind them. He stopped them to ask if one of them would go back to the fair to buy some cigarettes for him. One of the girls, Louise, obliged, skipping back the way they had come. As soon as she had disappeared, Kürten picked up the other sister, Gertrude, and strangled her before slowly cutting her throat. When the other girl came back with his cigarettes, he strangled and decapitated her.

The following day, when he encountered a woman

and asked if he could have sex with her, she replied, 'I'd rather die.' He responded, 'Die then!' before plunging his knife into her. She survived, however, and managed to provide a good description of him.

Kürten was now out of control. September saw him committing a rape and murder and he also savagely beat a girl with a hammer. In October the hammer came in handy again when he used it to attack two women. On 7 November, he strangled a five-year-old girl and stabbed her thirty-six times with a pair of scissors. Following this murder, he sent a map to a local newspaper showing them where he had buried her body.

Meanwhile, the police received tip-offs from the public that pointed the finger at thousands of different people. An enormous manhunt was under way and the city was in a frenzy of terror and suspicion.

In 1930, he made numerous hammer attacks in February and March, none of which proved fatal.

His eventual arrest was the result of an accident. An unemployed and homeless domestic servant by the name of Budlick was picked up at Dusseldorf station by a man promising to take her to a hostel. As they walked into a dimly lit park, she remembered the stories of the killer who was on the loose and became reluctant to go any further. They argued, and another man approached asking if she was having problems.

The first man took off, leaving her alone with the second man. He was Peter Kürten. She went with him to his room on Mettmanner Strasse but she said she did not want to have sex with him, asking instead if he could take her somewhere that she could find a bed for the night. They took a tram and walked into the Grafenberger Woods where he grabbed her by the neck and asked her to have sex with him. 'I thought that under the circumstances she would agree and my opinion was right,' he said later. He took her back to the tram, saying later that he did not kill her because she had offered no resistance to him. He let her go, believing that she would never be able find his flat or him again

On 21 May, he was surprised, therefore, to return to his room to find her there. She had written a letter describing the incident to a friend who had immediately passed the letter to the police. Fraulein Budick did, indeed, remember the location of Kürten's flat and had led the police to it.

Seeing her, Kürten went into the flat and then swiftly re-emerged, walking out onto the street, but followed by plain clothes detectives. He knew that capture was now inevitable, but reasoned that for the moment, the only charge against him would be one of rape which would mean a sentence of about fifteen years. He was concerned about how this would leave his wife and resolved to tell her everything so that she could take the information to the police and claim the substantial reward that was being offered for information leading to the capture of the Vampire of Dusseldorf.

On 24 May, Frau Kürten went to the police with her story, informing them also that she had arranged to meet her husband outside St. Rochus Church at three that afternoon.

That afternoon, the area around the church was completely surrounded and as Peter Kürten appeared, four officers rushed towards him. He put his hands up, smiled and said, 'There is no need to be afraid.'

ADOLF HITLER

Adolf Hitler was born in an inn, the Gasthof zum Pommer, in Braunau am Inn, in the Austro-Hungarian Empire on 20 April 1889, the fourth of a family of six. His father Alois, a customs official, had to obtain papal permission to marry his third wife, Klara, who was also his half-niece. Only Adolf and his younger sister, Paula, survived to adulthood. Hitler's childhood was unhappy. His father was frequently violent towards him as well as to his mother to whom Hitler was deeply attached.

The family moved frequently but in spite of the disruption the young Hitler performed well at school until, aged around eleven, he had to repeat a year. He claimed he was rebelling against his father who wanted his son to follow in his footsteps as a customs official, but Hitler wanted to be a painter. His father died in 1903 and Hitler dropped out of school a couple of years later, aged sixteen.

He claimed his passion for German nationalism emerged around this time, when he read a book about the Franco-Prussian War and wondered why

German Austrians did not join with Prussia against the French.

In 1905, Hitler went to live in Vienna but was rejected twice by the Academy of Fine Arts and was told he was more suited to being an architect but he did not have the requisite qualifications to attend the architectural school. He struggled to make a living as a painter, copying postcards and selling to tourists. By 1910, he was living in a house for poor working men.

In 1913, he received money from his father's estate and was able to move to Munich which allowed him to escape military service in Austria. He was arrested eventually by the Austrian army but was deemed unfit for service and allowed to return to Munich. On the outbreak of World War I, however, he enlisted in the Bavarian army, serving in Belgium and France. At the end of the war, he held the rank of lance-corporal but his role in the war had been dangerous. He had been engaged as a runner, a position that exposed him regularly to enemy fire. He fought at Ypres, the Somme, the battle of Arras and at Passchendale and was twice decorated for bravery. His award of the Iron Cross, First Class, in 1918 was one rarely given to a soldier of his rank. It seems, however, that his superiors did not believe that he possessed sufficient leadership skills to be made full corporal. He was wounded in the leg in 1916, but returned to the front in March 1917.

Germany's surrender in 1918 was a great shock to him. He had become a fervent German patriot and believed in the Dolchstoßlegende (dagger-stab legend), that the army and the country had been stabbed in the back by the poiliticians and Marxists at home. The Treaty of Versailles did nothing to allay this feeling. It punished Germany severely for the war – depriving it of territories, almost totally demilitarising the German armed forces, demilitarising the Rhineland and imposing massive reparation payments. It would help Hitler later when he persuaded Germans that this must not be allowed to happen again.

Hitler remained in the army at the war's end, based in Munich. He became a police spy working for the Aufklärungskommando (Intelligence Commando) with responsibility for influencing his fellow soldiers and for infiltrating the German Workers' Party, founded by Anton Drexler. The party was anti-semitic, anti-Communist and nationalist and it immediately appealed to Hitler. Drexler, for his part, was impressed with Hitler and he was invited to become the party's fifty-fifth member.

He met a formative influence at this point – Dietrich Eckhart, one of the party's founders. He and Hitler exchanged ideas and Eckhart advised him on everything, even how to dress. He also provided him with introductions to many important people. Soon, the party changed its name to the National-sozialistische Deutsche Arbeiterpartei (the national Socialist German Workers Party).

Discharged from the army in March 1920, Hitler became fully involved with the party and they made full use of his greatest skill – his oratory. His audiences began to grow, on one occasion 6,000 turned up in Munich to listen to him rail against the Treaty of Versailles, Marxists and Jews.

In July 1921, Hitler staged a coup within the party, replacing Drexler as chairmen. At his first meeting as leader, he was introduced as 'der Führer', a name that would continue to be used until his death.

The party began to grow, attracting followers fired by Hitler's inflammatory speeches. Rudolf Hess, Hermann Göring and Julius Streicher were all early members. Hitler became accepted in Munich society and formed relationships with business leaders.

Hitler was very impressed by Mussolini's fascists and wanted to emulate the drama of their 'March on Rome', the *coup d'etat* that brought them to power. He had the support of a number of important people, including Gustav von Kahr, de facto ruler of Bavaria and General Erich Ludendorff, as well as leading figures in the army and the police.

On 8 November 1923, Hitler and his Sturmab-teilung (storm troopers) launched what has become known as the 'Beer Hall Putsch' when they stormed a public meeting in a large beer hall outside Munich. He proclaimed the establishment of a new government and demanded support of von Kahr and the local military leaders. The following day as Hitler and his group marched from the beer hall to the Bavarian War ministry to overthrow the Bavarian government, they were attacked and dispersed by the police who killed sixteen members of the National Socialist Party.

Hitler was arrested for high treason and became a national figure at his trial when he expressed his nationalist sentiments. Sentenced to five years in Landsberg Prison, he was released after serving just nine months as part of an amnesty for political prisoners.

In prison, Hitler had used his time to dictate his book *Mein Kampf,* an autobiography and a political manifesto to his deputy, Rudolf Hess. Published in two volumes, by the end of World War II, it would have sold around ten million copies.

Following his release, there was an attempt to unseat him as leader of the party and he reacted to this challenge to his authority with the introduction of the Führerprinzip (leadership Principle). By this, leaders were appointed by their superiors and were responsible to them while being accorded unquestioning obedience by those below them.

The Depression was a godsend to Hitler who, by

the time it struck Germany in 1930, was keeping within the law as he tried to gain power, while still appealing in his oratory to German nationalist sympathies. Meanwhile, the government of the Weimar Republic which had ruled the country since the war was deeply loathed by all, from the extremists on the right to the communists on the far left. In 1930, Chancellor Heinrich Brüning led a minority government and was forced to use emergency decrees to implement his measures. This was a form of government that endured for several parliaments and certainly prepared the ground for Hitler's authoritarian style of government.

In 1932, Hitler finally obtained German citizenship which rendered him eligible to run for the German presidency against the incumbent, Paul von Hindenberg. He lost.

Elections were called in July 1932 and the Nazis won 230 seats, their best result so far, making them the largest party in the Reichstag, the German parliament. The new Chancellor, Fritz von Papen, tried to get Hitler to become his Vice-Chancellor, but Hitler would accept nothing less than the top job. Soon, the von Papen government had collapsed and fresh elections were called. The Nazis remained the largest party with thirty-three per cent of the vote.

After several more attempts to form a minority

government had failed, President von Hindenberg had no option but to appoint Hitler Chancellor of a coalition government, but with politicians from other parties taking the key roles in the cabinet. On 30 January 1933, Adolf Hitler took the oath of office in von Hindenberg's office.

Again, as no party had a majority, the Reichstag was dissolved in readiness for new elections in March 1933, but on 27 February, the Reichstag building was the victim of an arson attack which was blamed on the communists. The government reacted by suspending basic civil liberties and by banning the German Communist Party. Communists were rounded up, fled or, in some cases, murdered.

The Nazis campaigned for the elections, building up anti-Communist hysteria and increased their share of the vote to forty-three per cent. Again, however, they had to form a coalition government. Hitler now introduced the Enabling Act which allowed the cabinet to introduce measures without first gaining the approval of the Reichstag. It was to last for four years and represented his first step on the way to total power. On 14 July 1933, the Nazi party was declared the only legal political party in Germany and the power of the state governments was abolished.

Between 30 June and 2 July 1934, Hitler carried out a purge of the leadership of his SA stormtroopers, in which a number of its members represented a threat to him. This became known as the 'Night of the Long Knives' and around eighty-five people are reckoned to have died during it, although the final death toll may actually have been in the hundreds.

When President von Hindenberg died in August 1934, the cabinet declared the presidency dormant and transferred the powers of head of state to Hitler as Fuhrer and Reichskanzler. He was now in command of the armed forces whose officers and men swore an oath not to Germany or the constitution but to Hitler himself. A plebiscite voted overwhelmingly in favour of the changes. Hitler was now unchallenged dictator of Germany.

Hitler implemented a massive expansion of industrial production as well as a huge campaign of improvement to Germany's infrastructure. Numerous dams, autobahns, railways and other civil works were constructed and he sponsored architecture on a massive scale. The 1936 Olympic Games gave him an opportunity to demonstrate so-called Aryan superiority to the world. Of course, he did not allow for the extraordinary feats of the black American sprinter, Jesse Owen, who disproved his theories by winning four gold medals and infuriating Hitler in the process.

Hitler had written about Germany's need for Lebensraum (living space) in the east in *Mein Kampf* and it was a critical element of his foreign policy. He also advocated Anschluss (merger) with Austria, restoration of the pre-World War I frontiers, abolition of the restrictions on the German armed forces, return of Germany's former African colonies and a German zone of influence in eastern Europe.

He tried to build an alliance with Britain with the aim of obtaining Britain's support for an increase in the size of army Germany was allowed, an increase that would help him in his plan to destroy Russia. However, Britain refused to be drawn in and said it would prefer to wait ten years before it could provide such support.

In March 1935, he rejected the part of the Versailles Treaty limiting Germany's armed forces, publicly announcing an increase in the army to 600,000, six times the number permitted. He also introduced the Luftwaffe and increased naval strength. The League of Nations condemned these acts, but no one did anything.

On 15 September 1935, Hitler made a speech at the Nuremberg party rally in which he announced new laws regarding Germany's Jewish population. The Nuremberg Laws banned sex and marriage between 'Aryan' Germans and Jewish Germans and deprived 'non-Aryan' Germans of German citizenship.

Germany and Italy declared an Axis in October 1936 and Japan entered the Axis later in the year.

In 1939, Hitler began systematically killing Jews in concentration or 'death' camps. He had already made efforts to purify the German race by killing children with physical and developmental disabilities in a programme known as T4. Between 1939 and 1945, somewhere between eleven and fourteen million people, including six million Jews, died in the camps, in ghettoes and in mass executions. The methods used were poison gas, starvation and disease while working as slave labourers.

In 1938, Anschluss happened when Hitler persuaded Austria to join together in a Germanic union. His next target was the German-speaking Sudetenland in Czechoslovakia. On 30 September 1938, a one-day conference in Munich between Hitler, British prime minister, Neville Chamberlain, French premier, Daladier, and Mussolini came up with the Munich Agreement which gave Hitler what he wanted – the Sudetenland. Chamberlain famously claimed that they had secured 'peace in our time'. Hitler ignored the agreement and invaded the Czech half of the country in March 1939.

Poland was next and German tanks rolled into western Poland on 1 September. Hitler had by this time made a non-aggression pact with Russia and the plan was to divide Poland between them. However, Britain had already guaranteed Polish independence and Chamberlain declared war on 3 September. Hitler at last had the war he had wanted all along.

In April 1940, German forces invaded Denmark and Norway. In May, they took Belgium, the Netherlands and Luxemburg and then attacked France which surrendered on 22 June by which time Mussolini's Italy had joined in on the German side.

Hitler planned to invade Britain, but first wanted to bomb the country into submission. It was not to be, however, and his Luftwaffe lost the Battle of Britain to the men Winston Churchill, by then Prime Minister of Britain, called 'the few'. Meanwhile, Hungary, Romania and Bulgaria joined Hitler and Mussolini's Axis.

On 22 June 1941, in Operation Barbarossa, Hitler launched an attack by three million German troops on the Soviet Union, tearing up the pact that Hitler had signed in 1939. He made huge gains – the Baltic States, Belarus and the Ukraine amongst them.

On 11 December, however, as his troops bore down on Moscow, he faced a new threat when the United States entered the war following Japan's bombing of Pearl Harbor. But by now, things were starting to go wrong. The Germans lost at the second Battle of El Alamein, and the German 6th Army was wiped out at Stalingrad. He then lost in the huge Battle of Kursk.

His military judgement was coming into question and seemed to be increasingly erratic. Meanwhile at home, the economy was deteriorating and Hitler's health was beginning to suffer. His left hand trembled noticeably and it has been suggested that he suffered from Parkinson's disease. Others say that he had syphilis.

By June 1944, the Russians were pushing his armies back west and the Allies were advancing on Berlin from east, west and south. In July, a group of officers tried to assassinate him in his headquarters at the Wolf's Lair at Rastenberg by planting a bomb under a table. Hitler survived and launched ruthless reprisals, around 4,900 people being executed. Later that year, it was clear that Germany had lost the war, but he refused to allow his troops to retreat. He still hoped that he could negotiate a separate peace with the British and the Americans, but he was becoming dangerously irrational in such beliefs.

In April 1945, as Soviet troops attacked the outskirts of Berlin, Hitler's followers, in his bunker, the 'Führer's Shelter', below the Reich Chancellory, urged him to flee into the mountains. He refused, however, preferring to make a last stand in the capital.

His colleagues were now plotting against him. On 23 April commander of the Luftwaffe, Hermann Göring, argued that with Hitler stranded in Berlin, he should assume leadership of the Reich. Hitler had him arrested and stripped of his government positions. On 28 April, Hitler was furious when he learned that SS leader Heinrich Himmler was trying to negotiate with the Allies. He ordered his arrest and had his representative in Berlin shot.

On 29 April, Hitler dictated his last will and testament. He had earlier learned of the shooting of Benito Mussolini earlier that day. The next day, when the Russians were only a few hundred metres from his bunker, Hitler committed suicide, shooting himself in the mouth while at the same time biting into a capsule of cyanide.

His body and that of Eva Braun, whom he had married the day before, was put into a bomb crater, doused with petrol and burned.

The Thousand Year Reich he had strived to create had lasted just twelve years.

JOSEPH STALIN

It was 1 March 1953 and the previous night had been a long one. Lavrentiy Beria, Georgy Malenkov, Nicolai Bulganin and Nikita Khruschev had dined with Joseph Stalin, leader of the Soviet Union since 1924. That morning, however, there was no sign of Stalin; uncharacteristically, he had not emerged from his room. No one was bold enough to knock on his door or enter his room until ten o'clock that night, by which time 'Uncle Joe' as the western press liked to call him, had been lying on the floor of his room for some considerable time, having suffered a stroke that had paralysed the right side of his body. Three days later, the 'Coryphaeus of Science', the 'Father of Nations', the 'Brilliant Genius of Humanity' and 'Great Architect of Communism' – who was also behind the deaths of anywhere between three and sixty million people – died, aged seventy-four.

His life had been extraordinary. He had been a trainee priest, a poet, a weatherman, a newspaper editor, a bank robber and, of course, an ardent revolutionary who had played a large part in introducing Communism to Russia. Then, as leader, he had eliminated all of his opponents to make his position at the head of his government unassailable, helped to defeat the Nazis – albeit, at huge cost to the Russian nation – and, after the war, had turned Russia into one of the world's two superpowers. Just four years after his death, the Soviet Union had put the very first artificial satellite into orbit around the Earth.

Despite the iron grip with which he held the country, the terrible gulags where more than 3 million opponents were incarcerated, the secret police, the denunciations and purges, a recent survey found that more than thirty-five per cent of Russians would vote for him if he were alive today and, in a national poll to find the most popular person in Russian history and culture, Stalin topped the list.

He was born in Gori, Georgia in 1878 to an Ossetian cobbler and his wife whose business and marriage fell apart when the father became an alcoholic. The young Stalin spoke Georgian for the first eight or nine years of his life, only learning Russian at the church school he attended and where he did well. Around this time, he was knocked down by a horse-drawn carriage, receiving permanent damage to his left arm, an injury that later exempted him from fighting in World War I.

In 1894, at the age of sixteen, he was awarded a scholarship to the Georgian Orthodox Deminary at Tiflis where the teachers tried to impose Russian language and culture on students. Stalin was drawn to Georgian nationalism at this period. He also became a well-known poet, his work appearing in local newspapers.

His rebellious nature began to show at the seminary where he was punished several times for reading banned material – both foreign novels and Marxist literature. It became elementary, however, when the seminary suddenly raised school fees to a level that Stalin and his mother could not afford. He left the seminary in 1899, shortly before the exams. A short while later, he discovered the writings of Vladimir Lenin and his life's path was chosen – he would be a revolutionary.

He found a job at the Tiflis meteorological Observatory that, although it paid badly, allowed him time to indulge in revolutionary activities, organising strikes, leading demonstrations, writing articles and delivering speeches. It was a dangerous time to be a revolutionary; the Tsar's secret police, the Okhrana, were always on the lookout for the ring-leaders and many were arrested. When they looked as if they were about to pick him up, he decided to go into hiding and from then on lived off donations from friends and associates in the movement.

He moved to Batumi and found employment at an oil refinery and is believed to have been involved in arson at the refinery in 1902. The bonus the workers should have received for putting out the fire, was not forthcoming, as the management were certain the fire had been started deliberately. Stalin led the workers in a series of strikes that escalated into street fighting with Cossack soldiers. In one action, thirteen striking workers were killed and Stalin portrayed them in pamphlets and speeches as martyrs. Eventually, he was arrested and exiled to Siberia for three years.

He arrived in December 1903 but just five weeks later, he escaped and travelled back to Tiflis. He was anxious to throw himself back into politics. The Social Democrats had now split into two factions – the Mensheviks and the Bolsheviks who were led by Lenin and behind whom Stalin put his support.

He founded a Georgian Social Democratic party and travelled the region holding meetings and giving speeches. He began to come to the attention of the Bolshevik leadership in Russia.

A revolution broke out in the Russian Empire in January 1905 following the slaughter of 200 workers taking part in a demonstration in Baku. Stalin led a group of armed Bolsheviks during this upheaval, running protection rackets to raise funds for the party and stealing whatever they could get, including printing equipment. When the revolution finally died out with the Tsar still in power, Stalin continued his activity, fighting against the Mensheviks from platforms and stages across Georgia. He organised armed militias that continued to extort money from the rich and waged guerrilla warfare on the Cossacks.

He was chosen to be one of the three Caucasus representatives at the Bolshevik Conference in Finland in January 1906 and it was there that he first met Lenin on whom he made a very good impression. Returning to Georgia, he resumed his work and helped to organise the assassination of a Cossack general as well as continue his fund-raising through robbing banks and extortion. He was at the Fourth Conference of the Russian Social Democratic Labour party in April 1906 where he was disappointed to hear the conference ban bank robbery as a means of raising party funds. In July 1906, he found time to get married, to Ekaterina Svanidze and she would give birth to their son, Yakov, the following March.

In 1907, he travelled with Lenin to attend the Fifth Congress of the Russian Social Democratic Labour Party which was important because it confirmed the Bolshevik supremacy in the party and discussed communist revolution in Russia. Stalin also encountered his great rival, Leon Trotsky, at this conference. It was a defining time for Stalin who began to shift his attention away from the more parochial atmosphere of Georgia towards Russia and, tellingly, he began to write in Russian. His ambitions lay elsewhere. He also staged a huge robbery - 250,000 roubles, worth around £1.5 million in today's terms. He and his gang ambushed a convoy carrying the money and the ensuing gunfire and explosion of home-made bombs killed around forty people. As for the party ruling that there should be no more bank robberies, Stalin had temporarily resigned from the party to carry out the heist.

Ekaterina, his wife, fell ill around this time, and died, leaving him so devastated that his friends, fearing he might kill himself, took away his pistol.

He continued to organise strikes and ordered the murder of many right-wing supporters of the Tsar. To the annoyance of the Bolshevik intellectuals, money still came from kidnappings and extortion, but by now he was too powerful and influential to be opposed. It came to an end, however, in April 1908 when the Okhrana eventually tracked him down. He spent seven months in prison and had a further sentence of two years in Siberia to serve, but after just seven months, he disguised himself with women's clothes and escaped to St. Petersburg, travelling back to Georgia a few months later.

In 1910, he was again apprehended and this time

he was banned from the Caucasus for five years and sent into exile again to complete his previous sentence. He was released in July 1911.

In 1912, the Bolsheviks left the Russian Social Democratic Labour Party and became a separate political grouping. Stalin was co-opted onto the party's central committee after a number of other members were arrested. He edited the Bolshevik newspaper, *Zvezda*, renaming it *Pravda*, but before long had been arrested and exiled yet again. He escaped after just thirty-eight days and returned to St. Petersburg.

He worked to bring the Mensheviks and Bolsheviks together, writing editorials and articles in *Pravda* supporting the idea, but Lenin was displeased and moved him from the editorship to leading the Russian Bureau of the Bolshevik Party. Around this time, he wrote an essay entitled *Marxism and the National Question* and for the first time published it under the alias Stalin. Until that time he had used the name 'Koba'. It was the name of a Robin Hood-type hero in a novel by Alexander Kazbegi.

A spy within the Bolshevik ranks betrayed almost the entire central committee of the party to the Okhrana and they were all arrested and exiled, Stalin to the isolated Siberian province of Turukhansk where he spent six months. The authorities learned, however, that he was about to escape and sent him to a hamlet on the edge of the Arctic Circle where he had to live by fishing and hunting. He also enjoyed an affair during his two years there with a thirteen-year-old girl with whom he fathered two children.

Following the February Revolution in 1917, Stalin was released from exile and, back in St. Petersburg, while the majority of the party leadership remained in exile, seized control of *Pravda*. To begin with he supported the government of Alexander Kerensky in its pages, but Lenin's return brought a change in party thinking and the paper began to call for the downfall of Kerensky's regime. In the meantime, he was elected to the Bolshevik Party's Central Committee.

Fighting broke out between Bolshevik militias and Kerensky's men and the offices of *Pravda* were surrounded. He ordered his men to surrender and then smuggled Lenin to Finland. With Lenin absent, Stalin assumed the leadership of the party, being re-elected to the Central Committee and being given the job of editor-in-chief of the party press.

Kerensky faced a threat from inside his own party in September 1917 and looked to the Bolsheviks for help, arming them and allowing them to recruit a small army. When the threat dissipated, however, Kerensky found himself with the problem of an armed and militant Bolshevik army commanded by Stalin. Lenin decided the time was ripe for a coup and by 8 November, Kerensky's cabinet was under arrest.

The Bolsheviks formed the Council of People's Commissars and Stalin was given the job of People's Commissar for Nationalities' Affairs, with the objective of winning over the myriad non-Russian ethnic groupings of the Russian Empire.

But soon, civil war had broken out, Lenin's Red Army facing the White Army, mostly made up of anti-Bolsheviks. Stalin was given control of Red Army operations in the Caucasus. His ruthlessness showed through. He was distrustful of many of the former Tsarist officers in the Red Army and had many counter-revolutionaries executed. Entire villages were burned to force the peasants into submission. He had dissenters and deserters from the Red Army publicly executed.

In the meantime, he had married again, to Nadezhda Alliluyeva.

Lenin died in January 1924 and Stalin, Kamenev and Grigori Zinoviev took over the leadership of the party that had won the civil war and now governed Russia. Stalin was well aware that whoever took over the party would have to show loyalty to the heritage of Lenin and he organised his funeral and made speeches displaying undying loyalty to the ideas of the late leader.

His first move was to eliminate Trotsky from the

leadership and then forced out Zinoviev and Kamenev, allying himself with other senior members of the party against them.

But by 1927, the people of Russia were tired of war and factionalism. Stalin's concept of building 'Socialism in One Country' appealed strongly to them and so did he, a straight-talking man of the people. A one-party state was effectively created as no one could voice opposition to the leader of the party and therefore, no one could create an opposition. By 1928, Trotsky had been exiled – he would be assassinated in Mexico in 1940 on Stalin's orders – and Stalin stood unchallenged as leader of the Soviet Union.

One of the ways in which he retained power was through his extensive intelligence network, both at home and abroad. He had spies in every major country in the world and the Soviet Union was a dangerous place to voice opposition because his spies were everywhere there, too.

He introduced a series of Five Year Plans, aimed at changing the country from an agricultural to an industrial economy. Agriculture was collectivised, producing a marked drop in living standards for millions of Russian peasants and foreign experts were brought in to teach the Soviet people and to improve manufacturing processes. The first two plans achieved their goals and the previously backward Soviet economy was radically modernised. However, it has been estimated that around five million Ukrainian peasants may have died as a result of famine caused by failed harvests and the ruthlessly enforced excessive demands of the state. Stalin refused to release grain reserves.

In the 1930s, Stalin achieved absolute power in Russia by simply purging – assassinating or sending to labour camps, gulags – all of his opponents. It began when Sergei Kirov, leader of the Communist Party in Leningrad, was assassinated. Some suggest that the carnage that followed may have originated from Stalin's fear that, although he had nothing to do with the murder, he might be next and so he removed all who might have considered killing him. Of course, he may just have seen the popular Kirov as a rival and wanted him out of the way. Stalin claimed at the time that Kirov was part of a larger conspiracy led by the hated Trotsky. Other supposed conspirators, Zinoviev, Kamenev and fourteen other senior members of the party were assassinated in 1936. Show trials were held and many politicians and military leaders were convicted of treason, the military leaders being especially missed when World War II broke out. No section of society was left untouched by the great purge and people would inform on others to deflect blame from themselves and it took very little to be named an 'enemy of the people'. Around 700,000 people were executed during this period – the majority peasants and workers – and by the end of it, only three of the 'Old Bolsheviks' remained – Stalin, Mikhail Kalinin and Vyacheslav Molotov.

At the same time, history was re-written to remove the purged Communists from textbooks and photographs.

The world was surprised when Stalin signed a non-aggression pact with Hitler in 1939 but he had been offered eastern Poland by the Nazis to stay out of the war that began with Germany's invasion of Poland on 1 September 1939. On that day, Soviet troops crossed Russia's eastern frontier with Poland. In November, Stalin invaded Finland, anticipating an easy victory, but finding the Fins determined and resolute and ceding only a small part of their territory in exchange for almost 400,000 Soviet casualties. In March 1940, in an incident known as the Katyn Massacre, Stalin approved the order for the execution of 25,700 Polish nationalists and 'counter-revolutionaries' in the sections of the Ukraine and Belarus that had been annexed from Poland.

In June 1941, Hitler invaded Russia, launching what Russians call 'The Great Patriotic War'. The Soviet Union was not expecting the attack and the

Germans made huge initial gains, capturing and killing millions of Red Army troops. Just in case the political prisoners held in the gulags helped the Germans, Stalin at this point ordered their deaths and around 100,000 were bayonetted to death or horrifically blown up by grenades in their crowded cells. Stalin's troops forced the Germans back at Moscow in December 1941 and for the first time he began to appear on the world stage, being seen in newsreels at the Moscow, Teheran, Yalta and Potsdam Conferences with Churchill and Roosevelt.

Meanwhile, any Soviet soldier who retreated or surrendered was declared a traitor and many were sent to the gulags on their release from prisoner of war camps. But 3.5 million Russian troops never made it back to Russia from the camps.

The war won, Stalin's early collaboration with Hitler was swiftly forgotten and Russian propaganda created a surge of nationalism. In the fallout from the war, Stalin surrounded the Soviet Union with 'satellite states' and entered into a long period of tension and distrust – the cold war – when the USSR and the USA, the world's two great powers would often come into conflict, but never armed conflict. In 1948, Stalin tested the patience of the Americans when he blockaded Berlin, the former German capital, now split into four occupied zones governed by each of

France, Britain, the United States and Russia. Only the Berlin Airlift of goods and products kept the city going in the year before Stalin lifted the blockade. He then tested the Americans in North Korea, helping the North Koreans to fight the Korean War.

It may be that elements within the Soviet Union had finally had enough of Uncle Joe by that dinner in 1953 because there have been strong suggestions that he was assassinated. In 2003, a group of Russian and American scientists announced that he had swallowed warfarin, a flavourless, powerful rat poison. The truth will never be known and his body lies buried by the Kremlin wall, having been moved from its original resting place in Lenin's Mausoleum in Red Square. De-Stalinisation had begun.

ANDREI CHIKATILO

CITIZEN X

Only bones remained. A few pieces of skin clung here and there and patches of matted black hair hung from the skull. It lay amidst the spindly trees of a lesopolosa, a forested strip of land, not far from the village of Novocherkassk in the Rostov-on-Don area of the USSR. The corpse lay on its back, the head turned to one side. The victim was a female. She had been stabbed many times in an apparently frenzied attack, and had been gouged with a knife in the pelvic area. Disturbingly, she had also been stabbed in the eyes.

Major Mikhail Fetisov, the region's chief detective, determined that the victim was a missing thirteen-year-old girl, Lyubov Biryuk. Unfortunately, that was about as much as could be gleaned from the scene. It looked like that most difficult of cases – a random attack.

The police started to look for suspects amongst the usual groupings; people suffering from mental illness and known sex offenders. One man, learning that he was a suspect, promptly hung himself and the police breathed a sigh of relief, believing they had their man.

Two months later, however, another pile of bones was discovered.

It was near the railway station at Shakhty. The victim, a woman, had received multiple stab wounds and once again, the killer had attacked the eyes.

A month passed before a soldier, gathering firewood, stumbled across the body of yet another woman. She had been mutilated in the same way.

There was little doubt that a serial killer was on the loose. But this was the Soviet Union and such things did not happen there. Serial killers were a manifestation of western decadence, after all. Consequently, the press were not briefed and no warning was given to people to take precautions. Instead, a special task force was assembled. It included a second lieutenant from the criminology lab, thirty-seven-year-old Viktor Burakov, an expert in the analysis of crime scenes and physical evidence. This case would consume him for the next few years.

Victim number four turned up that same month, although she had been killed about six months previously. The body, a woman again, bore the same wounds as the others.

What was the issue with the eyes, Burakov and the team wondered? What it did suggest is that the

Maniac, as they had started to call him, did not just kill and run; he spent time with the victims after they were dead. He was sexually-motivated and his hunger for the kill seemed to be increasing. Still only a very few in the police force and high-ranking officials were aware of what was really happening.

Ten-year-old Olga Stalmachenok had gone missing in the town of Novoshakhtinsk, on her way to piano lessons. Now when someone went missing, everyone feared the worst and sure enough it happened. It took four months for her body to turn up. This attack had been particularly frenetic, the knife having been pushed into the girl's body countless times, to the extent that it moved her internal organs around inside the body. The heart, lungs and sexual organs had received particular attention and, as usual, the eyes were gouged. Olga's parents had been sent a card while she was missing, signed 'the Black Cat Sadist' and police began to check the handwriting against everyone in the town, a thankless, and, ultimately, pointless task. They looked yet again at sex offenders and the mentally ill.

Nothing happened for four months, but a group of boys playing in a lesopolosa close to Rostov, found the remains of a thirteen-year-old girl who had suffered from Down's Syndrome, in a gully. As if things had not been bad enough; to harm a child with such a condition seemed to take this killer's cruelty to a new level of degradation.

Suddenly, however, someone was arrested. Nineteen-year-old Yuri Kalenik had spent years in a home for children with special needs, but now worked in the construction industry. He was arrested on the basis of an accusation by an inhabitant of the home, and everyone was convinced they had the Maniac. Kalenik, at first, denied the charges. Then, in order to stop the beating he was taking, he confessed to all the murders, even adding some others that had been carried out locally.

Burakov interrogated Kalenik. He seemed a likely candidate. After all, he had a history of mental problems and also used public transport, just like the Maniac. He also led the team to the sites of several of the murders, but as far as Burakov could make out he was almost being guided to them by a team of policemen willing him to be their murderer. Burakov was convinced Kalenik was responding to coercion.

In the meantime, the body of another young woman was discovered. The mutilation of the body and the eyes were similar, but this time, her nipples had been bitten off. She had been there for several months. So, Kalenik could have murdered this girl, but, unfortunately for the police, not the one found on 20 October. She had been killed three days earlier, while the boy had been in custody. This woman had been disembowelled, but, strangely, the organs were nowhere to be found. He had taken them away with him. Unusually the eyes had not been attacked. Was it the same killer?

A few weeks later another body was found, she had been killed months before and the killing bore the hallmarks of the Maniac. Number ten was a fourteen-year-old boy, found near railway lines. He had been stabbed no fewer than seventy times and he had been castrated and raped. During it all, the killer had gone to a place nearby and had a bowel movement. Kalenik was in the clear.

Another boy, another former pupil of a home for children with special needs, had apparently taken the same train as the dead boy. Mikhail Tyapin was a big and powerful young man who could barely speak. Nonetheless, the police got him to talk and obtained yet another confession. Tyapin, like Kalenik, had a violent fantasy life and, like him, claimed responsibility for other murders in the area. What he failed to mention, though, was the damage to the eyes.

Semen found in the murdered boy's anus provided them with a break. They could find the killer's blood type from it. Now they were able to eliminate all the suspects they had had so far; their blood did not match. The lab, however, announced that it had mixed up the sample and that it did, indeed, match Mikhail Tyapin. Now they were convinced they had their killer.

Or at least, they would have, if the killer had not carried on killing.

Throughout 1984, woods in the region disgorged bodies, lots of them. And they all bore similar wounds.

One of them was an eighteen-year-old and on her clothing were semen and blood, left, presumably by the killer who, it seems had masturbated over her dead body. A forensics expert from Moscow confirmed that two semen specimens found on different bodies were type AB and that immediately eliminated every suspect to date. He was still out there.

And, in March, he struck again, killing ten-year-old Dmitri Ptashnikov. He cut off the tip of his tongue and his penis. Close to the body was a large footprint, the same size thirteen that had been found at an earlier scene. For the first time, however, he was seen. A tall, hollow-cheeked man with a stiff-kneed gait and wearing glasses had followed the boy.

Victims followed in quick succession, one killed by a hammer blow, another stabbed thirty-nine times with a kitchen knife; a mother and daughter killed at the same time; the eyes were stabbed and now sometimes the upper lip and nose were cut off and deposited in the corpse's mouth or stomach. The death toll rose to at least twenty-four.

The police were lost and confused. They split into factions and Burakov argued with his superiors. Two hundred officers were by this time working on the case. They worked undercover at bus and train stations, they walked the streets and parks on the lookout for the tall, hollow-cheeked man.

At Rostov bus station an older man was spotted taking an interest in a young girl. The undercover officer became suspicious and brought him in for questioning. It was a man called Andrei Chikatilo, the manager of a Shakhty machinery supply company. When questioned about his behaviour, he told police that he had once been a teacher and missed the company of the young. They let him go.

He was followed however, and when he continued to act suspiciously, accosting women and even receiving oral sex from a prostitute in the street, he was picked up. In his briefcase were a jar of Vaseline, a long knife, a length of rope and a grimy towel. Hardly the accoutrements of a businessman.

But his blood type was A and not AB. They held him for a few days, but he persisted in his denials. There was nothing untoward in his background and he was a member of the Party. He was released again.

Burakov, in the meantime, asked a psychiatrist, Dr

Bukhanovsky, to create a profile of the killer. He was a sexual deviant, the psychiatrist said, twenty-five to fifty years old and around five feet ten in height. He was sexually inadequate to the extent that he had to mutilate the corpses to achieve arousal. He was a sadist. He damaged the victims' eyes to stop them looking at him. He was a loner and he definitely worked alone. Bukhanovsky named him 'Citizen X'.

The pressure was on the officers, but all went quiet. Only one body in ten months, a woman killed near Moscow. Had the Maniac moved there?

Then, in August 1985, a dead woman, bearing the usual marks, was found near an airport. Officers checked flights and tickets, but found nothing. Checking other murders in the capital, however, they found three murders of young boys that seemed in all likelihood to have been committed by the man they were looking for – all had been raped and one had been decapitated.

But soon they were back at Shakhty where another young woman was found near the bus station, her mouth stuffed with leaves in the same way as one of the dead women in Moscow.

Officers continued to work the train and bus stations, but without success.

Another profile of the killer provided some stark facts. Stabbing his victims was for him a way to enter them sexually. He might masturbate, either spontaneously or with his hand. He might damage the eyes because he believed the old superstition that the image of a killer is left on his victims' eyes. He cut women's sexual organs as a means of establishing control over them. Organs were often missing; he might have eaten them. He cut boys' sexual organs off to make them appear feminine. He would have had a difficult childhood and had a vibrant fantasy life and a perverse response to sexuality.

Nothing happened until July and August 1986, when a couple of women's bodies turned up, the second buried with only a hand pointing up out of the earth.

Burakov cracked under the pressure towards the end of 1986 and spent time in hospital. The killer, too, took a rest and no bodies were found until April 1988. A woman was discovered, the tip of her nose sliced off and her skull smashed. Her eyes had not been touched, however. Then a nineteen-year-old boy was found in May with his penis cut off. He had been seen entering the woods with a middle-aged man with gold teeth and a sports bag. Even with that lead, they turned up nothing and in April 1989 another boy's body was found and in July an eight-year-old boy. Elena Varga was killed in August and that same week, ten-year-old Aleksei Khobotov went missing, his body showing up four months later. A ten-year-old boy was found with his tongue bitten off; in July 1990, a thirteen-year-old was discovered mutilated in the Botanical gardens.

Thirty-two victims in eight years.

The fall of Communism meant newspapers were now free to report on the case and there was a feeding frenzy with officials threatening each other and people becoming desperate for the case to be solved and the killing to stop. When an eleven-year-old was stabbed forty-two times and castrated, the public were outraged.

Another couple of sixteen-year-old boys were murdered before Burakov's work at the stations, checking the names of passengers began to bear fruit. Over half a million people had been investigated up to this point, but one name stood out.

Andrei Chikatilo had been at the station the day one of the recent murders had been carried out nearby. He had been seen emerging from the woods and washing his hands. On his cheek had been a red smear, his finger had been cut and his coat was covered in twigs.

When checked out, it turned out he had resigned from a teaching job after molesting students. His travel records coincided with several murders and there had been no deaths while he had spent time in prison in 1984.

Chikatilo was arrested and a search of his house revealed twenty-three knives, but nothing linking him with his victims. At first, Chikatilo denied everything, but then he began to admit to 'sexual weakness' and 'perverse sexual activity'. He admitted he was impotent.

He was persuaded that it would be best for him to admit everything but claim insanity. Days passed while Chikatilo considered this, still denying he was the killer. Finally, however, he confessed, going through each of the thirty-six murders in detail. He explained that he was clearing the world of undesirables – vagrants, runaways and prostitutes. These were the people he killed. He told how he could not achieve an erection and used the knife as a penis substitute. He had also believed the story of the killer's image being imprinted on the victim's eyes, but had stopped believing it which explains why he stopped damaging the eyes at one point. He told how he could only get gratification if he committed violence. 'I had to see blood and wound the victims.' He talked about placing his semen inside a uterus that he had just removed and as he walked back through the woods, he would chew on it; 'the truffle of sexual murder,' as he described it. He would tear at his victims' mouths with his teeth. He said it gave him an 'animal satisfaction' to chew or swallow nipples or testicles.

In all, he confessed to fifty-six murders and said

that being caught was a relief. Why had he done it? Perhaps because of his chilling childhood; father a POW during World War II and desperate famine in Russia, a famine so bad that there were reported instances of cannibalism. Human flesh was bought and sold and Chikatilo was told by his mother that his ten-year-old brother had been taken and killed and eaten.

He was examined and found to be sane before being brought to a court in Rostov where he was kept in a large iron cage. The court was full, some 250 people screaming at him when he was brought in. The trial was a fiasco and there was little doubt from day one that Chikatilo would be found guilty. His efforts at pretending to be mad, drooling and rolling his eyes, singing, speaking nonsense and claiming that he was being 'radiated' were to no avail.

He was found guilty on fifty-two counts of murder and five of molestation. The people in the courtroom cried out for him to be handed over to them so that they could do to him what he did to his victims and it is reported that the Japanese offered a million dollars for his brain so that they could study it.

However, on 15 February, he was taken to a sound-proofed room, told to face the wall and not turn round. He was then executed with a shot behind the right ear.

PART SIX

PSYCHOPATHIC KILLERS FROM THE REST OF THE WORLD

IDI AMIN

In the house of Idi Amin, military dictator and President of Uganda during most of the 1970s, sat a freezer. Every now and then, Amin, in the midst of one of his frequent diatribes on any number of subjects – internal opposition, the Israelis, the Zionists who ran America, or the former British colonial powers – would stroll over to the freezer and open a drawer. He would then deliver a lecture to the drawer's contents – the heads of some of his most distinguished victims, men such as his former Chief Justice.

This story may or may not be apocryphal, but there is no denying the brutality that Amin unleashed on the country under his control. It made people terrified of the late-night knock on the door or the sound of a car pulling up beside them in the street – those bundled into the car by members of Amin's hated and murderous State Research Bureau, were never seen again.

The number of deaths in Uganda while Amin was in power can only be estimated. The International

Commission of Jurists suggested a death toll of at least 80,000, but estimated that it was more likely to be closer to 300,000. Amnesty International reckoned that as many as 500,000 Ugandans were killed. Amongst the dead were many high-profile Ugandans, such as former Prime Minister, Benedicto Kiwanuka, the Anglican Archbishop, Janani Luwum, former Governor of the Central Bank, Joseph Mubiru, Vice Chancellor of Makerere University, Frank Kalimuzo, playwright, Byron Kawadwa and two cabinet ministers, Erinayo Wilson Oryema and Charles Oboth Ofumbi.

The rest of the world watched in horror, powerless to act against the increasing madness and destructiveness of Amin's depraved regime. Closing the American Embassy in Uganda due to concern about Amin's increasingly erratic behaviour, US Ambassador Thomas Melady did not mince his words when he described the dictator as 'racist, erratic and unpredictable, brutal, inept, bellicose, irrational, ridiculous, and militaristic'.

Idi Amin Dada's rise to power was extraordinary. He was born in either 1924 or 1925 in Koboko in Uganda, the son of Andreas Nyabire a member of the Kakwa tribe, who converted to Islam from Catholicism in 1910, changing his surname to Amin Dada. He abandoned his family, however, and Idi

Amin was brought up by the family of his mother, Assa Atte, an ethnic Lugbara who was a practitioner of herbal medicine, treating members of the then-ruling Buganda royal family. When Amin left school in 1941, he had a series of odd jobs before enlisting in the Ugandan army as an assistant cook. It was a lowly starting point from which to launch an attempt at leading his country.

His records show that he joined up when the war was already over, but, ever willing to make grandiose claims for himself, Amin always claimed that he was forced to enlist during the Second World War and that he fought in the Burma Campaign.

He served as a private in the King's African Rifles, part of the British Colonial Army, in Kenya from 1947 until 1949 when his unit was deployed in Somali to fight Somali Shifta rebels who were engaged in banditry there. In 1952, he fought against the Mau Mau rebels in Kenya, by this time promoted to corporal, but making sergeant in 1953.

At the time, a black African could achieve no more than the rank of warrant officer in the British Colonial Army and Amin was promoted to that rank in 1954, returning to Uganda that same year. By 1961, things had changed slightly and he rose to lieutenant, a signal honour as he was one of the first two Ugandans to achieve the status of commissioned officer. He was a captain by the following year and then major the year after that. In 1964, he became Deputy Commander of the Ugandan Army.

Meanwhile, Idi Amin's prowess as a sportsman was being noted. He had been Ugandan light-heavyweight boxing champion for ten years and was also very good at swimming and rugby.

His real rise to power came through his association with Prime Minister Milton Obote. With Obote, he devised a scheme whereby they would secretly supply Congolese rebels with arms in exchange for gold and ivory. When, in 1966, the Ugandan Parliament demanded an investigation, Obote seized power, abolishing the purely ceremonial presidency held by the Kabaka – or King – Edward Mutesa II of Buganda. Obote became President while Amin, who had personally led an attack on the Kabaka's palace, was promoted to Colonel and given command of the Ugandan Army and Air Force.

Inevitably, Amin and Obote became enemies. In October 1970, Obote demoted Amin and when Amin heard that he was about to be arrested for misappropriating army funds, he used the power he still had over the army, to stage a military coup, seizing power while Obote was at a Commonwealth summit meeting in Singapore.

Initially, Amin claimed to be a soldier and not a

politician. His regime was merely there in a caretaking capacity, he claimed, until elections could be held. He released political prisoners and allowed the remains of the late Kabaka, who had died in exile in London, to be brought back to Uganda for burial, cleverly appeasing the former regime's supporters. It was a popular coup amongst foreign powers, the British Foreign Office labelling him 'a splendid type and a good football player'.

Nonetheless, the killing began within a few days of him taking office.

A week after the coup, he declared himself President and Commander-in-Chief of the Armed Forces. He suspended bits of the Ugandan Constitution, giving military tribunals precedence over courts of law. Government House in Kampala was renamed 'The Command Post' and he replaced the previous internal security bureau with the sinister State Research Bureau, gangs of uniformed men who wore dark glasses even at midnight and whose business of death and horrific torture was fully endorsed by Amin. Before long, 20,000 Ugandan refugees had joined Milton Obote in exile in neighbouring Tanzania. A failed attempt by these exiles to restore Obote to power in 1972 unleashed a bloodletting as Amin purged his armed forces of supporters of the former President, principally those who were of the Acholi or Lango tribes. By early 1972, at least 5,000 of these troops had been killed and twice as many civilians had disappeared never to be seen again.

He also began to order the deaths of people regardless of ethnic groupings – journalists, lawyers, judges, students, intellectuals, criminals and foreign nationals. Entire villages were massacred and so many people were killed and thrown into the River Nile that the Owen Falls Hydro-Electric dam in Jinja was blocked on several occasions, allowing the crocodiles to feed at their ease.

The crocodiles were lucky to be able to come by their food so easily because food was not quite so easy to come by for his people. Amin drove the country into the ground economically, his actions depriving the country of the production expertise needed to both grow food for internal use and to earn much-needed foreign income from exports. For example, when he came to power in 1971, Uganda was a net exporter of sugar but he decided to expel all the Asians who ran the country's sugar mills and, without the necessary expertise in production and organisation, the sugar industry collapsed. The result was that Uganda became an importer of sugar. The tourist industry collapsed due to neglect and lack of foodstuffs and the coffee industry stalled while the instant-coffee processing facilities waited, like most other Ugandan factories, for spare parts or repair.

Much of the money that did come into the country from foreign earnings was squandered by the government on tax-free luxuries to keep Amin's soldiers happy. The Boeing 707 and Hercules C130 that made up the entire fleet of Ugandan Airlines, made regular trips to London's Gatwick Airport where it would load up with radios, whisky, cars and other luxury items for Amin's 21,000 army officers.

His 'Economic War' launched in August 1972, included the taking by force of properties owned by Europeans and, particularly, Asians. There were some 80,000 Asians in Uganda, people who had immigrated from the Sub-Continent when Uganda had been a colony of the British. They were good business people and ran many successful concerns in the country, efficiently and profitably. Amin announced the expulsion of the 60,000 Asians in Uganda who held British passports, a decree later changed to the expulsion of the country's entire Asian population of 80,000, apart from professional people such as doctors, lawyers and teachers. Many of them came to Britain.

The businesses the Asians left behind were gifted by Amin to his supporters but mismanagement and poor organisation led to entire industries collapsing and had a disastrous effect on the increasingly weak Ugandan economy.

Amin's hatred of Israel knew no bounds. Following the massacre of Israeli athletes at the 1972 Munich Olympics, he sent a letter to UN Secretary-General, Kurt Waldhiem, in which he applauded the massacre, saying that Germany was the most appropriate locale for this because it was where Hitler burned more than six million Jews. In June 1976, he astonished the world when he permitted an Air France plane, originating at Tel Aviv in Israel, that had been highjacked by members of the Popular Front for the Liberation of Palestine and a German terrorist group, the Revolutionäre Zellen, to land at Entebbe Airport, on the shores of Lake Victoria, not far from Kampala. All the non-Jews and non-Israeli citizens on board were released, leaving eighty-three Jewish hostages and twenty others who refused to leave the plane. In the subsequent Israeli rescue operation in which all the hostages were freed by Israeli commandos, forty-five Ugandan soldiers died. In the shocking aftermath, he ordered the summary execution of air-traffic controllers, policemen and other airport officials who had been on duty at the airport. It was, ultimately, one of the most humiliating episodes of his entire rule.

In the few years he had left in power, his behaviour became increasingly strange. When Britain broke off diplomatic relations with Uganda in 1977, he retaliated by declaring that he had defeated the British. In celebration, he awarded himself the CBE (Conqueror of the British Empire). His new title, as announced on Ugandan radio, was 'His Excellency President for Life, Field Marshal Al Hadji Doctor Idi Amin Dada, VC, DSO, MC, CBE'.

He praised Nazi leader, Adolf Hitler, in speeches, promising to create a memorial to him in Kampala. On one occasion, he arrived at an event on a sedan chair carried by four local British businessmen, describing himself as 'the new white man's burden'.

Worst of all, gruesome rumours began to be substantiated that Amin indulged in cannibalism.

Things had eventually begun to conspire against him by 1978. There was increasing anger at his actions within Uganda and a number of his ministers fled into exile. In an attempt at deflecting attention away from the deteriorating situation at home, he sent troops into Tanzania. The Tanzanian President Julius Nyerere mobilised his army and retaliated, supported by Ugandan rebels, opponents of Amin. Despite aid from Libya's President Gaddafi, his army was pushed back and defeated. Amin fled on 11 April, 1979 as Kampala fell to the Tanzanians, firstly to Libya and then to Saudi Arabia.

He made one attempt to make a comeback in 1989

when he reached Kinshasa at the head of an armed group, but Zairian President Mobutu forced him to return to exile.

Idi Amin Dada died, almost unnoticed, and without expressing remorse for the hundreds of thousands of deaths for which he was responsible, in Saudi Arabia on 16 August, 2003 after slipping into a coma. His wife pleaded with Ugandan president Museveni to let him go back to Uganda to die. Museveni told her that he would be forced 'to answer for his sins the moment he was brought back'.

POL POT

He called himself 'Brother Number One' when the
Khmer Rouge captured Phnom Pen, the Cambodian
capital, on 17 April 1975. As his *nom de guerre*,
however, the name by which history would remember
him, he coined Pol Pot – a shortened version of the
French words *Politique Potentiale* that the Chinese had
used for him.

From 1975 until 1979, Pol Pot, leader of the
communist Khmer Rouge, imposed a kind of
collective national psychopathic behaviour on his
country in pursuit of political ideals. It was a
programme of extermination, torture and ethnic
cleansing that resulted in the deaths of somewhere
between 750,000 and 1.7 million people, around
twenty-six per cent of the entire Cambodian
population. In fact, some estimates put the numbers
even higher – it may, according to these sources have
been as many as three million.

Interestingly, although Pol Pot attempted to
impose an agrarian and social revolution on

Cambodia, of which the peasant class was the heart, he was himself a member of the landowning class, having been born as Saloth Sar in 1925, in Kampong Thom Province, to a fairly well-off family of Chinese-Khmer origins. He attended a Catholic school in Phnom Penh but was often a visitor at the royal palace where his sister was a concubine of the king, Sisowath Monivong.

He was not the best of students during his time at an exclusive school in the capital and moved to a technical school where he earned a scholarship that sent him to France to study radio electricity in Paris. He remained in France from 1949 until 1953 during which time he joined the French Communist Party (FPC), espousing its anti-colonial stance.

Once again, he did not progress in his studies, returning to Cambodia in 1954. In France he had become a member of a secret Marxist cell that had taken control of the Khmer Student's Association. On his return to his homeland, he began working for this fledgling Cambodian Communist group, evaluating groups in South-east Asia engaged in rebellion against their governments.

When Cambodia was given independence by the 1954 Geneva Conference, the Cambodian King Norodom Sihanouk began playing the different parties off against each other, suppressing what he believed to be extremist groups with force. The elections of 1955 were corrupt and many leftists realised that they would never gain power by peaceful means. While teaching French history and literature at a private college, Saloth worked closely with the parties of the left.

A purge by the king of elements of the left, put Saloth in a position where he could become leader of the party. In 1963, he was elected Secretary of the Central Committee and was forced into hiding. He hid on the Vietnamese border, making contact with North Vietnamese units who were fighting the war against South Vietnam.

The Vietnamese helped Saloth establish a base camp where he worked with his lieutenants on devising an ideology for the Khmer Rouge, as he called his party. To some extent, he followed the example of Chinese leader, Mao Zedong, declaring the rural peasant farmer to be the true working class proletarian and the starting point of the revolution. His movement increased its membership as the king imposed more and more repressive sanctions on the country.

In January 1968, Saloth launched a national uprising, attacking an army base at Battambang. The attack was seen off by the Cambodian army but Saloth's men captured a number of weapons.

His leadership style began to change at this point.

Decisions were no longer made on a collective basis. He began to act like an absolutist ruler of his party and had his own compound and private staff.

In 1970, Sikanouk was removed by his government as head of state but the North Vietnamese persuaded him and Saloth to work together to bring down the government. The North Vietnamese played a large part in the insurgency, invading Cambodia with 40,000 men and advancing to within fifteen miles of Phnom Penh. Saloth and his men did not participate in a major way in North Vietnam's war against the Cambodian government, but while it was going on, he was building his own army and carrying out political indoctrination and education programmes in Cambodian villages. By early 1972, he had an army of 35,000 troops that could be supplemented by 100,000 irregulars, funded with $5 million a year provided by the Chinese.

The first signs of his need for absolute control became evident around this time when he forced minorities to abandon their traditional styles of dress and adornment in favour of Cambodian styles. He also endorsed a programme of making all land holdings the same size. All means of public transport were banned, such as bicycles and mopeds. They were policies designed to please the peasants who had none of these things anyway and to disenfranchise the wealthier town and city dwellers.

As the Vietnamese began to withdraw, the Khmer Rouge began to make progress. Many lives were lost during efforts to capture Phnom Penh in 1973 but by the middle of the year, he controlled two-thirds of the country. He besieged the city and launched a series of purges of government officials and educated people.

An uprising by the Cham minority in regions the Khmer Rouge controlled was followed by Saloth's orders to torture rebels. It was an experiment that would later be extended to the entire population of the country.

Between 1969 and 1973, the Americans had been bombing Vietnamese bases in eastern Cambodia, the result of which was an influx of hundreds of thousands of Cambodian peasants into Phnom Penh. It played into Pol Pot's hands, of course, as the country became increasingly destabilised, both economically and militarily. When the Americans finally withdrew from Vietnam, the corrupt and incompetent Cambodian government also lost its American support. Pol Pot and his army of teenage peasant guerrillas marched into the capital. On 17 April 1975, the Khmer Rouge seized control of Cambodia and, renaming the country the Democratic Republic of Kampuchea, Pol Pot began his revolution.

His first step was to declare: 'This is Year Zero'. He announced that he was going to purify Cambodian society. Where once western cultural influences, city life, religion and capitalism had featured, he was introducing an extreme form of peasant communism.

Foreigners were immediately expelled from the country, embassies closed, religion banned, and all foreign medical and economic aid was prohibited. Newspapers, radio, and television stations were closed and mail and the use of the telephone were limited. Money was withdrawn from circulation and businesses were wound up, education halted, health care banned and parental authority was done away with.

As he had been taking over the country, Pol Pot had discovered that it had been difficult to force the inhabitants of towns and cities to adhere to socialist tenets. They would quickly revert to their old capitalist habits. He concluded that the only answer was to send the entire populations of the country's conurbations into the countryside to work. Remarkably, all of Cambodia's towns and cities were forcibly evacuated. The 2,000,000 inhabitants of Phnom Penh were sent into the countryside on foot and at gunpoint. It was done under the pretext of a threat of American bombing raids and it is thought that in this one action, Pol Pot was responsible for around 20,000 deaths.

The fields in which these vast numbers of people had to work became known as the 'Killing Fields'.

They effectively became slaves and overwork, malnutrition and disease accounted for tens of thousands of deaths. People had to survive for two days on just a 180-gram tin of rice. Work began at four in the morning, ending at ten at night, with little rest and armed guards watching over them, ready to open fire at the slightest opportunity. They were allowed a day off every ten days. They were often harvesting fruit and rice, but were forbidden to eat any.

But life was cheap to the Khmer Rouge. To build their new agrarian communist utopia, they estimated they would need around two million people. The rest were superfluous. As they chillingly announced, 'To keep you is no benefit; to destroy you is no loss.' Hundred of thousands were forced to dig their own graves in shackles and were then beaten to death with iron bars and farming implements. The soldiers had been warned not to waste bullets.

Pol Pot now launched a series of purges in an effort to exterminate remnants of the society that had existed before Year Zero. Before his seizure of power, he had compiled a list of people to be killed following a Khmer Rouge victory. It originally contained seven names and then expanded to twenty-three, incorporating all senior government leaders and the leadership of the army and police force. It spread much wider, however. The wealthy and the educated were killed. Buddhist monks, teachers, doctors, lawyers and government officials were murdered alongside their families. The crippled and disabled were targeted and he even had many of his own colleagues, who had fought alongside him, shot or axed to death.

People were forbidden to gather in groups of more than two and children were taken from their parents and forced to live in communes. Mass arranged marriages were held.

As many as 20,000 people were tortured at a school in Phnom Penh, but often just being a suspect was enough to have someone shot, without the need for any questioning. Victims suffered the removal of toenails, suffocation and the horror of being skinned while still alive.

Ethnic groups fared just as badly just for being different. Of the 450,000 people of Chinese origin living in Cambodia at the time, fifty per cent were killed.

By 1977, relations with Vietnam had begun to deteriorate, leading to clashes along the two countries' border. In May, Vietnamese planes attacked Cambodia and in the autumn Cambodian troops were making forays into Vietnamese territory. In December, 50,000 Vietnamese troops invaded but were driven back. Negotiations broke down and Vietnam invaded again in late 1978 with the objective of unseating the Khmer Rouge government. When the Cambodian army was defeated, Pol Pot fled from Phnom Penh to the border with Thailand where he lived for the next six years, trying to regroup.

He resigned from the party in 1985, due to asthma, but remained de facto leader of the Khmer Rouge. Day-to-day power was transferred to the successor he had hand-picked – Son Sen. In 1986, Pol Pot, now sixty-one years old, had to travel to China for treatment for cancer of the face. Returning to Cambodia, he refused to talk peace and continued the struggle against the coalition government now ruling the country. In 1995, he had a stroke that left him paralyzed down his left side.

The government had a policy of encouraging individuals in the Khmer Rouge to defect or make peace. When Son Sen tried to make a settlement with the government in 1997, Pol Pot had him executed and also ordered the killing of eleven members of his family.

Eventually, he was arrested in November 1997, presented to the world in a show trial and sentenced to house arrest for life.

On 15 April, it was announced that the Khmer Rouge had agreed to hand Pol Pot over to an international tribunal. Later that same night, he died in bed. It was claimed that his death was due to heart failure, but there were inevitable suspicions that he had either committed suicide or been poisoned. No one would ever find out. He was cremated within days of his death before his body could be inspected.

IVAN MILAT

AND THE BACKPACKER MURDERS

Englishman Paul Onions was one of the thousands of backpackers who arrive in Australia annually from around the world, eager to explore its vast wastes and exciting cities. He was having the time of his life, but despite living modestly and staying in a backpacker's hostel in Sydney's Kings Cross area, his funds were disappearing fast and casual work was not easy to find. Someone told him that fruitpicking paid good money and, determined to prolong his stay in the country, he headed for the Riverina area, a few hundred miles southwest of Sydney. To save money, he took a train to the city of Liverpool and started hitchhiking from there. The Hume Highway that runs for around 550 miles from Sydney to Melbourne would take him where he wanted to go and before long he was standing by the side of the road, sticking his thumb out.

After a while he walked to a small shopping centre to buy a drink. As he was standing there a fit, well-built man approached and enquired whether he wanted a lift. Paul climbed into the stranger's four-wheel drive and they headed south. The man told him his name was Bill and asked him a lot of questions about his trip and where he was from. He was pleasant enough at first, but as the journey progressed, he seemed to become angry, making racist comments. Then he turned morose and clammed up.

After they left the town of Mittagong, Paul noticed that Bill's driving was becoming erratic and became edgy when he saw him constantly looking in his rear-view mirror. Bill suddenly brought the vehicle to a stop, announcing that he was going to get some cassette tapes from the back. Paul was puzzled because there were tapes in a space between the seats. He decided to get out as well, but as he did so, Bill snarled menacingly at him to get back in the car. He did so but when Bill climbed back in he reached down beneath his seat and pulled out a large black revolver which he pointed at the Englishman. 'This is a robbery,' he said, also pulling out a length of rope. Paul asked him what he thought he was doing before grabbing the door handle, throwing open his door and jumping out.

He ran out into oncoming traffic, cars swerving to avoid him. A van approached and he threw himself in front of it, forcing the driver, Joanne Berry to stop. He jumped in beside her, shouting that the guy in the four-wheel drive had a gun. She thought for a moment – she had her sister and her four children in the back of the van, after all – but seeing the terror in the Englishman's eyes, she put her foot down on the pedal and sped off in the direction of the nearest police station.

Astonishingly, no one acted on Paul Onions' story. He made a statement and waited to hear something, but no one contacted him and he returned to England where he tried to forget about the day a gun was pulled on him.

He had been lucky, though. The man who had given him a lift was Ivan Milat, one of Australia's most prolific serial killers, a man known to have killed seven times, but actually believed to have possibly been responsible for around thirty.

Ivan Robert Marko Milat was born in 1944 into a large Yugoslavian immigrant family. Not much is known about his childhood, apart from the fact that his family life was isolated and rural and he had thirteen siblings. He developed a love of hunting and guns from an early age and along with his brothers gained a reputation in the neighbourhood for wildness and lawlessness. The local police became very familiar with the road to the Milat farm.

In 1971, Ivan was charged with the rape of two female hitchhikers, but when the prosecution failed to produce enough evidence, he was acquitted.

However, he had, undoubtedly, got a taste for the kidnapping and assaulting of backpackers. By the early 1990s, it was a taste he was indulging in regularly.

Belango State Forest is located south of Berrima in the Southern Highlands, a couple of miles west of the Hume Highway. On 20 September 1992, two men taking part in an orienteering competition were running near a spot called Executioner's Drop when they both noticed a terrible smell. They had a look at what appeared to be a pile of debris and to their horror found human remains.

There was immediately speculation that the two bodies that were uncovered might belong to some of the backpackers who had mysteriously vanished during the past few years. There were four Germans missing, a couple of British girls and two Australians, from Victoria.

Police confirmed that the bodies were actually those of the English girls, Caroline Clarke and Joanne Walters who had disappeared in Sydney's Kings Cross district in April. Joanne had been viciously stabbed in the heart and lungs. The killer had been powerful; her spine had been cut and two ribs had been completely severed. As well as being stabbed, Caroline had also been shot in the head a number of times. It was later established that the bullets in her skull had been fired from three different directions. The killer, it seemed, had used her head for target practice.

A fireplace had been built with bricks and six cigarette butts were found; the killer had spent a considerable amount of time there. They were certain that the killer was familiar with the area and was, therefore, likely to be a local man. The killing of Caroline was not sexual, but more like an execution, carried out by someone who liked to exert control over people. They also believed that there might have been more than one person involved. Joanne's attack, however, had been frenzied and was thought to have had more of a sexual element – her shirt and bra had been pushed up and, strangely, the zipper of her jeans was undone, but the button was still fastened. Her underwear was missing, believed to have been taken as a 'trophy' by the killer. Chillingly, the profiler involved believed that the girls had been killed for pleasure.

A massive search of the area revealed nothing further and the police stated that they were confident there were no more bodies in the forest.

A few months later, as the investigation was scaling down without any further developments, Bruce Pryor was driving on an unfamiliar road in the forest. He came to a bare, rocky area where he noticed a small fireplace built from rocks. Getting out to have a look, he was shocked to see a bone lying on the ground that looked surprisingly like a human thigh-bone. Investigating further, he noticed something white in the undergrowth. It was a human skull.

There were two bodies, a man and a woman, police thought. A black floppy felt hat found in the vicinity told them that the victims were most likely James Gibson and Deborah Everist, a couple from Victoria who had been missing since 1989. Curiously, however, Gibson's backpack and camera had been found seventy-eight miles north of the Belangalo Forest. It seemed that the killer had been trying to divert their attention from the forest in their search for the young Victorians.

Although only the couple's skeletons remained, it became apparent that both had been stabbed a number of times. Deborah Everist's skull had been fractured several times and she had slash marks on her forehead. A bra was found with a stab wound through one of the cups and it looked as if a pair of tights that were found had been used as a restraint of some kind.

The forest was now exhaustively searched by forty officers as well as specially trained sniffer dogs.

Meanwhile, it was established that bullets and casings found at the scene were from a Ruger repeating rifle but it was estimated that there were probably around 50,000 such rifles in Australia at that time. Gun clubs and local gun-owners were questioned. One man contacted them and gave a detailed description of two vehicles that he had seen in the forest the previous year. In them, he claimed he had seen a man and a woman who appeared to be bound. The man's name was Alex Milat.

Twenty-six days after the discovery of the bodies of Everist and Gibson, a search team reached a small clearing where they found a pair of pink women's jeans and a length of blue and yellow rope. They also found a fireplace, as in the other two locations. An officer stopped and raised his arm above what looked like a bone lying on the ground. A little further on lay a human skull, wearing a distinctive purple headband.

Simone 'Simi' Schmidl was an adventurous German backpacker who had travelled the world and had then fallen off the edge of it on 20 January 1991, last seen hitchhiking out of Liverpool in the direction of Sydney.

She was partly clothed, her shirt and underclothes were pushed up around her neck and she had multiple stab wounds. Strangely, the pink jeans belonged not to her, but to another missing German girl, Anja Habschied, and it was not long before they found her, as well as another body, that of her companion, Gabor Neugebauer. The two had gone missing from Kings Cross just after Christmas 1991.

Gabor had been strangled and shot with the same type of bullets used in the other murders, but there was one striking difference with Anja's remains. Her head and top two vertebrae were missing and she had no other wounds. Forensic scientists chillingly concluded that her head had been cut off using a sharp instrument like a sword or machete. She had been kneeling when it was done and they concluded that the killer had attempted to re-create a ritual execution of some kind.

It was an extraordinary case in which it seemed almost as if the murderer was experimenting with different types of torture and killing. The seven victims had died in a variety of ways – beaten, strangled, shot and decapitated. Both men and women victims had been sexually assaulted in some way – often their zippers were down although the top buttons of their trousers were always fastened. The killer also seemed to spend time with his victims. Police described the killer as cruel and sadistic as well as calculating and confident.

The authorities were swamped with information, but gradually they began to develop suspicions about the Milat family. Then, they got the break they had been waiting for when Paul Onions' escape from a gun-wielding man in 1991 emerged. They flew him over from Britain and he identified Ivan Milat as his attacker.

In the early hours of 22 May 1994, police surrounded Milat's property and ordered him to come out. Inside they found a huge amount of evidence linking him to the killings – sleeping bags, clothing and camping equipment belonging to the victims. They also found an arsenal of weapons and ammunition. A long, curved cavalry sword was discovered in a locked cupboard at Milat's mother's house. It was probably used to behead Anja Habschied.

Before long, ballistic results proved that one of his guns had been used in the attacks and Milat was charged with the seven murders as well as with the attack on Paul Onions.

At his 1996 trial, the most sensational in Australian history, Milat took the extraordinary step of claiming that he had been set up by other members of his large family. The jury did not believe him, however, and, found guilty on all charges, he was sentenced to seven life sentences.

Incarcerated in the maximum security wing of Goulburn prison, Milat swore that he would seize every opportunity to escape, almost succeeding in May 1997. The prison authorities foiled the breakout and Milat's accomplice was found mysteriously hanged in his cell the next morning.

It is thought that Milat started killing long before 1989 and he has been questioned about many other disappearances although no charges have yet been brought in those cases. Nonetheless, his brother, Boris, in hiding from the other members of his violent family, has told the media, 'the things I can tell you are much worse than what Ivan's meant to have done. Everywhere he's worked, people have disappeared, I know where he's been.'

JAVED IQBAL

In just five months, Javed Iqbal lured 100 boys to his run-down three-bedroom apartment in Lahore. There, he raped them, strangled them using an iron chain and then disposed of their bodies by dumping them in a vat of acid.

The worst thing is hardly anyone even noticed they had disappeared and only twenty-five were ever reported missing. It seemed that no one cared. The first the authorities knew of it was when Iqbal wrote to them to tell them what he had done. He had already confessed to a newspaper. But still nothing happened because the police were incompetent and unable to locate him. Eventually, he walked into a police station and handed himself over to them.

It was a terrible indictment of Pakistani society. Bad enough to have nurtured a psychopathic killer like Iqbal, the worst paedophile and serial killer in Pakistan's history, but worse still to have created a society that let such a thing happen unchecked. That uncaring society and its bungling, corrupt police force were accused of being complicit in the murders of his hundred young victims.

Javed Iqbal was well-known in the markets, a twice-divorced man in his mid-forties with white hair and glasses. He would take teenage boys back with him to his flat to work as servants and even lovers, a practice not uncommon in the subcontinent, although homosexuality is forbidden by the Koran.

Iqbal called himself a journalist and a social worker and insisted that he was looking for boys because he was lonely and that he did not take them home for sex, but in order for them to work in his flat. He said that he felt sorry for them, wanted to help them. But he had also been exploited by them. He claimed in a statement following his arrest that a couple of street kids had brutally beaten and almost killed him. His memory had been affected by the beating, he claimed, and he had to go into hospital to undertake surgery on his head. During that time, he said, he lost his home and his car. His mother had become ill with worry about him and had died. The police refused to help him and instead accused him of practicing sodomy.

With no help available, Iqbal decided to take matters into his own hands and wreak the most terrible vengeance on the streetkids and on Pakistani society. He recruited four young men to help him in his gruesome task – Nadeem, Shabir, Sajid and Ishaq Billa.

In early November 1999, a good-looking young boy named Ijal was plying his trade, offering massages to the men in the square. The earnings were meagre but it was the only way he knew to make enough to enable him and his younger brother, Riaz, to eat.

That day, he was approached by Iqbal and a couple of his cohorts. Iqbal offered him fifty rupees for a massage, a king's ransom to Ijal who considered it a good day if he earned twenty rupees. Iqbal said he suffered from paralysis and hoped that a massage could ease it a little. The two brothers followed him and his friends along the Ravi River to a dark building with a courtyard. Arriving at the house, Ijal sent his brother home, arranging to meet him later. The younger boy's last view of his brother was of him lounging in his tattered white shirt in the house's front room.

Ijal did not come home that night and when Riaz went to Iqbal's house the next morning, he was told that he had left immediately after the massage.

Of course, Ijal never left the house and the next time Riaz saw his brother was in a photograph Iqbal had taken of him. He was proudly wearing a new blue shirt and on the picture was written 'Number 57'. A few minutes after it had been taken, Iqbal had strangled him after giving him a sedative and quizzing him exhaustively about his family. Iqbal was different to most serial killers who tend to objectify their victims, removing all thought of them as people from their minds. He wrote down all the details he could glean from them. It has been suggested that he did this simply to make the victim let down his guard. After a life of not being of particular interest to anyone, the boy would be flattered to be so interesting to this man. Others say that it was just an example of the depraved nature of the man – a cruel travesty that he perpetrated just before murdering his victim. He, himself, would claim that he was preparing a document that would detail the abuses and deprivation suffered by these children, and allowed to continue by an uncaring society.

He detailed every killing he carried out in a diary. The method was always the same. After the victim had become groggy from the drug he had fed him, he would rape him. As the boy lay on the floor, he would wrap the iron chain around his neck and gradually pull it tight, slowly strangling his victim. The corpse would then be dissected and the pieces would be submerged in a vat of hydrochloric acid. He even costed the killings, claiming to police later that each murder cost around 120 rupees, or about £1.70.

He was unhurried and always waited until every last piece had been dissolved – hair and bone took longer to dissolve than flesh. The liquid was initially poured down a drain, but when neighbours began to complain about the smell, he had his young friends pour it into the river.

When Iqbal had sexually assaulted and murdered his hundredth victim, he sent a copy of his confession to an Urdu-language newspaper, having already delivered it to the police. He had also ensured that the remains of two of his last victims were not poured away. They stayed at his house, as proof of his horrific activities. Astonishingly, the police disregarded his confession. It was only when they heard that the press had received a copy that they made their way to Iqbal's house.

It was a horrific scene at the house and even hardened journalists were horrified by what they saw. Blood stained the walls and floor and the iron chain lay there. A gallery of photographs of Iqbal's victims decorated the walls, victims, some as young as nine, snapped smiling, moments from death. A bag in a corner contained eighty-five pairs of shoes as well as children's clothing. A card on the wall, near to the bubbling tank of acid explained in Iqbal's handwriting that 'The bodies in the house have deliberately not been disposed of so that authorities will find them.'

The police were themselves put in the dock again when it emerged that Javed Iqbal had been arrested three times for sexually abusing young boys, but on each occasion had bribed his way out of any charges being brought. In June 1988, for instance, he had paid two boys for sex. He was immediately freed on bail but it is unlikely anything further would have happened if his murders had not come to light a year later. His neighbours had ganged up on him, trying to persuade him to control his lust for young boys, but he had simply moved to another part of town where nobody knew him.

The one thing missing when reporters and police officers arrived at his house was Iqbal himself. He had left a note claiming that he was going to tie a rock around his neck and throw himself into the Ravi River but after the river had been dragged, it seemed obvious that his suicide threat had been an empty one.

The biggest manhunt in Pakistani history was launched and before long it unearthed his four accomplices who were taken as they attempted to cash a traveller's cheque for 18,000 rupees in Sohawa. When one was reported to have committed suicide by jumping from a third-floor window, many did not believe it and there was more public outrage and a shake-up of the Lahore Police Force followed.

Pressure mounted but suddenly, out of the blue, Javed Iqbal walked into the offices of the Urdu newspaper, Jang. He and his three accomplices were charged with murder and the trial that followed was surrounded by a media frenzy.

It was all very surreal. His three young helpers giggled as they were led into the closed courtroom, pointing at newspaper photos of themselves. Iqbal, meanwhile, maintained that he was innocent and that he was the real victim in this case. He claimed to have staged the entire affair to highlight the plight of Pakistan's street-children and poor families who become victims of evil, corrupt individuals. He said that the missing boys were all actually alive, some living with people and some returned to their families. He claimed he had confessed because he was afraid that he too would be thrown from a window.

Nonetheless, he and his three accomplices were found guilty after a grueling trial featuring 102 witnesses. Two of the younger boys were sentenced to life imprisonment, but Iqbal and Sajid, who was now twenty, were sentenced to die in a way that the judge thought best suited their crimes.

He ordered that they be taken to the market square and there, in front of the families of their victims, they were to be strangled with the same iron chain that had been used to dispatch the boys. Their bodies would then be chopped up and dissolved in acid. The punishment would, indeed, fit the crime.

There was outrage around the world at the barbarity of the sentence but before it could be carried out it was announced that Iqbal and Sajid had been found dead in their adjoining prison cells. One version has it that they had been poisoned. Another says that they had been beaten and then strangled with their bedsheets.

The plight of Pakistan's streetkids remains unchanged.

PART SEVEN

PSYCHOPATHIC CHILD KILLERS

GILLES DE RAIS

Gilles de Rais learned from experts. Following the death of his father, Guy de Rais, he was brought up by his grandfather, the ruthless, scheming nobleman, Jean d'Craon who had fought to have the right to care for Gilles and his brother, not because he cared what happened to them, but because he wanted to get his hands on the property that they had inherited on their father's death.

True to form, d'Craon was a bad influence. The boys were taught the things necessary to being a young lord – morals, ethics, religion and the humanities, but beyond that, they were given little guidance and were allowed to run free with little supervision. D'Craon was an arrogant man who believed himself to be better than any other man and certainly above the law, traits that the young Gilles appropriated from him.

Not long after his arrival at d'Craon's chateau at Champtoce, d'Craon negotiated a marriage between the thirteen-year-old boy and Jeanne de Peynel, daughter of the Norman Lord de Hambye. It was a marriage that would bring together two wealthy families and that would make the d'Craons the most powerful family in France. That proved too much for the Parlement de Paris, the governing body of the region. It ordered that the marriage be postponed until Jeanne was older. Jean d'Craon could not wait that long. Ten months later, Gilles was betrothed to Beatrice de Rohan, niece of the Duke of Burgundy, another marriage that did not come to pass. Eventually, aged sixteen, Gilles was married to Catherine, daughter of Milet de Thouars, whose family owned estates that neighboured the de Rais lands. She had to be kidnapped first and three of her uncles were thrown into Champtoce dungeons, but the young couple were married in 1420.

By 1429, a remarkable figure had emerged in France. A nineteen-year-old girl, Joan of Arc, who seemed to possess magical powers of leadership and was given an army of 10,000 men by French King, Charles VI, with which to fight the English. Beside her rode Gilles de Rais, now a general in the French army and principal adviser to Joan. They liberated Orleans from the English and conducted the Dauphin – the heir to the French throne – to Reims for his coronation, Gilles de Rais charged with carrying the holy chrism, or anointing oil from Paris to the site of the coronation.

De Rais was appointed France's highest-ranking soldier when he was promoted to Marshal of France. He remained in that position for only two years, however. When Jean d'Craon died in, expressing remorse for all his evil deeds, de Rais effectively removed himself from public life and began to indulge the fantasies of his private life. In 1432, he killed a child for the first time. He would carry on killing for some time.

His first victim was a twelve-year-old apprentice furrier who was carrying a message from de Rais' cousin, Gilles de Sille, to the chateau at Mahecoul on France's west coast. He disappeared and his master, Guillaume Hilairet, approached de Sille, to be told that he had been taken by thieves in the village of Tiffauges. De Rais would later be charged with the boy's death. He kidnapped him, with the help of an accomplice, Etienne Corrillaut, raped him and then hung him by the neck on a hook. As he was dying, de Rais took him down, raped him again and then either killed him himself or ordered someone else to kill him.

On other occasions, victims were decapitated, or had their throats cut. They were sometimes dismembered and at other times their necks were broken with a stick. His henchman, Poitou, would later testify that de Rais often sodomised the children shortly after they were dealt the fatal blow. He raped them as they died.

De Rais later told how he much admired the most handsome of his child victims, having their bodies cut open so that he could look at their internal organs. He was also said to have often sat on the stomachs of the children as they died, laughing at them as they breathed their last. The bodies were then cremated, the ashes being disposed of in a cesspit or the moat of the castle.

De Rais did not kill alone. In fact, as the death tally rose, it became impossible for him to do so. His cousins, Gilles de Sille and Roger de Briqueville, were early participants in his deadly sport, providing him with his first two victims and although they did not take part in the sexual part of the acts, they were very active in planning and disposing of the evidence of his crimes.

As children began to disappear from the vicinity of the castle, the inhabitants of the nearby village naturally became suspicious of de Rais, but there was little they could do. They lived in fear of what he would do if they voiced their suspicions or complaints publicly. At the very least they would face imprisonment. Rumours about the village spread far and wide and its reputation grew. One man from a neighbouring village was heard to say to a man he encountered from Machecoul, 'They eat little children there!'

One of de Rais' princial helpers was a woman called Perrine Martin who was nicknamed 'La Meffraye' (the Terror). She was reputed to wander the countryside looking for any children out tending their family's animals or working alone in the fields. She would convey them to the castle. One witness at the later trial testified that he bumped into La Meffraye one day and she was accompanied by a young boy. She told him they were going to Machecoul. When the man met her again a few days later she was alone. When he asked about the boy, he was told that she had left him with a 'good master' in Machecoul.

Eventually, the disappearances were becoming so commonplace that de Sille was forced to invent an explanation for them. He admitted that the children had indeed been kidnapped, but it had been done by order of the king. They were handed over to the English, he added, to train as pages. It is unlikely that the parents of his victims were taken in by this obvious nonsense.

Gilles de Rais also began to take an unhealthy interest in the black arts. He had dabbled in alchemy and had even been conned out of substantial sums of money in his pursuits of the transmutation of base metals into gold and summoning the devil. He became involved with a twenty-two-year-old French conjurer and charlatan, Francois Prelati, who claimed to have control over the netherworld.

One of their many failed efforts to raise the devil saw de Rais bring into their presence a large, leather-bound book of spells and incantations that was sealed with a huge metal lock. Inside the pages were covered with writing in red ink, that was rumoured not to be ink at all, but blood, the blood of de Rais' many young victims. On another occasion, Prelati told de Rais that the devil had asked for the sacrifice of a child's heart, eyes and sex organs. De Rais had little trouble in providing him with what he asked for.

Soon, however, things began to get tricky for him and his henchmen when his brother began to take an interest in his affairs. René became very concerned about his brother's spending and succeeded in getting the King to issue an edict preventing Gilles from selling off any of the family property. In the process, René gained control of the estate of Champtoce. Gilles began to worry that soon René would move to take over Machecoul as well. This would be disastrous for him as he had over forty children's bodies hidden in one of the castle's towers. He immediately sent two of his men to clear them out and dispose of them, but as they were doing so, they were seen by two noblemen. Incredibly, they failed to report what they had seen, considering the victims to be merely peasant children who were not worth bothering about.

Several weeks later, René and a cousin, André de Laval-Loheac, occupied Machecoul castle as Gilles had anticipated, but the clean-up operation had been botched by de Sille. Two children's skeletons were discovered in the grounds of the castle and the men that de Rais had sent to clean up the tower, Poitou and Henriet, were interrogated about them. Naturally, they denied that they knew anything about the bodies, but by this time the family, fearing disgrace, had decided to erect a wall of silence.

The problem was, however, that Gilles was quite mad and, feeling cornered, reacted violently. One Sunday in 1440, during High Mass, he and a gang of outlaws burst into the church of St. Etienne de Mermorte. De Rais was in a state of high anxiety, wild-eyed and carrying a double-headed axe. The priest was the brother of the treasurer of Brittany who had occupied a castle owned by Gilles and the murderer kidnapped him demanding that the property be returned to him.

At last, some action was taken against a man who was clearly out of control and highly dangerous, as everyone already knew. Some of his most powerful enemies came together to bring him down. Jean V, the Duke of Brittany, who had long cast coveting glances at de Rais's land, allied himself with the Bishop of Nantes, Jean de Malestroit, another enemy of the de Rais family. Of course, the deaths of so many peasant children never entered into their considerations. Their decision to act was made for purely financial reasons.

The Bishop began by gathering information about de Rais. He was horrified by what he heard. Witnesses came forward in droves to testify about missing shepherd boys and sinister men, their faces hidden behind dark veils prowling the countryside and kidnapping innocent children. The Bishop published his evidence, asserting in the document that 'Milord Gilles de Rais, knight, lord, and baron, our subject and under our jurisdiction, with certain accomplices, did cut the throats of, kill and heinously massacre many young and innocent boys, that he did practice with these children unnatural lust and the vice of sodomy, often calls up or causes others to practice the dreadful invocation of demons, did sacrifice to and make pacts with the latter, and did perpetrate other enormous crimes within the limits of our jurisdiction.'

De Rais was unmoved. He was, after all, Marshal of France, an important and powerful man. He could not conceive of anyone accusing him of heresy or murder. Soon, however, he found himself distressingly alone as his accomplices de Sille and de Briqueville fled, not sharing his confidence.

In August, 1440, the Constable of France seized de Rais' castle at Tiffauges. Meanwhile, the King of France was hearing the evidence against him and prepared the documents to have him arrested and brought to justice. Finally on 14 September, Bishop Malestroit issued a warrant for the arrest of de Rais and his henchmen – Poitou, Henriet, Prelati and Blanchet. De Rais was conducted to Nantes where he appeared initially before the secular court on the charges connected with his attack on the church at St. Etienne. At this point his black magic experiments and the murders were not dealt with.

The investigation into the murders began a few days later. One mother told of handing her young son over to de Rais who said he would care for him and provide him with an education. She never saw the boy again. In all, ten families who suspected de Rais of killing their children, gave evidence. On 13 October, he was formally charged with thirty-four charges of murder, sodomy, heresy and the violation of the sanctity of the church. It was said that, in reality, de Rais and his gang had murdered 140 children in the past fourteen years.

When asked to make a plea, de Rais ranted at the

court, calling the judges names and saying he would rather be hanged than answer to them. The Bishop of Nantes excommunicated him and adjourned the hearing. A few days later, it was a different Gilles de Rais who appeared before the court. This time, he was contrite, having realised that he was being denied Communion and all other rites of the Church. He feared for his soul. He confessed to his crimes and asked forgiveness for his earlier behaviour. He was readmitted into the Church.

He then went on to make a full confession of everything apart from his efforts, with others, to summon Satan. His lie was exposed, however, by the testimony of his accomplices and it was decided to torture him to make him confess. The judges ordered that he be taken to the torture chamber in the dungeon at La Tour Neuve. Before he got there, however, he agreed that he would answer whatever questions they had for him. He could use torture but was reluctant to be on the receiving end of it.

He made a full, detailed and explicit confession before the Bishop and Pierre L'Hopital, the Chief Justice of Brittany. Interestingly, heresy was considered a more grievous crime than murder. His confession, therefore, was at pains to emphasize that he killed purely for pleasure and carnal delight rather than as a sacrifice to the devil. He could be pardoned for murder – even 140 murders – but not for heresy.

He was eventually sentenced to death, following another excommunication that was rescinded after he fell to his knees and pleaded with the Bishop. Poitou and Henriet received the same sentence.

When they went to the gallows on 26 October 1440, de Rais gave a long speech to the large crowd that had gathered to witness the spectacle, admitting his sins and at last displaying the humility he had so clearly lacked throughout his life.

ALBERT FISH

It was probably a good job that Delia Budd was illiterate because, in 1934, six years after her daughter, Grace, had been abducted, she received a letter containing these chilling words:

On Sunday June the 3, 1928 I called on you at 406 W 15 St. Brought you pot cheese–strawberries. We had lunch. Grace sat in my lap and kissed me. I made up my mind to eat her. On the pretense of taking her to a party. You said yes she could go. I took her to an empty house in Westchester I had already picked out. When we got there, I told her to remain outside. She picked wildflowers. I went upstairs and stripped all my clothes off. I knew if I did not I would get her blood on them. When all was ready I went to the window and called her. Then I hid in a closet until she was in the room. When she saw me all naked she began to cry and tried to run down the stairs. I grabbed her and she said she would tell her mamma. First I stripped her

*naked. How she did kick – bite and scratch. I
choked her to death, then cut her in small pieces so I
could take my meat to my rooms. Cook and eat it.
How sweet and tender her little ass was roasted in
the oven. It took me 9 days to eat her entire body. I
did not fuck her tho I could of had I wished. She
died a virgin.*

The letter had been written by Albert Hamilton
Fish, the man who had taken and killed Grace Budd.
Fish, then fifty-eight years old, had arrived on the
Budds' doorstep in May 1928, pretending to be Frank
Howard, a farmer from Farmingdale, New York. He
was calling in response to an advert placed in the *New
York World* by Edward Budd, Grace's eighteen-year-
old brother. It read:

*Young man, 18, wishes position in country. Edward
Budd, 406 West 15th Street.*

Fish spun a story that he needed someone to work
on his farm and Edward was eager for the work. Fish
returned a few days later to confirm that Edward had
the job and was asked to stay for lunch. While there,
Fish befriended Grace. She sat on his lap at the dinner
table. As he was about to leave, he said he was on his
way to a children's birthday party at his sister's house

and wondered whether Grace would like to accompany him. Grace's mother was unsure, but her husband Albert thought it would be fun for the girl and off Grace went with Albert Fish. It was the last they saw of their daughter.

Albert Fish was born Hamilton Fish in 1870 and his father was forty-three years older than his mother. When his father died in 1875, the five-year-old Hamilton was put into St John's Orphanage by his mother. It was there that he changed his name to Albert to avoid the nickname 'Ham and Fish' that he had been given by the other children.

Life in the orphanage was harsh and cruel. There were regular beatings and whippings, but, perversely, Albert grew to enjoy the pain. He enjoyed it so much, in fact, that he would have erections for which the other children mocked him. His mother was able to look after him again when she found employment in 1879, but Albert was already scarred by his experiences at St John's. By the age of twelve, he was engaged in a homosexual relationship. His partner, a telegraph boy, introduced him to perverse practices such as coprophagia and drinking urine. He spent his weekends watching boys undress at the public baths.

Fish claimed that by 1890 he was working as a male prostitute in New York City and that he was raping young boys on a regular basis. In 1898 he married and six children followed. He was working as a house painter but was also molesting countless children, mostly boys under the age of six. At this time, he developed an interest in castration and tried it out on a man with whom he had been having a relationship; the man fled before Fish could carry it out.

In 1903, he was charged with embezzlement and was sent to Sing Sing. But it wasn't that much of a hardship for him as he could have sex with other inmates.

His life changed completely, in 1917, when his wife ran off with another man. Fish began to behave even more strangely than before. He claimed to hear voices and once wrapped himself up in a carpet, saying he had been ordered to do so by Saint John. His children reported seeing him beat himself on his nude body with a nail-studded piece of wood until he was covered with blood. Once they saw him standing alone on a hill with his hands raised, shouting: 'I am Christ.'

He inserted needles into his body, in the area of the groin – twenty-nine were discovered by an X-ray following his eventual arrest – and inserted alcohol covered balls of cotton wool into his anus; he would then ignite them. In this way, he thought he could cleanse himself of his sins.

Some four years prior to the abduction of Grace Budd, seven-year-old Francis McDonnell was playing with some friends near his home on Staten Island. His mother saw a man behaving oddly. He walked up and down the street, wringing his hands and talking to himself. She thought no more of him and went indoors. Later that same day, the same man lured Francis into some nearby woods. The next day his body was discovered, sexually brutalised, mutilated and strangled. It would be another ten years before they would discover who the killer was.

A year before Grace's murder, Fish abducted, tortured and killed another child, Billy Gaffney. Fish later confessed:

I brought him to the Riker Avenue dumps. There is a house that stands alone, not far from where I took him. I took the boy there. Stripped him naked and tied his hands and feet and gagged him with a piece of dirty rag I picked out of the dump. Then I burned his clothes. Threw his shoes in the dump. Then I walked back and took the trolley to 59 Street at 2 a.m. and walked from there home. Next day about 2 p.m., I took tools, a good heavy cat-o-nine tails. Home made. Short handle. Cut one of my belts in half, slit these halves in six strips about 8 inches long. I whipped his bare behind till the blood ran from his legs. I cut off his ears, nose, slit his mouth from ear to ear. Gouged out his eyes. He was dead then. I stuck the knife in his belly and held my mouth to his body and drank his blood. I picked up four old potato sacks and gathered a pile of stones. Then I cut him up. I had a grip with me. I put his nose, ears and a few slices of his belly in the grip. Then I cut him through the middle of his body. Just below the belly button. Then through his legs about 2 inches below his behind. I put this in my grip with a lot of paper. I cut off the head, feet, arms, hands and the legs below the knee. This I put in sacks weighed with stones, tied the ends and threw them into the pools of slimy water you will see all along the road going to North Beach. I came home with my meat. I had the front of his body I liked best. His monkey and pee wees and a nice little fat behind to roast in the oven and eat. I made a stew out of his ears, nose, pieces of his face and belly. I put onions, carrots, turnips, celery, salt and pepper. It was good. Then I split the cheeks of his behind open, cut off his monkey and pee wees and washed them first. I put strips of bacon on each cheek of his behind and put them in the oven. Then I picked 4 onions and when the meat had roasted about 1/4 hour, I poured about a pint of water over it for gravy and put in the onions. At frequent intervals I basted his behind with a wooden spoon. So the meat would be nice and juicy. In about 2 hours, it was nice and brown, cooked through. I never ate any roast turkey that tasted half as good as his sweet fat little behind did. I ate every bit of the meat in about four days. His little monkey was a sweet as a nut, but his pee-wees I could not chew. Threw them in the toilet.

Ultimately, it was Fish's arrogance that betrayed him. The letter he wrote to Mrs Budd was delivered in an envelope that bore the logo of the New York Private Chauffeur's Benevolent Association. It turned out that a janitor of the association had left some stationery in a boarding house when he had moved out. Albert Fish had moved in after him but, the landlady told police, he had also since moved out. However, he had been expecting some money to be sent and had asked her to hold on to the cheque for him until he could call round to collect it. Detective William F. King waited at the house and when Fish arrived, asked him to accompany him to police HQ to answer some questions. Fish lunged at King with a razor, but the policeman easily overpowered him and arrested him.

Fish confessed to the pre-meditated murder of Grace Budd launching a debate as to whether he was sane which raged both before his trial and throughout it. However, he was found to be both sane and guilty and was sentenced to death. He thanked the judge for his death sentence and after sentencing confessed to the murder of Francis McDonnell. It is speculated that as well as the three murders that can be ascribed to Albert Fish with certainty, he may actually have murdered at least fifteen children and assaulted hundreds more over the years.

At Sing Sing on 16 January 1936, at 11.06, he was strapped into 'Old Sparky', the electric chair, and three minutes later, was dead. He is reported to have said that the execution would be 'the supreme thrill of my life'.

Ian Brady and Myra Hindley

THE MOORS MURDERERS

Rejecting an appeal for their early release of Ian Brady and Myra Hindley in 2000, the House of Lords described their crimes as 'exceptionally wicked and uniquely evil'. The country agreed, disgusted by the depravity of their deviant sexual relationship, and Brady and Hindley became possibly the most despised people in Britain in the last forty years.

They met in January 1961, when he was twenty-one years old and Hindley was nineteen. He was working as a clerk at a Manchester chemical company where she got a job as a secretary. Their attraction to each other was immediate.

Myra Hindley was from Gorton in Manchester, the oldest child of Bob and Nellie Hindley. She was brought up, however, by her grandmother. Her childhood was fairly uneventful and she was thought of as a reliable girl who could be trusted, ironically, given her later acts, to babysit. Not considered bright enough to take O Levels, she left school at the age of fifteen and started working as a clerk at an electrical engineering firm. She was engaged at seventeen, but she called it off shortly after, taking fright at the type of life that would lie ahead of her. She wanted something a little more exciting than a mortgage, kids and a husband who spent his wages in the pub.

Ian Brady was certainly that. By the time she met him he was already a disturbed young man. He had been born out of wedlock in the rough Gorbals area of Glasgow and his mother had given him up for adoption. He became increasingly difficult as he got older, having terrible tantrums during which he would bang his head on the floor. At school, he was a loner who did not take part in the games the other boys played and he hated sport.

He was an intelligent boy, however, doing well enough to gain entrance to a good school, Shawlands Academy, at the age of eleven. But he never fulfilled his potential and was constantly in trouble. He also developed an unhealthy fascination with the Nazis, devouring books about them and collecting Nazi memorabilia. He began to get on the wrong side of the law and was charged with housebreaking three times between the ages of thirteen and sixteen. Eventually, he was ordered to leave Glasgow to live with his mother or be given a custodial sentence. He chose his mother and Manchester, moving to Moss Side.

With his Glasgow accent, Brady found it even more difficult to fit in in Manchester and became even more of an outcast. His mother had re-married a man named Brady and he took his name. His stepfather found him a job as a porter at the local market and he then found work at a brewery. Before long, however, he was arrested for stealing lead seals from his employers and sentenced to two years in a young offenders institution. However, there was no room for him and the first few months of his sentence were spent in Strangeways Prison where he had to grow up fast.

Released in November 1957, he got a job at Millwards where he met Myra Hindley.

She fell head over heels in love with him, seeing him as silent and aloof whereas others just thought he was sullen. To her, he was enigmatic and very different from anyone else she had ever gone out with. He rode a motorbike and she would comment in her diary about how he looked and what he was wearing. Nonetheless, it took him a year to ask her out – their first date was spent watching the film, *Judgement at Nuremberg* – and pretty soon they were an item.

He initiated her into his world, making her read his favourite books – *Mein Kampf, Crime and Punishment,* and the works of the Marquis de Sade. He persuaded her to bleach her hair blonde and to dress differently, wearing leather skirts and high boots. She allowed him to take pornographic pictures of her and he photographed them having sex. Some of the photographs show the marks left by a whip across her buttocks. She had always been a churchgoer, but when he told her there was no God, she stopped going. She believed everything he told her.

Within six months, he had moved in with her at her grandmother's house where the elderly lady spent most of her time in bed. Her devotion to him was now total and as she was about to prove she would do anything to please him.

On the night of 12 July 1963, sixteen-year-old Pauline Reade was on her way to a dance. Some friends of hers had been forbidden to go as alcohol was going to be served, but they were curious to see if she would actually go on her own as she had said. Wearing a pretty pink dress, she did indeed set out for the dance, but she never arrived. Her friends followed her and then took a shortcut to surprise her outside the club. They waited but there was no sign of her.

At midnight, her parents went out looking for her and the next morning, having found no trace of her, they informed the police that she was missing.

Hindley had apparently intercepted Pauline and

asked for her help in finding a glove that she had lost on Saddleworth Moor, an isolated and windswept area of the Peak District National Park. Once they were on the moors, Brady turned up on his motorbike. According to Hindley, he went off with the girl to search for the glove while Hindley waited at the car. She claimed that Brady raped Pauline and cut her throat before coming back to enlist her help in burying the body. Brady disagrees, saying that Hindley took an active part in sexually molesting Pauline.

On 11 November of the same year, they killed again. Twelve-year-old John Kilbride had gone with a friend to the cinema and had afterwards walked to the Ashton-under-Lyme market where there was sometimes money to be earned helping stallholders pack up. His friend left John at the market to catch a bus home and it was the last time he was seen alive.

A massive search was launched, involving thousands of police and volunteers but, as before, not a trace was found.

That day, Hindley had hired a car that was used to abduct John Kilbride. It was returned covered in mud and according to Hindley's sister, Brady and Hindley shopped at Ashton market every Saturday.

In May 1964, Hindley bought a white Mini van and on 16 June, another child went missing. Twelve-year-old Keith Bennett stayed at his grandmother's house every Tuesday evening while his mother went to bingo. That night when he failed to turn up, his grandmother just thought that his mother had decided not to send him over. The next morning when she turned up at her daughter's door without Keith the police were called and another massive, but ultimately fruitless, search was launched.

Meanwhile, Brady and Hindley had joined a local gun club and would often go up onto Saddleworth Moor for target practice. Chillingly, they would also visit the graves of their victims, photographing each other kneeling on them.

Their fourth victim was ten-year-old Lesley Ann Downey. On Boxing Day 1964 she went to a local fair with her two brothers and some friends. They had soon spent all the money they had been given and decided to go home. Lesley Ann decided to stay, however. She was last seen by a schoolmate, standing alone next to one of the rides.

Again, a huge search was initiated with thousands of people being questioned and hundreds of posters being put up. Yet again it was all to no avail.

Lesley Ann's abduction and subsequent torture was about as depraved as two human beings could get. Photographs were later found of the little girl, naked and bound, posing for pornographic photographs. They tortured her, callously making a recording of her screams as she died. On the tape, the voices of both Hindley and Brady could be heard threatening and abusing her.

Brady, like the true psychopath he was, thought of himself as invincible and all-powerful. He now attempted to gain another recruit for his depraved acts, trying to corrupt Myra's seventeen-year-old brother-in-law, David Smith. He gave him his beloved books and made him write some quotations in a notebook – 'Murder is a hobby and supreme pleasure' and 'People are like maggots, small, blind, worthless fish-bait.' He boasted to an incredulous Smith about the murders he had already committed and then decided to involve him in a murder. It would be his and Hindley's undoing.

On 7 October 1965, Smith turned up at Hyde Police Station and told an astonishing story. He said that the previous night, his sister-in-law, Myra Hindley had told him that she was too afraid to walk home alone and had asked him to accompany her. On arriving at her house she invited him in to pick up some miniature bottles of wine that her boyfriend, Ian Brady, had left for him.

As he stood in the kitchen, however, he heard a loud scream coming from the living room, followed by a yell from Myra for him to come through. He rushed to the room wondering what he would find.

On entering he saw Ian Brady holding what he at first thought was a life-size doll. He realised with a start, however, that it was actually the body of a young man. Brady stood up and straddled him, an axe in his hand. The young man on the floor was moaning and Brady raised the axe and brought it down on the man's head. As the groans subsided, Brady swung the axe down on his head again and the groans changed to gurgles. Brady threw a cover over the youth's head and wrapped a piece of electrical cord around his neck, pulling it tight and repeating the words 'You fucking dirty bastard' over and over again. The man on the floor stopped making any noise and Brady then turned to Hindley and said calmly, 'That's it, the messiest yet.'

While they had a cup of tea, Hindley and Brady joked about what had just happened. But Smith was horrified, and also very afraid of what might happen if he made the wrong move. He stayed long enough to help them clean up the mess and truss the body up for removal and disposal. He then went home and was violently sick.

The police were just as incredulous as Smith had been about Brady's bragging, but they went round to Hindley's house to check. Sure enough, there in the back bedroom they found the body of the young man they had murdered the previous evening, Edward

Evans, a seventeen-year-old homosexual that Brady had picked up in a pub in Manchester.

When confronted, Brady admitted to killing Evans but said that it happened during an argument. He also tried to implicate David Smith, something he consistently did during interrogation. Hindley was not initially arrested, but four days later, a three-page document turned up in her car that detailed how she and Brady were going to carry out the murder and clean up afterwards. Critically, however, they also found a mention of Hindley's prayer book. Examining that, they discovered a left luggage ticket between its pages. In the locker at Manchester Piccadilly station they made a horrific find. There were two suitcases containing pornographic books and magazines. But there were also pictures of Lesley Ann Downey, naked and gagged, as well as the tape of her screams as they brought her young life to a cruel end.

The trial was a procession of perversion and cruelty. It seemed that Myra Hindley was turned on by watching Brady perform homosexual acts on his victims but throughout the trial the pair said nothing and showed no remorse.

They were each sentenced to life, Brady refusing to appeal while Hindley did, but her petition was rejected. For seven years they corresponded with each other in prison before Hindley stopped. She took a university degree and helped police with information about the whereabouts of their victims' bodies.

As the years passed, Hindley made many attempts to obtain a release from prison, but Brady constantly countered her moves by revealing more about her involvement in the murders. It all became academic in 2002 when she died in prison. Brady, meanwhile, has never sought release and has been trying to starve himself to death for a number of years.

Keith Bennett's body remains undiscovered forty-six years after his murder.

ARTHUR GARY BISHOP

You would never have been able to predict that Arthur Gary Bishop was a monster who would grow to be Utah's most notorious killer of the 20th century.

Born in 1951 in the small town of Hinckley in Utah, and raised by God-fearing Mormon parents, as a child he was a high-achieving student and an Eagle Scout. Following his graduation from high school, like most Mormon kids, he served as a missionary, his service taking him to the Philippines. Returning to America, he enrolled at a Utah business school and graduated from there with good grades.

Success in high school and college, a solid, religious background; all seemed normal in Bishop's world. But he was far from normal. He had grown addicted to pornography, but not just any old pornography – it was pornography involving children.

It was not that, however, that brought his first contravention of the law. In 1977, to the surprise of his family and everyone who knew him, he was accused of embezzling almost $9,000 from a used-car dealership where he had been employed as a bookkeeper for a year. He pled guilty and was given a suspended five-year prison sentence on condition he repaid all the money. He seemed to show the appropriate remorse, but it turned out to be a sham. Before long, he had disappeared, spending the next five years on the run, using false names, finding work wherever he could and stealing money to live on when he could not.

His flight from justice did not take him very far. He went to Salt Lake City, about 100 miles northeast of Hinckley, calling himself Roger W. Downs. That was the name he used when he enrolled with Big Brothers Big Sisters, a non-profit organisation designed to help children reach their potential through one-to-one relationships with mentors. It was the last place that a man with the proclivities of Bishop should have been and it later emerged that during his time with the organisation, he molested at least two young boys. The tragedy is that both incidents were reported to the police and nothing was done about them.

Meanwhile, he worked in odd jobs, continuing to molest boys whenever he had the opportunity. In October 1979, however, molestation turned into something altogether more serious.

On 14 October, four-year-old Alonzo Daniels was approached by Downs who lived in the apartment across the hall from his own. He told him he could have some candy but it was in his apartment. Once there, Downs undressed and fondled the frightened boy, panicking when Alonzo began to cry and said that he would tell his mother. Bishop grabbed a hammer and bludgeoned Alonzo with it. Still failing to stop the boy crying, he carried him into the bathroom, turned on the taps and drowned him in the bathtub. Putting the corpse into a large cardboard box, he carried it out to his car. As he walked through the courtyard, he passed Alonzo's mother who was calling her son's name.

When the police arrived, they started door-to-door enquiries, Downs being one of the first to be questioned. He was, of course, unable to help them. Meanwhile, the search for the boy escalated and carried on for several days, with hundreds of police officers and civilians involved. Photographs were distributed and thousands of people were questioned, but he seemed to have vanished without a trace.

On the night of the fourteenth, Bishop drove out to the desert, twenty miles outside Salt lake City and buried Alonzo's body near the town of Cedar Fort.

It seemed for a while as if Bishop tried to subvert his urge to murder children by focusing instead on killing puppies. He adopted around twenty from shelters over the next year, killing all of them by bludgeoning them with hammers, by strangulation or by drowning. He later claimed that it was like killing Alonzo. 'It was so stimulating,' he told a detective. 'A puppy whines just like Alonzo did.' The strange thing is that nobody seemed to notice, or if they did, they chose to take no action.

He was still molesting young boys but they were allowed to live if they promised not to tell anyone. It was not until November 1980 that his murderous urge took over again.

He met an eleven-year-old, Kim Peterson, at a roller-skating rink and agreed to buy his skates from him. The boy left home the following day, telling his parents that he had found a buyer for the skates and was going out to meet him. It was the last time they would see him. When he failed to return home in time for dinner that night, the police were called and another search was launched, with similar results to the one for Alonzo. This time, however, there were some witnesses who provided a description of a man aged between twenty-five and thirty-five who was seen talking to Kim at the rink. He was wearing, they said, glasses, jeans and an army-style jacket. A couple of skaters at the rink agreed to be hypnotised and provided more details, including the fact that the man drove a silver Chevrolet Camaro with an out-of-state registration. This last fact was, of course, incorrect and misled the police for some time. Critically, however, they failed to connect the case of Kim Peterson's disappearance with that of Alonzo Daniels.

Meanwhile, Kim who had also been bludgeoned to death, was also buried out in a remote part of the desert. Now Bishop realised that although he had killed both boys to prevent them from exposing him as a child-molestor, he had actually enjoyed it. He wanted more.

First, however, he had to find some cash without working too hard to get it. He took a job as a bookkeeper at a ski shop, under the name Lynn E. Jones. One day he simply failed to return from his lunch-break and neither did $10,000 he had removed from the shop safe, along with his personnel file.

A few weeks later, on 20 October 1981, he spied what he later sickeningly described as 'the most beautiful little boy' in a local supermarket. He approached the boy, four-year-old Danny Davis, who was fiddling with a bubble gum-machine and offered him sweets. Danny had been well-taught, however, and refused the offering. Bishop gave up, deciding to leave the shop. But the boy followed him, and, once outside, Bishop led him towards his car.

In the shop, Danny's grandmother realised Danny was missing and raised the alarm. The shop-workers and customers quickly searched the shop and the surrounding area but Danny was long gone by that time. The authorities looked everywhere for him, police divers searching ponds and lakes, the mountains and desert being combed in the most intensive search in Salt Lake City's history. A $20,000 reward was offered for information and the FBI became involved. No trace of the boy was uncovered.

Roger Downs, living close to the scene of Danny's disappearance once again answered the door to a policeman, but satisfied them once again that he knew nothing. What the police did not know, however, was that Bishop had smothered the boy by pinching his nostrils and covering his mouth with his hand when he would not stop crying. Once again he drove out to Cedar Fort and disposed of the body.

When a fourth child, a girl this time, four-year-old Rachel Runyan, disappeared from a school playground in August 1982, in the town of Sunset, north of Salt Lake City, there was uproar. The public was outraged that the authorities appeared powerless against this maniac who was on the loose. When her body was found, strangled, a short time later, the state passed a new piece of legistlation, making their law on child abduction the strictest in the United States. Abductors could now be sent to prison for up to fifteen years depending on the seriousness of their crime.

The police deduced that there was no connection between Rachel Runyan's death and the disappearance of the three boys in Salt Lake City, but by now, people were panicking and reports of suspicious strangers in parks and playgrounds flooded in. As Halloween approached, rumours started to circulate that the missing boys had been kidnapped by occultists who had sacrificed them. When Halloween 1982 passed without incident, the rumours died down.

Police were baffled, however. There seemed to be no pattern to the disappearances. The boys had been taken at different times, on different days and they had been different races – Alonzo Daniels was African American and the other two Caucasians with blond hair. Neither was age consistent – Kim Peterson was eleven and the other two boys were four.

Two years passed before Bishop gave vent to his urges again. It was Troy Ward's sixth birthday and he was playing in a park close to his home. He failed to turn up to meet a family friend at four o'clock on a corner near the park to be taken home for a birthday party.

There was no delay in summoning the police who immediately launched a search. They found a witness who recalled seeing a boy matching Troy's description, leaving the park with a man just before four.

Once again, Bishop's charm and ease with children persuaded Troy to go home with him. The usual ritual of molestation followed and then the hammer and the bathtub after the distraught boy threatened to report what had occurred. He then drove Troy's body to Big Cottonwood Creek, in the Twin Peaks Wilderness Area where he buried him.

Just a month later, he struck again. He was going to be taking two junior high school boys on a camping trip. One of the boys disappeared before they left, however. Thirteen-year-old Graeme Cunningham disappeared from his neighbourhood on the afternoon of Thursday 14 July. Incredibly, while the disappearance was being flagged up on the news and the state began to fear that the maniac had struck again, the killer, Roger Downs, was knocking on the door of the boy's mother offering any help he could.

The police again went through the motions, door-to-door questioning, dragging lakes, rivers and ponds and scouring the surrounding desert and mountains. This time, however, someone noticed something strange. A man called Roger Downs had been questioned each time one of the five boys went missing. Furthermore, he lived close to four of the boys and knew the parents of the fifth.

A couple of detectives returned to Bishop's apartment and asked him some more questions. This time they felt sure he was being evasive and they invited him to police headquarters for further questioning. Experienced detective Don Bell interrogating him and soon began to squeeze the truth from him. He confessed to his real identity and before the day was out, he had also confessed to all five murders.

The following day, he took them to the sites where he had buried his victims, at Cedar Fort and Big Cottonwood Creek.

As the days passed, they strived to establish what motivated him to kill the boys. At first, he claimed that he killed them only because they threatened to expose him, but as time went on, it became obvious that although that had initially been his reason, he had grown to enjoy killing and would have carried on until stopped or arrested. 'I'm glad they caught me,' he said, 'because I'd do it again.'

The floodgates opened following the announcement of his arrest. Numerous parents telephoned the police accusing Bishop of molesting their child or friends' children during the past ten years. Police were baffled as to why they had not called earlier and possibly prevented Bishop from killing. The horror mounted when it emerged that his younger brother, Douglas, had been arrested for also sexually abusing young boys in Provo, a town south of Salt Lake City.

Arthur Bishop was charged with five counts of murder, five of kidnapping, two of forcible sexual assault and one of sexually abusing a minor.

Like all psychopaths, Bishop was found to have what the Desert County Attorney described as 'a scheming, calculating, cunning mind,' and his defence team played on his 'emotional and psychological deficits', trying to obtain a manslaughter rather than a murder conviction. They blamed his addiction to pornography, claiming that it had warped his mind and he himself agreed that porn had desensitized him to normal feelings. Eventually, the images of young boys naked had been insufficient for him and he required more to stimulate him sexually. 'Finding and procuring sexually arousing materials became an obsession,' he said. 'For me, seeing pornography was lighting a fuse on a stick of dynamite. I became stimulated and had to gratify my urges or explode. All boys became mere sexual objects. My conscience was desensitized and my sexual appetite entirely controlled my actions.'

None of it mattered, however. He was found guilty on charges of murder, kidnapping and sexual abuse of a minor and was sentenced to death.

As was the law in Utah, he was given the choice between dying in front of a firing squad or by lethal injection. He chose the injection and sat on Death Row for four years, during which time he is said to have read the *Book of Mormon* ten times from cover to cover.

By the 10 June 1988, the date of his execution, Arthur Bishop was being described by a Mormon bishop as the most 'sorrowful and repentant and remorseful' of the thousands of inmates he had visited in the past thirty-three years.

ROBERT BLACK

It was a very strange sight. A man swimming up and down the pool, with a broom-handle protruding from his anus where he had earlier inserted it. By day he worked as a lifeguard and at night he broke in and swam. He loved swimming. He also loved little girls.

Robert Black had been unloved from almost the minute he was born on 21 April 1947. His mother, Jessie, was not prepared to face the stigma that being an unmarried mother brought in those days and having already refused to name her baby's father on his birth certificate, gave the child up for adoption as soon as she could, at six months. Within a year, she was long gone, married and living in Australia where she had four children, none of whom was told about the half-brother they had back in the old country, Scotland.

Meanwhile, the boy, christened Robert, was fostered out to the Tulip family who lived in the town of Kinlochleven in the West Highlands. He would spend the next eleven years of his life there. He was serially unlucky in his choice of parents, however. His foster-father, Jack, died when Robert was only five and his foster-mother, Margaret, passed away when he was just eleven. During those years, however, life was no bed of roses for Robert. Friends and neighbours remember him being covered in bruises and he was often beaten with a leather belt when he misbehaved. He was known as 'Smelly Robert' to schoolmates and, indeed, Robert Black had a problem with body odour that remained with him.

He is reported to have been an aggressive lad who did not mix well with children his own age, preferring instead to hang around with a gang of younger kids that he could boss about. He was a bully and one friend recalls a particularly savage beating he gave for no reason at all to a boy with an artificial leg. However, he never got into any really serious trouble.

He did confess after his eventual arrest, to an unnatural fixation with his anus and his urge to see what he could fit in it. He said that he would put a little piece of metal up there, but photographs recovered following his arrest show him with such items as a telephone hand-set and a table leg inserted.

When Margaret Tulip died in 1958, Black was sent to a children's home near Falkirk and a year later, at the age of only twelve, he made his first attempt at rape. He and a couple of other boys from the home, took a girl into a field, lifted her skirt and tried to rape her. When the girl informed on the boys, it was decided that Black needed a home with stricter discipline. He was sent to the all-male Red House children's home near Musselburgh on Scotland's east coast. Unfortunately, he became the subject of repeated sexual abuse by a member of staff.

Aged fifteen, he left the Red House, the authorities finding a job for him as a delivery boy while he lived in a rented room in Greenock in Glasgow. It was while doing his deliveries that he began to live some of his fantasies, molesting around forty girls as he did his rounds. Incredibly, no one reported him at the time. A year later, however, he was convicted for 'lewd and libidinous behaviour'.

Black, now aged seventeen, had met a seven-year-old girl in a park and asked if she would like to go with him to see some kittens. He led her to a disused building where he held her down by the throat until she was unconscious and removed her underwear. He then assaulted her and masturbated over her unconscious body. When he left her, he had no idea if she was alive or dead. Neither did he care.

She was later found wandering in the street, distraught and bleeding.

Astonishingly, Black was merely admonished for this act, the psychiatric report suggesting that this was no more than 'an isolated incident'. Nonetheless, Social Services sent him back to his home-town of Grangemouth, hoping that he would make a fresh start to his already troubled life.

He found a job with a builders' supply company and seemed to settle down. He even had a relationship with a woman, Pamela Hodgson, that looked as if it might result in marriage. But rumours about his sexual predilections began to circulate before long and Pamela ended it. They were more than just rumours, however. He had been up to his old tricks again with the nine-year-old daughter of his landlord and landlady. They did not involve the police, not wanting to put their daughter through the anguish of an investigation but word soon got out and Black lost his job. He returned to Kinlochleven, renting a room in a house. Unfortunately, there was a seven-year-old girl in the house and Black was soon caught molesting her. The police were called this time and in March 1967 he was sent to Borstal at Polmont for indecent assault.

On his release, he decided to head for the anonymity of the big city and moved to London. He managed to stay out of trouble throughout the 1970s, but fuelled his sexual urges, instead, with child pornography magazines. He also used his time working as a swimming pool attendant, watching little girls as they swam. It was around this time that he would break into the swimming pool and perform his weird swimming ritual with a broom-handle. He was also reported for touching a little girl again but the police did not pursue the case, fortunately for him.

He began taking an interest in photography, but his snaps and videos were only of little girls.

In 1976, he found work as a driver for a company called Poster Dispatch and Storage, delivering posters to depots all over the country. He loved the work. Very much a loner, it allowed him to be on his own all day and to keep to his own schedule. For ten years he worked for the company, frequently doing the longer runs for other drivers who did not like to be away from home for so long. What they did not know was that in the back of his van were various masturbatory implements that he would insert into his anus. Sometimes he would dress up in girls' clothing or swimming costumes in the back of the van while he fantasized about touching little girls.

He finally killed one hot summer's afternoon in July 1982.

Eleven-year-old Susan Maxwell lived in a farm-house just outside the town of Cornhill-on-Tweed, on the English side of the border. She had gone to play tennis with a friend in Coldstream, just on the other side of the border. When her mother went to collect her after the game, she was nowhere to be found. A phone call to her friend confirmed that she had left to walk home, in which case her mother should have passed her on the road.

The police were called and it emerged that Susan, dressed in bright yellow and holding a tennis racket, had been seen by a number of people until she crossed the bridge over the River Tweed at which point she seems to have vanished.

Two weeks later, her body was discovered in a ditch beside a lay-by on the A518 at Loxley, near Uttoxeter, 250 miles from her home. She had been there a while and her body had badly decomposed in the summer heat. They identified her from her dental records but it was difficult to conclude how she had died. Her underpants had been removed and folded beneath her head and her shorts had been replaced. There was no doubt that, however she died, the motive for the attack was sexual.

The investigation into Susan's death lasted for a year, but came to no conclusion, in spite of 500,000 hand-written index cards that had been compiled. It was the days before computer databases made crime-fighting much easier.

He struck again on 8 July 1983 in his old haunt, Portobello, a seaside resort just outside Edinburgh. Five-year-old Caroline Hogg had attended a party that day and had gone out to play before bedtime. The playground was only a few minutes away and her mother had seen no harm in letting her daughter out for five minutes.

When fifteen minutes had passed and she had not returned, her mother sent her brother out to find her. When he came back saying there was no trace of her, panic set in and the police were called. They immediately established that Caroline had been seen by numerous people holding hands with what was described as a 'scruffy man'. He had taken her to a nearby fairground, 'Fun City', where he had paid for her to go on a ride. They were last seen walking out of the entrance, still holding hands.

A massive search was instigated, the largest ever in Scotland, while her parents, like the Maxwells, spoke to the press, her mother weeping as she explained how much she missed her beloved daughter.

They found Caroline's body on 18 July in a lay-by at Twycross in Leicestershire, close to the A444, a road that stretches from Northampton to Coventry. She was 300 miles from home, but within just twenty-four miles of the location of Susan Maxwell's body. She was identified from her hairband and a locket and this time, the body was completely naked.

The police, naturally, linked the two cases and the Deputy Chief Constable of Northumbria, Hector

Clark was put in overall charge of the joint operation that now involved a number of police forces. Clark set about computerising all the data gathered thus far. The police had learned from the Yorkshire Ripper investigation just how valuable computers could be in the hunt for a murderer.

They interviewed witnesses and made house-to-house enquiries. They sat for weeks on the A444 taking down registration numbers of passing cars and checking them out. Police forces all over the country were asked to provide the names of possible suspects and holiday-makers from around the world sent in rolls of film taken at Portobello on the night in question. They found nothing, however. Once again, they had no leads.

There was a gap of three years before the next incident. On 26 March 1986, ten-year-old Sarah Harper went to a local shop for a loaf of bread and never returned to her home in Morley in Leeds. Within an hour the police were called and an intensive search was launched. Her body was found on 19 April by a man walking his dog by the River Trent in Nottingham. It was estimated that she had probably been dumped in the river at Junction 24 of the M1 while she was still alive. Her injuries were described as 'terrible'.

At first they thought that her death was not linked

to the Maxwell and Hogg killings. There were differences – Susan and Caroline had been much younger than Sarah and had been dressed in bright summer clothes. They had both been taken near main roads. Morley was out of the way and you did not go there without a reason. However, there were also similarities. All three were abducted for sexual purposes and driven south to the Midlands where their bodies were dumped. Admittedly, Sarah's injuries were more extreme than the others, but it is thought that the offender tends to escalate the violence he perpetrates, the more murders he or she commits and the more confident he or she becomes.

In July 1990, Robert Black was finally caught. Six-year-old Mandy Wilson was walking to a friend's house in the village of Stow in the Scottish borders. A neighbour, David Herkes, watched her walk past as he cut his grass. He later explained that as he bent down to look at the blades of his lawn-mower he noticed her feet standing next to a man's. 'Suddenly they vanished,' he said, 'and I saw him making movements as if he were trying to stuff something under the dashboard. He got into the van, reversed up the driveway the child had just come from and sped off towards Edinburgh.'

He quickly memorized the car's registration as it disappeared and ran indoors to call the police. The number was radioed out to every police car in the vicinity, but as he stood explaining what had happened to a police officer, Robert Black's van suddenly appeared again. The policeman ran into the road and the car swerved to avoid him before stopping. The officers dragged Black out and handcuffed him. In the back of the van they found the little girl, wrapped in a sleeping bag with tape over her mouth to prevent her calling out.

When questioned about the girl, Black displayed the true characteristics of a psychopath. He was completely disassociated from her, saying 'I wasn't thinking about her at all . . . like, you know, what she must be feeling.' If she had died, he added, 'it would have been a pure accident.'

Robert Black was sentenced to life imprisonment for Mandy Wilson's abduction and, later received sentences of thirty-five years for the other murders. He will be eligible for parole in 2029 when he will be eighty-two years old. It is thought that he might be responsible for a great many more murders of little girls, such as the unsolved killing of thirteen-year-old Genette Tate who disappeared in Devon in 1978. So far, he has not been willing to talk about these deaths.

As he was taken down after sentencing, Black turned to the twenty-three police officers there to hear the verdict and said with a smile, 'Well done, boys.'

MICHEL FOURNIRET

They called him the 'Ogre of the Ardennes' when they finally caught him. He confessed to ten murders but some put the probable total closer to forty and when he was arrested, police forces across Europe re-opened unsolved murders to establish whether Michel Fourniret might have been responsible.

He was in prison already, in Belgium, having been caught trying to abduct a thirteen-year-old girl of Congolese origin who had managed to run away from him. If she had not escaped, there is little doubt that she would be dead. His wife, Monique Olivier, had been closely following the paedophile murder case that had been horrifying Belgium, that of Marc Dutroux. She had what you might call a professional interest in the case. When she saw Dutroux's wife being sentenced to thirty years imprisonment for 'trying to cover up her husband's crimes', she took fright, realising that she had actually done a lot more than cover up her husband's crimes – she had helped him to trap his unfortunate victims. She would ride in the car with him when they went out 'hunting for virgins', as they called it. When potential victims were approached, they were reassured by the sight of a woman in the car and thought nothing of climbing in. Worse still, Monique Olivier sometimes took along with him the couple's young son, Sélim, to reassure victims even more. No one knows what horrors those young eyes had to witness.

Fearing her fate at the hands of the courts, she denounced her husband to the police, naming him as the murderer of nine people – mostly girls – in France and Belgium. She initially claimed that she played no part in the crimes but that she was fully aware that when he told her he was 'going out to hunt' that he was going out in search of a victim. It emerged before long, however, that she was often intrinsic to the success of the 'hunt' and, often, he would order her to watch as he raped and killed his victims.

Fourniret had been a qualified draughtsman and by his early thirties, was running his own tool-making business near Paris. He was an expert handyman. However, he was already well known to the police. He was twenty-four years old when he was first convicted, for abducting and abusing a ten-year-old girl in his hometown of Sedan in the Ardennes. After a further two convictions, he was picked up and put in preventive detention in 1984 for a series of kidnaps and sexual attacks on teenage girls and young women in the Paris area. At this time, he placed an advert in a weekly Catholic magazine, looking for a penpal. Monique Olivier, who had already been married twice and had two children, from whom she was estranged, answered the ad and they began to write to each other. It was an intense correspondence. She called him 'My Dear Shere Khan' – from the Jungle Book and 'my beast'. In the letters, they discuss raping virgins and Fourniret, in one letter, gruesomely describes virgins as 'membranes on legs'.

He was tried in June 1987 for eleven sexual assaults and sentenced to seven years in prison for rape and indecent assault on minors. Unfortunately, he was released after only four months for good behaviour and because he had already spent three years in custody awaiting trial. When he walked out of the prison gates, Olivier was waiting for him. They moved to the village of St. Cyr-les-Colons in northern Burgundy.

It had not been his first offence. His convictions for sexual assault and rape stretched back as far as the 1960s. In 2006, there was speculation that he might have been the real perpetrator of one of France's most controversial crimes of the second half of the twentieth century – the murder of eight-year-old Marie-Dolores Rambla, killed at Marseille on 3 June

1974. Christian Ranucci had been convicted of the crime and guillotined for it in 1976, one of the last people to be guillotined in France.

That day, Marie-Dolores was out with her brother when a man came up to them asking them to help him find his lost dog. The girl climbed into his car and they drove off. An hour later, the car was in collision with another vehicle, but the kidnapper quickly drove off. He was followed by an elderly couple who saw him later with a large package. A huge search was launched for the missing girl who was found a little later, stabbed to death, in some bushes. Ranucci was arrested and charged simply because he had been in an accident that day and had also been spied carrying a large package. In his car, police found a pair of trousers that had on them traces of dried blood that turned out be the same blood type as that of Marie-Dolores.

At first Ranucci confessed, but the next day, he retracted his confession and it has, in fact, been suggested that his file was altered and evidence tampered with so that it fitted what he confessed. The bloodstains have been found to have been much older than the day of the murder and were due to a motorcycle accident Ranucci had. Unluckily for him, he had the same blood type as the dead girl. The evidence of the elderly couple has also been doubted by commentators and, crucially, a red pullover that was found at the scene did not belong to Ranucci, as was originally thought.

Chillingly, it emerged that Michel Fourniret had been holidaying in Marseille at the time of the murder. Furthermore, the car he was driving at that time was the same colour as the one described by witnesses. Crucially, his modus operandi – the lost dog – was identical to the one that Fourniret would use in later killings. Marie-Dolores showed no sign of sexual assault. Fourniret often did not assault his victims, but masturbated over them instead.

It did not take long for him to claim his first victim in St. Cyr-les-Colons. Seventeen-year-old Isabel Laville was snatched on her way home from school on 11 December, just six weeks after his release. Olivier later told police that she was picked because she resembled her when she was young and still a virgin. She had pulled up alongside the girl and asked her for directions, persuading her to get into the car to show her the way. Further along the road, they came upon Fourniret who posed as a stranded motorist who had run out of petrol. She stopped for him and, sitting in the back seat, he reached over and put a cord around Isabel's neck. They drugged the unfortunate girl and drove her back to their house. When Fourniret found himself unable to rape Isabel, Olivier stimulated him with oral sex. Isabel was buried at the bottom of a deep, disused well in the countryside.

In August 1990, Fourniret was involved in a bizarre incident that he was lucky to get away with. His van was parked at the side of the road, near Reims. A passing female motorist, believing him to have broken down, stopped to ask him if he needed help. He ignored her question and blurted out that he wanted to sodomise her. She put her foot down hard on the accelerator and sped off to the nearest police station. He followed her and made excuses for his behaviour. He was let off with a caution.

Fourniret confessed to the murders of six girls and women – thirteen-year-old Marie-Ascension Kirombo, twelve-year-old Elisabeth Brichet, thirteen-year-old Natacha Danais, seventeen-year-old Isabelle Laville, twenty-two-year-old Jeanne-Marie Desramault and Farida Hellegouache, whose age was unknown.

In July 2004, he further admitted the murders of Celine Saison and Manyana Thumpong. He denied the murder of the au pair employed by him and his wife. Monique had claimed that when she came home to find her husband and the girl naked, he killed the au pair to prevent her telling anyone. The number of murders he had now admitted came to nine after he claimed to have shot dead a man at a motorway rest stop in order to rob him.

He would look specifically for virgins, digging a three-metre deep grave in the grounds of his house in the Ardennes before setting out on one of his excursions. One exception was a woman that Fourniret killed for money.

While incarcerated in a French prison he encountered an inmate named Pierre Hellegouache. Hellegouache, who had been imprisoned for being a member of a far-left urban guerrilla group called Action Directe, that had set off a number of bombs in France in the 1980s, let slip to Fourniret that his wife, Farida, was looking after the organisation's war chest of gold coins, worth £20,000. Released from jail, Fourniret decided to get his hands on this money. He traced Farida Hellegouache, forced her to tell him where the money was hidden and killed her. He proceeded to use it to buy an 18th century farmhouse set in thirty-two acres of land in Donchery in the French Ardennes, just over the border from Belgium. It was from there that he would launch his hunts and it was to there that he would bring the bodies of a number of his victims. In July 2004, he led the police in a search of the grounds, clad in a bullet-proof vest, showing them the burial sites of twelve-year-old Elisabeth Brichet and French student Jeanne-Marie Desramault. As police uncovered the remains of the two girls, it was reported, Fourniret showed no emotion whatsoever.

He was sixty-five years old by the time he bought the farm. Fourniret and Olivier were thought of as quiet by locals and they even found work in the local primary school, working as playground and canteen supervisors

When Monique Olivier was interrogated by two French detectives in Belgium in February 2005, the plump, dowdy fifty-six-year-old was silent for hours, refusing food and drink. She had said nothing about the killings for seven months. Suddenly, however, she opened up, describing to the two men the 1988 murder of nineteen-year-old Marie-Angèle Domece. She said that her husband had stalked the girl for weeks before the two of them had persuaded her to get into their car. Her husband had disposed of the body, she told them. Then, however, she started describing another killing in Burgundy, informing them first of all that it was one of which they knew nothing about, as yet. It turned out to be the 1990 murder of a young British girl, Joanna Parrish. Joanna's death had been the subject of one of France's longest-running murder investigations.

Joanna, from Gloucestershire, was a student of Modern Languages at Leeds University and part of her course was to teach in France. She had found a position at a secondary school in the town of Auxerre and was in the last week of her time there.

She had placed an advert in a local paper offering English lessons and a local man had, it seems, responded to the ad. She arranged to meet him in a square in Auxerre at seven one evening. She went to Auxerre with a friend and then the two separated and Joanna set off to meet the man. She was never seen alive again.

On the morning of the next day, 17 May, a fisherman saw her body floating in the Yonne River, not far from Auxerre. She had been drugged, tied up, raped, beaten and strangled before her killer had thrown her into the Yonne.

It turned out to be a case that was thoroughly bungled by the police. They failed to search all the land in the vicinity and then allowed the public on to it too soon after her body was found, contaminating the crime scene. Critical evidence such as bite marks on the body seem to have been ignored and the police failed to hold DNA tests of the local male population. Neither did they allow any media appeals.

Olivier confessed to driving the van into which they had thrown Joanna to an isolated spot in the countryside. As she drove, her husband savagely beat Joanna 'until she spoke no more', as she described it. She was thrown into the nearby river when he had finished with her, Olivier went on.

Fourniret denied it the next day when they

confronted him with what his wife had described. It was not the first time he had denied murders that he later admitted to, however, and the detectives knew it might only be a matter of time before they had him for these murders, too.

Both Fourniret and Olivier were sentenced to life imprisonment. Judges stipulated that she should serve at least twenty-eight years before being considered for release. He is unlikely ever to be freed.

PART EIGHT

PSYCHOPATHIC WOMEN KILLERS

BELLE GUNNESS

At close to six feet tall and weighing in at more than fourteen stone, Belle Gunness was a big woman, a big woman who killed at least twenty people and is estimated by some commentators to have actually dispatched close to a hundred, a number of them – in particular her own immediate family – killed for insurance policies.

Although, like most details of her life, knowledge about Belle's birth is sketchy, most agree that she was born as Brynhild Paulsdatter Størseth, in Selbu in Norway in 1859. While still a young woman in Selbu, an incident is said to have occurred that was to change her personality, and her life, forever. It seems she got pregnant, although we do not know who the father was. Attending a dance, she was attacked and kicked in the stomach, losing her baby. Belle was never the same again and resolved to go to America to seek her fortune, as her sister, Nellie, had done some years previously. She worked for three years as a servant and saved enough to pay her passage to the New World.

She left Norway in 1881 and, at this point, changed her name to the more American-friendly 'Belle'. In the beginning, she worked, as she had in Norway, as a servant, but she was very ambitious and always wanted more.

In 1884, she married a man called Mads Albert Sorenson in Chicago. They opened a confectionery store, but it proved a flop. A year after it opened, it mysteriously burned down. According to Belle, a kerosene lamp exploded, but no evidence was found to support that claim. Nonetheless, the insurance money was paid out.

They used the insurance money to buy another house, in the suburb of Austin, but in 1898, that, too, burned down. Once again, the insurance money for that went towards the purchase of another house.

Insurance was proving pretty lucrative to the money-hungry Belle and she picked up even more when her husband, Mads, died suddenly in July 1900, coincidentally the day that two insurance policies overlapped. The doctor initially suspected that his death was due to strychnine poisoning, but he had been treating Mads for an enlarged heart and eventually concluded that he had died of heart failure. Luckily for Belle, there was no autopsy.

Belle's in-laws were both appalled and suspicious when she applied for the insurance money just one day after Mads' funeral. It was $8,500, a tidy sum in those days. Whispers began that she had poisoned him and they started to agitate for the body to be exhumed and an inquest to be carried out. It is unclear whether this actually happened, but what is known is that the insurance companies coughed up yet again and Belle bought a farm just outside the town of La Porte in Indiana into which she moved with her children in 1901. Some researchers assert that the couple actually had four children, but two, Caroline and Axel, had died in infancy of acute colitis. Interestingly, the symptoms of that illness match perfectly the symptoms of many forms of poisoning. Needless to say, both children had been insured.

Shortly after she moved in, there was the customary fire. The boat and carrriage houses were destroyed and Belle collected more insurance money.

She met Peter Gunness and married him in April 1902, but tragedy struck when his young daughter died of unknown causes just one week after the wedding. When she died, she had been alone in the house with Belle. And then, before too long, it was time for Peter Gunness to take his leave. His demise was extremely suspicious, especially to the neighbours who began a whispering campaign against Belle. According to her, he was working in the shed when a heavy part of a sausage-grinding machine fell off a shelf above him onto his head, split his skull open, killing him and earning Belle $3,000 in insurance. The neighbours found it hard to believe that Gunness could have made such a mistake and the district coroner who reviewed the case announced that he thought Gunness had been murdered. An inquest was convened to investigate the death. Matters were made worse when Jennie, one of Belle's children, told a friend at school that her mummy had killed her poppa with a cleaver.

The child denied having said this when she was brought before the inquest and Belle swayed the jurors herself with a bravura performance in the dock, playing the role of a woman left all alone to bring up her family. It helped that she was heavily pregnant and she was released.

Rather than re-marry immediately, she now hired a series of men to help run the farm and by 1906, a man called Ray Lamphere was installed as her handyman. Around this time, Jennie, the child who had given evidence at the inquest, disappeared, Belle explaining that she had gone to a Lutheran college in Los Angeles. Needless to say, Jennie had actually been killed.

Belle decided that she was now ready for marriage again and placed an advert in a number of newspapers, saying: *Personal – comely widow who owns a large farm in one of the finest districts in La Porte County, Indiana, desires to make the acquaintance of a gentleman equally well provided, with view of joining fortunes. No replies by letter considered unless sender is willing to follow answer with personal visit. Triflers need not apply.'* It should probably have read: 'Anyone wanting to survive need not apply'.

Well-off suitors started to arrive at the farm and almost as quickly disappear. John Moo came from Elkhart lake, Wisconsin, willing to pay off Belle's mortgage in exchange for wedded bliss. He disappeared a week after arriving. George Anderson, another Norwegian immigrant, from Tarkio, Missouri, wisely did not bring his money with him, and although Belle had turned out to be not quite as attractive as he had hoped, he agreed that he would pay off her mortgage if they married. He would return to Tarkio, get the money and come back and marry her. That night, he awoke in the farm's guest-house to see Belle standing by his bed with a strange, sinister expression on his face. He let out a yell and she fled from the room, almost dropping the candle she was carrying. Anderson leapt out of bed, put his clothes on as quickly as he could and ran for his life down the country road that led to La Porte, all the while expecting her to come after him. In La Porte, he jumped on the first train to Missouri.

Nevertheless, they kept flooding to the farm, lonely, middle-aged and older men with sizeable wallets. But none of them ever left. A widower from Iola, Wisconsin, Ole B. Budsburg, was seen at the La Porte Savings Bank on 6 April 1907. There, he signed over the deed to his land in Wisconsin and walked out with several thousand dollars in his wallet. When his sons found out where he had gone, they wrote to Belle, enquiring as to his whereabouts. She wrote back saying she had never seen him.

Puzzlingly, Belle began to have large trunks delivered to the farm which she manhandled herself. The shutters of the house were closed all day and night and when darkness fell, Belle could be seen digging away in the pig-pen. Passers-by noticed that there was a lot of digging at the farm, some of it done by Lamphere.

The suitors kept arriving . . . and disappearing. Andrew Helgelien turned up after an amorous correspondence with the widow Gunness. He brought with him his savings of $2,900 and it was duly cashed by him a few days after his arrival. Then, a few days later, she began to visit the bank to make deposits, firstly of $500 and then $700.

But things were starting to go wrong. Ray Lamphere was in thrall to Belle, deeply in love with her. He would do anything for her and was insanely jealous of the men who came with the intention of marrying her. Things became fraught between them and she fired Lamphere. Then, possibly worried that he would go to the authorities and tell them what she had been up to, she made an appointment at the courthouse in La Porte. There, she declared that Lamphere was not right in the head and represented a danger to the public. They summoned Lamphere to a hearing but found him to be of sane mind. Unperturbed, Belle had him arrested a few days later for trespassing.

Lamphere began to threaten Belle with exposure, even confiding in one farmer that Helgelien would not be a problem; 'We fixed him for keeps,' he said.

They may have 'fixed' Helgelien, but his family were troubled by his disappearance and his brother, Asle, wrote to Belle. When she replied, saying that he had probably gone to Norway to visit family, Asle did not believe her. He said that he believed his brother was actually still in the La Porte area. She persuaded him that if he came to La Porte and instigated a manhunt, it could be expensive for him. He delayed his visit for some months.

Belle began to panic. There were now two people who could, conceivably, expose her and send her to the gallows. She took steps to neutralise one of them, informing a lawyer – not the police – that Lamphere had threatened to kill her and burn her house down. She told him she wanted to make a will and left everything to her children. She then went to the bank and paid off her mortgage, having withdrawn all her money.

A man called Maxon, who had replaced Lamphere at the farm, awoke on the morning of 28 April with the smell of smoke in his nostrils. The house was on fire. He screamed Belle's and her children's names, but there was no response. Flames blocking his escape down the stairs, he jumped from the window of his room which was on the second floor and ran to town to get help. But, by the time they arrived at the farmhouse it was little more than a smouldering ruin. They searched the property and found four bodies in the cellar. One, that of a woman, was headless and so, could not be positively identified as Belle, although it was presumed it was her. The bodies of her children were lying next to her.

Lamphere was, of course, suspected and was picked up immediately. Unfortunately for him, a witness was found who said that he had seen Lamphere running down the road from the farm just before the fire broke out. He was charged with murder and arson. Meanwhile, the sheriff and his deputies began a careful search of the ruins, looking for evidence.

Was it the body of Belle Gunness that was found?

When the remains were measured, it strangely proved to be the corpse of a woman only five feet three inches tall, eight or nine inches shorter than Belle. Further complicating matters was the fact that she weighed just under eleven stone, some three stone lighter than Belle. Either being burnt to death is very slimming or this was not Belle Gunness. Her friends certainly did not think it was her. Several neighbouring farmers looked at the corpse and said it was not her. Some friends who arrived from Chicago said it could not be her. The La Porte clothiers who made her dresses and other garments categorically stated that it was not her.

Then, the case was thrown wide open when the doctor examining the dead woman's internal organs, found that she had died of strychnine poisoning.

However, on 19 May, Louis 'Klondyke' Schultz, who had been detailed to sift through the debris to try to find some dental evidence from the headless corpse, that would link it to Belle, discovered two human teeth. They were identified as two porcelain teeth and a gold crown on some bridgework that had belonged to Belle. That was enough proof for the coroner and at a subsequent inquest it was declared that the body found in the ruins was, indeed, that of Belle Gunness.

Meanwhile, Asle Helgelien had arrived on the

scene, insisting that a search be carried out for his brother. On 3 May, the first of a series of grisly finds was made – the body of Belle's daughter, Jennie. Then, one after another, the bodies began to be pulled from the earth in the pig-pen – Ole B. Budsberg, Thomas Lindboe of Chicago, who had been one of Belle's handymen, Henry Gurholdt of Scandinavia, Wisconsin who had brought $1,500 to Belle with the intention of marrying her, Olaf Svenherud of Chicago, John Moo, Olaf Lindbloom from Iowa and many more whose remains could not be identified. More than forty men and children were discovered buried in shallow graves around the farm.

Ray Lamphere admitted to arson, but denied the murder of Belle and her children. He was found guilty of arson, but acquitted on the charge of murder and was sent to jail for twenty years, dying in prison in 1909.

He made a deathbed confession, claiming that, although he helped Belle to bury a number of her victims, he had not taken part in their murders. He explained her method. She would welcome her guest with a hearty meal and a cup of drugged coffee. When the man had fallen asleep she would come up behind him and split his head with a meat cleaver. Or sometimes she would chloroform her victim when he was in bed asleep before carrying the body to the basement where she would dissect it. The remains were buried around the farm or sometimes they were fed to the pigs.

He also shed some light on the headless woman, he explained that she had been lured to the farm believing she was going to be Belle's housekeeper. But Belle, of course, had other plans for her. She had drugged her, killed her and cut her head off, throwing it into a nearby swamp. Then she chloroformed her children, suffocated them and put them in the basement. She dressed the woman in her clothing, set fire to the house and fled, leaving her false teeth behind. Lamphere had been part of the plan, but she had evaded him after the fire and disappeared.

He said that by this time she was rich. He estimated she had murdered forty-two men and each of them had brought with him at least a couple of thousand dollars. By the time she disappeared, he reckoned that she had saved around $250,000.

Belle Gunness became an American Lord Lucan. Sightings were reported for decades. She was seen in Chicago, San Francisco, New York. She was reported to be living in Mississippi as a wealthy landowner. Nothing was proved, however.

Interest grew in her case once again, in 1931, when a woman named Esther Carlson was arrested in Los Angeles for poisoning a suitor, August Lindstrom, for money. Some said she looked like Belle, but before they could confirm whether or not it was her, up to her old tricks, she died while awaiting trial.

In November, 2007, the body of Belle Gunness was exhumed. Tests are being undertaken to prove once and for all whether it was her body that was found without a head in the basement in Indiana all those years ago.

MARY ANN COTTON

How did she get away with it? A bit of stomach pain and an unexpectedly sudden death. She did it twenty times. Husbands, children, it did not matter. If they got in her way, she would dispatch them without a second thought.

Of course, in those times – the late nineteenth century – poison was easy to come by. They used arsenic, for instance, for all kinds of things, including, when mixed with soap, for killing bed-bugs. All you had to do was extract it from the soap in which it was mixed and it was so easily confused with gastric fever. The symptoms – violent sickness and diarrhoea – were exactly the same and who would suspect arsenic to be the culprit? She killed very young babies and in those times, one form of baby food was flour mixed with water which often upset the baby's stomach. So, when one of Mary Ann Cotton's babies was sick, a doctor would not think it unusual or suspicious. Infant mortality was a huge problem in Victorian times. Therefore, no one thought there was anything wrong when Mary Ann's babies died. After all, twenty-five per cent of all babies did not live beyond their first year. She was just unlucky, they thought, if they thought about it at all. Also complicating matters was the fact that she moved around a great deal and married several times, taking a different name each time. No one linked Mary Ann Cotton with Mary Ann Mowbray, Mary Ann Ward or Mary Ann Robinson.

She was born the daughter of a miner in 1832, in the village of Low Moorsley in County Durham and her father died before she was fifteen. It was a tough life. Her father, staunchly religious and a rigid disciplinarian, had barely been able to earn enough to feed his family. When she was eight, they moved to the village of Murton. She went to a new school but suffered greatly from being unable to make friends. The family was then devastated by the death of her father in a tragic accident when he fell 150 feet down a mineshaft.

A few years later, her mother re-married but Mary Ann did not get on with her step-father. The family was better off, however, and although she did not like him, she liked the things that his money could buy. Nonetheless, aged sixteen, she moved out, finding work as a nurse in a nearby village. Three years later, she returned home to train as a dress-maker.

She met and married William Mowbray, and they moved to Plymouth in Devon. They had five children, four of them dying from gastric fever. Moving back to the Newcastle area of the northeast, Mary Ann gave birth to three more children, all of whom died. William worked as a foreman at South Hetton Colliery and then got a job as a fireman on a steam ship. Not long after, though, he also died of gastric fever. Some said that Mary Ann was not terribly upset about it, especially when she received the £35 she had insured him for with the British and Prudential Insurance Company.

Finally, out of eight children born to her from her first marriage, only one was left alive.

She moved to Seaham Harbour in County Durham where she began a relationship with a man called Joseph Nattrass. Unfortunately, however, Nattrass was engaged to another woman and Mary Ann left Seaham when she realised that her relationship with him was doomed. Meanwhile, another of her children died, aged three.

Returning to Sunderland, she became a nurse at the Sunderland Infirmary, House of Recovery for the Cure of Contagious Fever, Dispensary and Humane Society. Her one surviving child, Isabella, was sent to be looked after by Mary Ann's mother while she worked there. Soon, she had fallen in love with one of her patients, George Ward. They married in August 1865, but George did not survive long, dying following a long illness characterised by the intestinal pains that seemed to dog everyone associated with Mary Ann Cotton. Once again, she collected on an insurance policy she had taken out on her husband. She was thirty-three years old and had murdered ten people.

James Robinson was a widower, a shipwright and the father of five children with whom she obtained a position as housekeeper. When she had been there only a month, his youngest child died of gastric fever. He was heartbroken and she comforted him. She comforted him so well, in fact, that she became pregnant. When her mother became ill and looked like she might need looking after, Mary Ann paid her a quick visit and after nine days her illness became terminal. Nothing and no one was allowed to get in the way of Mary Ann's happiness.

Next, her nine year-old daughter, whom she had brought back to live with her and Robinson, died, but she was not alone. Another two of her new paramour's children also passed away suddenly, all of the same painful condition – gastric fever. They buried three children in the month of April 1867. Four months later, a child she had with Robinson lasted only two weeks before dying.

Now married to Robinson, she tried to persuade him that he needed insurance. So ardent was she in her efforts to get him to insure himself that he became suspicious. When he heard that she had tried to insure him herself and when he realised that she was spending his money faster than he could earn it, he threw her out.

She became a prostitute and was getting desperate but it was not long before another sucker turned up – Frederick Cotton, another recent widower with two sons, a pitman who lived in Walbottle in Northumberland. Mary Ann was introduced to him by Margaret, his sister. Unfortunately, Margaret, who had helped bring up Cotton's children, died of an undetermined stomach ailment shortly after. Mary Ann moved in and comforted Cotton. Soon she was pregnant again, for the eleventh time. The fact that she was still married to James Robinson did not prevent her from marrying Cotton in September 1870. A son, Robert, was born in early 1871.

When Mary learned that her former lover, Joseph Nattrass, was living nearby and that his marriage was over, she persuaded her husband to move closer to him. Then she got rid of him altogether in December of that year in the customary manner. The insurance money came in very handy.

Nattrass moved in with her immediately and she

found work as a nurse to John Quick-Manning, an Excise Officer who was recovering from smallpox and who was the next man to take her fancy. First, of course, she had to dispose of the baggage she had brought with her. Cotton's oldest son and the baby she had with him were in the ground within a few weeks. Joseph Nattrass also became surplus to requirements. Gastric fever again – a terrible illness. She was now left with just two children – seven-year-old Charlie Cotton and a baby she had with Quick-Manning.

When Charlie came down with a painful gastro-intestinal illness, suspicions were raised. She had been asked by a parish official to nurse a woman who was suffering from smallpox. However, she complained that she could not as she had to look after Charlie. She suggested to the parish official that Charlie be committed to the parish workhouse. He told her that was impossible – she would have to accompany the boy to the workhouse. Undaunted, she told him that it would not be a problem for very long, suggesting that 'he'll go like the rest of the Cottons.' Five days later, Charlie, who had been a healthy boy, had died of what looked like gastric fever. The parish official went to the police and an autopsy was held. The doctor found signs of malnutrition and then the contents of Charlie's stomach were re-tested. They found arsenic.

Mary Ann, meanwhile, had paid a visit to the insurance office to claim on the policy she had taken out on her son.

The newspapers latched on to the story and began to investigate Mary Ann Cotton. They uncovered her movements around northern England and learned how she had lost three husbands, a lover, a friend, her mother and a dozen children. They had all, it seemed, died of the same thing – gastric fever.

Finally, the game was up for Mary Ann. She was arrested shortly before taking John Quick-Manning as her fifth husband.

Even under arrest, she gave birth. This daughter would be out of her reach and would survive. She was tried only for her last murder, that of Charlie, but the other murders soon became apparent and the verdict was inevitable. She was found guilty and sentenced to death. *The Times* reported, 'After conviction the wretched woman exhibited strong emotion but this gave place in a few hours to her habitual cold, reserved demeanour and while she harbours a strong conviction that the royal clemency will be extended towards her, she staunchly asserts her innocence of the crime that she has been convicted of.' She had claimed that Charlie had arsenic in his body because he had inhaled it from wallpaper in which it was used as a dye.

No pardon materialised, despite several petitions and on 24 March 1873, she felt the hood being placed over her head, followed by the rough texture of the noose. Hers was not an easy death, however, somewhat like the deaths she had inflicted on her victims. The hangman botched it, getting the length of the drop wrong and after the trapdoor on the gallows was opened, she struggled for a full three minutes before her neck snapped.

NANNIE DOSS

If you were invited to dine at her table, best not to choose the prunes. Arsenic Annie, as they would later call her, was partial to sprinkling a little rat poison or arsenic on them to give you a little kick. If the flavour was too strong she would just add a little more sugar. She poisoned eleven people and giggled all the way to prison.

Born Nancy Hazle in 1905, her childhood was harsh. Her parents were poor farmers in a tiny town called Blue Mountain in the hill country in northeast Alabama. Her father, James, was an angry man who ruled his family with a rod of iron. The kids were forced to work in the fields from an early age, missing school to do so and if they cut up rough, they would suffer the pain of a beating. By the age of five, she was clearing and ploughing fields and cutting wood. None of the children was allowed, or indeed had time to have friends.

When she was young, Nannie received a serious head injury while visiting a relative. She was on a train which had to make a sudden stop. Nannie jolted forward and banged her head on the iron frame of the seat in front of her. She experienced blackouts and pain for months afterwards and had headaches for the rest of her life as a result. Some suggest that this might have been the cause of what happened later, but others claim that she was just bad from the start.

Her only relief as a child was the romantic story magazines her mother bought. Nannie loved to leaf through them during any spare time she got. However, she had no opportunity for romance in her own life. Her father prohibited his daughters from attending social events such as barn dances in the area. They were not allowed to wear make-up, silk stockings or tight dresses. It did not stop Nannie from having a good time, however. She would often sneak away to enjoy the company of boys in haylofts or corncribs.

James Hazle had always said that he would find husbands for his girls and he found one for Nannie. Charlie Braggs was a co-worker at the Linen Thread Company where she worked from the age of sixteen. He was tall and good-looking and he seemed to dote on Nannie. James liked the fact that Charlie was devoted to his mother and not as footloose as most of the young men in the area. Four months after they met for the first time, Nannie and Charlie were married. She barely knew him.

Charlie's mother was not unlike her father – domineering and demanding. However, they got on with married life and Nannie had four daughters in four years. However, the pressures of family life and, in particular, of sharing a home with her mother-in-law, drove Nannie to drink. She also developed a smoking habit that would have been extreme in a man. She began to find her amusement elsewhere, consorting with men in the gin palaces of Blue Mountain. As for Charlie, he was too drunk himself, to even notice that she was not at home. At other times, he was out chasing women in another part of town.

In early 1927, the two middle daughters of the Braggs family mysteriously died. They sat down to breakfast, perfectly well, and by noon they were dead. The doctor described their deaths as accidental, but Charlie was not so sure. He fled the marital home, taking his eldest daughter, Melvina, with him, but leaving the youngest, Florine, behind.

Braggs later described how afraid he was of his wife. Her mood swings were extreme and he refused to eat or drink anything she had prepared when she was in a bad mood. He was gone for a long time, almost a year, finally turning up again in summer 1928 but in the amorous company of a divorcee and her child. Nannie got the message and left. Charlie remained behind, the only one of her husbands to survive marriage to her.

She moved back in with her parents and found work at a cotton mill in Anniston, not far from Blue Mountain. She still enjoyed the romantic magazines and decided to try her luck in the lonely hearts column she liked so much. She wrote to a number of men who had advertised, but one stood out for her. Frank Harrelson was a handsome, twenty-three-year-old factory worker who lived in Jacksonville. He fell for her and they were married in 1929. Unfortunately, Frank was an alcoholic who had also served a jail term for assault. He was not quite what he said he was and the regular visits from the Jacksonville police to let her know that her husband was in jail for drunkenness again confirmed this fact. He was abusive, just like her father, but she persevered with the marriage for sixteen years.

Her daughter, Melvina, had one child, Robert, and was pregnant again in 1945. Nannie was present for the birth and nursed the baby when it finally arrived. However, Melvina later told how, as she lay semiconscious from the anaesthetic in bed, she saw Nannie with the newborn baby cradled in her arms. She then thought she saw Nannie produce a long and very sharp hatpin and drive it into the child's head. The doctors, however, were astonished and could not discover what the baby girl had died of. Six months later, Robert, Melvina's son, died while in Nannie's care. The doctors diagnosed asphyxia from unknown causes. Nannie, meanwhile, seemed distraught at the graveside, but was less distraught when she picked up a cheque for $500 from an insurance policy she had taken out on her grandson.

In August 1945, it was the turn of her husband Frank. On 15 September, he went out celebrating the end of the war, welcoming home some friends who had been fighting overseas. He came home drunk and insisted on having sex. She was furious and determined to take action. The next day, she found his corn-liquor jar hidden in the garden, poured out some of its contents, filled it with rat poison and replaced it where she had found it. That same evening, Frank Harrelson had a drink, was suddenly consumed with excruciating stomach pains and died, aged thirty-eight. Naturally, she rinsed out the jar shortly afterwards.

Her life for a short while after this incident is vague. She seems to have travelled extensively and some suggest that she was married to a man called Hendrix. Whether he survived the marriage is unknown.

In Lexington, in 1947, within two days of meeting him, she married a man called Arlie Lanning that she had met through a lonely hearts column. He was another philanderer and drinker but when it got too much, Nannie would take off, sometimes for months on end. Whenever she returned home, he would promise to stop the womanising and the drinking but his promises did not last long. When she was there, however, she presented to the world a picture of a devoted wife. Her absences were explained as visits to her sister who had cancer or to look after Arlie's eighty-five-year-old mother. Neighbours gossiped, however, about Arlie who could often be seen in Lexington's red light district.

Arlie died suddenly of heart failure, or, at least, that is what the doctor concluded. No autopsy was carried out due to the fact that he was a heavy drinker and that it was thought that he had been suffering from the virulent flu bug that was rampaging across the state.

Nannie said, 'He just sat down one morning to drink a cup of coffee and eat a bowl of prunes I especially prepared for him.'

Curiously, the house that Nannie and Arlie had shared, burned to the ground not long after his death. It had been left to his sister in his will, but Nannie got the insurance money. She had also managed to get her beloved television out of the house before the fire, ostensibly to take it to be mended. Nannie had moved in with Arlie's mother but left suddenly after Mrs Lanning died in her sleep.

She went to her sister's house but Dovie's condition seemed to deteriorate from the moment that Nannie arrived. She died on 30 June in her sleep.

For $15 a year, you could be a member of the Diamond Circle Club, a lonely hearts organisation that sent out a monthly newsletter. In 1952, she used this group to find another husband. She was forty-seven years old now and beginning to lose her looks. Therefore, it seemed sensible to look for a more mature sort of man. Richard L. Morton of Emporia, Kansas, was just such a man. He had been a salesman but was looking for a woman and Diamond Circle provided him with Nannie. She moved to Emporia where they were married in October 1952.

He was a handsome older man, half Native American and he treated her well at first, buying her presents and jewellery. Eventually, however, she realised that it was all being done on credit. He owed everyone. Not only that – he was also dallying with other women in town. Marrying him, she realised, had been a big mistake. But for Nannie, of course, that was no problem. His demise was delayed, however, by a visit from her mother following the death of her father. Time, of course, was money, and Nannie could not wait. Her mother died, suffering chronic stomach pains not long after arriving at her house. Morton followed a short while later.

Her fifth husband was fifty-nine-year-old state highway inspector, Samuel Doss, a God-fearing individual who, unlike her other husbands, did not drink, smoke or chase women. He was thrifty and loathed frivolity. Unfortunately, he was also deadly boring. The couple married in June 1953 but she was soon fed up. Sex was pre-scheduled and the romance novels and stories she adored were banned. The electric fan was only switched on when temperatures were extreme and lights had to be religiously switched off when leaving a room. She was fed up but delighted to discover that he had made a couple of fundamental mistakes. Firstly, he had given her equal access to his bank account. Secondly, he had taken out two insurance policies of which she was the beneficiary.

If only he had known about the prunes. One evening, following a delicious prune cake, he experienced severe stomach pains. He was taken to hospital where he stayed for twenty-three days to recover. They said he had suffered a severe infection to the digestive tract. On being released from hospital, Nannie served him up a cup of coffee and a pork roast. Unfortunately for him, the coffee was laced with arsenic. By midnight he was dead.

This time, however, the doctor was perturbed. He ordered an autopsy and arsenic, in horse-killing quantities, was discovered.

Nannie was arrested and police began to look back at her history, learning that four of her husbands had died suspiciously. She confessed all, giggling all the while and was sentenced to life imprisonment.

She died in the Oklahoma State Penitentiary of leukemia in 1965, still looking for eternal love, by all reports.

VELMA BARFIELD

Poor Velma Barfield. She had endured more than her share of grief over the years. So many people in her life had died. The problem was, of course, that she had killed them all.

She had been born Margie Velma Bullard in rural Carolina in 1932, the second of the nine children of Murphy and Lillie Bullard. They were poor, living in a wooden house with no electricity or running water. The cramped house was shared with Murphy's parents and his sister Susan Ella who had been disabled by polio. Murphy gradually improved his family's situation, working as a logger and then finding work in a Fayetteville textile mill. He was a heavy drinker and a strict disciplinarian and did not hesitate to beat his children when he thought they had overstepped the mark. But Velma was adept at talking back to her father and along with her older brother, Olive, was the child who became most familiar with his belt or the back of his hand. Velma, meanwhile, became resentful of the way her mother sat back and submissively watched her husband beat both her and her children. Lillie Barfield, for her part, was also often on the receiving end of her husband's bad temper and was well aware that he was a serial womaniser.

At least at school Velma could escape the tensions of the Barfield family home, but she was often picked on due to the second-hand clothes she wore and the simple food she had in her lunchbox every day. She began to steal money from her father to pay for sweets and then was caught stealing $80 from an elderly neighbour. Murphy used his belt to cure her of that habit.

Velma later claimed that her father raped her and had been touching her inappropriately for years. It was a claim disputed by other members of the family as an attempt to gain sympathy, and, of course, Velma was a practiced liar.

At high school she started going out with a boy named Thomas Burke who, at seventeen, proposed to her. She accepted but Murphy Bullard hit the roof. Nonetheless, they married and left school, living in a small house in Parkton, Thomas working in a number of different jobs – as a delivery driver, a farm labourer and in a cotton mill. Velma found work in a drugstore but Thomas did not like her working and she was persuaded to give up the job.

In December 1951, Velma gave birth to a son, Ronald, and two years later, a daughter, Kim, was born. She was a good mother, taking her children to the local Baptist church and becoming involved in school activities. She started to work again, working the night shift at a textile plant while Thomas worked as a delivery man for Pepsi Cola. They were making more money and moved to a better house, still in Parkton.

In 1963, Velma had to have a hysterectomy and it seemed to affect her badly. She became moody and was often depressed, especially when her husband went out at night. She resented his drinking, having had enough of drunken violence from her father. In 1965, when Thomas was involved in a car crash, she blamed it on drink, but he denied that he had been drinking. He suffered from concussion and endured painful headaches for the remainder of his life.

Her nagging about his drinking began to badly affect their relationship and arguments raged on a daily basis. However, Thomas never resorted to violence.

Eventually, he was arrested for drunk-driving in 1967 and lost his licence and his job. He became depressed and resorted to booze even more. Although he found work in a mill, the tension in the house was palpable. Velma was prescribed sedatives for her own depression and became addicted to

Librium and Valium. She began using a number of doctors from whom she would be given prescriptions for her drugs, none of them knowing about the others. She was often groggy and dazed at home, behaving like the drunkard she accused her husband of being.

In April 1967 their house caught fire with only Thomas at home. He died of smoke inhalation. Then, shortly after her son had graduated from high school, the house caught fire again, being destroyed this time. She and her children moved in with her parents while they waited for the insurance company to pay out.

She began dating a widower, Jennings Barfield. Barfield had been forced to take early retirement due to ill health – he suffered from diabetes and emphysema and had a bad heart. They married in August 1970 and she and the kids moved into Barfield's home in Fayetteville that he shared with his teenage daughter, Nancy.

It was not long, however, before Velma's pill habit began to damage their relationship. They split up and then got back together again when she said she would stop taking the pills. The marriage, however, had been a mistake for both of them and looked like it was going to be short-lived.

Before things really came to a head, however, Jennings died, finally a victim, it appeared, of the heart trouble that had plagued him for years. Velma sunk into drug-enhanced oblivion and took to her bed. She was still using a number of doctors to keep up her pill intake but they did not prevent her from sinking into an even deeper depression.

She found work in a department store but became frantic when her son Ronnie enlisted in the army to go to fight in Vietnam. In the midst of this, the house caught fire again and she was forced to move back in with Murphy and Lillie. Then in quick succession, she lost her job and her father died of lung cancer aged sixty-one. She was thrown into an even blacker mood when Ronnie told her he was getting married. She became unnaturally jealous of her son's new wife.

In March 1972, she was charged with forging a prescription but got away with a suspended sentence and a small fine. But things were looking up as Ronnie came home from Vietnam. At home, though, life was hard. Lillie and Velma argued constantly and Velma was irritated by the way her mother bossed her about. Lillie, meanwhile, gave her a hard time about the number of pills she was consuming.

In the summer of 1974, Lillie became very ill with severe stomach pains. She was vomiting and suffering from violent diarrhoea. In hospital, the doctors were puzzled but she recovered after a few days and was sent home.

Velma, meanwhile, came into some money - $5,000 from an insurance policy on a man she had been dating who was killed in a traffic accident.

Just after Christmas 1974, Lillie became ill again, vomiting and suffering from terrible pains in her stomach and back. She was rushed to hospital and died there a few hours later.

In 1975 Velma was jailed for six months for passing dud cheques and on her release, looked for work caring for the elderly. In 1976 she was looking after Montgomery and Dollie Edwards who were ninety-four and eighty-four, respectively. Velma moved into their well-appointed brick ranch-house and for a while all was well. As time wore on, however, Dollie began to scold Velma for the quality of her work. The two quarrelled regularly. Montgomery died in January 1977, but Velma continued to look after Dollie. In late February, Dollie became ill, vomiting and suffering from diarrhea. She thought she had flu, but her condition got worse and she was taken to hospital. She died a few days later.

She moved on to another elderly couple, eighty-year-old John Lee and his seventy-six-year-old wife, Record. Velma did not like Record much. She talked incessantly and often fought with her husband.

Record caused trouble over a cheque she was certain had been forged. Her name was signed on it but she could not remember signing it. The police were even called, but no one could think of how it had come to be forged and who would have done such a thing. A quick look at Velma's criminal record might have clarified things, of course, but no one bothered.

Towards the end of April, John Lee became ill with the customary stomach pains and diarrhoea that seemed to follow Velma around. He went to hospital but recovered and was released. Doctors were puzzled and unable to find out what had caused the illness. They put it down to a virus.

At home, however, he continued to have relapses, getting better and then becoming ill again. It continued throughout May but everyone agreed that Velma was doing a wonderful job caring for him.

In early June, however, he was worse than ever and returned to hospital where he died on 4 June.

Now forty-six years old, Velma moved in with a farmer, fifty-six-year-old Stuart Taylor, shocking her children by living in sin. Taylor, however, had found out about her criminal record and, as a result, refused to marry her. One night they drove to a revival meeting in Fayetteville, featuring a famous preacher. As the service got under way, Stuart suddenly complained of feeling ill. He had awful stomach pains and felt sick. He left the hall and went outside to lie down in his truck, parked outside.

Back home, his pain and nausea continued into the night and Velma phoned his daughter to let her know her dad was ill. They agreed that it was probably just flu. When his condition had not improved next morning, she drove him to the hospital where doctors diagnosed his illness as gastritis. He was given some medicine and sent home where he gradually got better.

The next day, however, he took a turn for the worse and was taken by ambulance to hospital with sirens blaring. An hour after his arrival at the hospital, he died.

The doctors were mystified by his illness and sudden death and an autopsy was called for. Stuart's children agreed to it and everyone wondered how all these tragedies could keep happening to a devout, God-fearing woman like Velma Barfield.

That same day, Lumberton Police Detective Benson Philips received an incoherent anonymous phone call. A woman's voice ranted on the other end of the line: 'Murder! . . . I know who did it! . . . You've got to stop her! . . . You've got to stop her!' He suggested she call him at the station, and when she did, she offered much more information, although she remained anonymous. She told him she was calling from South Carolina and that Velma Barfield had murdered her boyfriend, Stuart Taylor in the same way as she had killed her own mother. She intimated that they were not the only ones. People had a habit of dying around Velma Barfield.

The police began to check the death certificates of the people who had died when Velma was around. They found that no one had tested for poison in any of the cases, but that they had all died of gastroenteritis. It had happened too often to be a coincidence and they realised that they were looking at a serial killer, a psychopath who killed without remorse.

Velma was picked up, ostensibly for questioning about dud cheques, but they surprised her by telling her that Stuart had been killed by a dose of arsenic, as the autopsy had discovered. She denied any involvement, claiming that they had been in love and were planning to marry. She had nursed him when he became ill, she said. Why would she have wanted to kill him?

She went home, and the next day when it was inevitable that she was about to be arrested for murder, she confessed to Ronnie, telling him that she only intended to make him sick. She had never meant for him to die.

Soon, however, Ronnie learned the worst. She had also poisoned John Lee, Dottie Edwards and her own mother, he was told.

Velma was put on trial on one count of first-degree murder, that of Stuart Taylor. She was found guilty and sentenced to death.

While waiting for the sentence to be carried out, Velma seemed to really become a Christian. She had always gone to church but now claimed to have heard the voice of God. She was visited by the famous evangelist Billy Graham and was allowed to mix with other prisoners because she was such a positive influence on them.

Her appeals lasted six years, during which time she admitted that she had also been responsible for the deaths of both Thomas Burke and Jennings Barfield. Finally, they were exhausted and at 2.15 am on 2 November 1984, she lay down on a gurney and lethal poison was pumped into her veins.

AILEEN CAROL WUORNOS

'I'd just like to say I'm sailing with the Rock and I'll be back like Independence Day with Jesus, June 6, like the movie, big mothership and all. I'll be back.' Aileen Wuornos's last words were certainly not a reflection of the terrible hand of cards she had been dealt by life. She died as she lived – alone and unloved.

She was born on the last day of February, 1956 as Aileen Carol Pittman. Her mother, Diane Wuornos, had married Leo Dale Pittman when she was fifteen and gave birth to a son, Keith, in 1955. A year later, Aileen was born, but by then the marriage was over and Diane had divorced Pittman who would go on to become a psychopathic child molester who hanged himself in prison in 1969. He was never any good. One story tells how, as a boy, he liked nothing better than to tie two cats together by the tail, hang them over a clothes-line and watch them fight.

In 1960, Diane handed her two children into the care of her parents, Lauri and Britta Wuornos, who adopted them and brought them up as their own in Troy, Michigan. Aileen would not discover until the age of twelve that they were not her real parents.

Life with the Wuornos's was harsh and very strict and Aileen and Keith became increasingly hard to control. It was not helped by the fact that Lauri was a drinker with a terrible temper. He was not afraid to use a belt to discipline the kids and on many occasions Aileen would be bent over a wooden table in the kitchen or flat on her front on her bed to be whipped on her bare buttocks. It is unsurprising that with so little love at home, the teenage Aileen sought it elsewhere and she was sexually active from an early age. Inevitably, at the age of fourteen, she became pregnant and was sent to live in a home for unmarried mothers. Her son was adopted in 1971.

Britta Wuornos died of liver failure in July of that year, Diane contending that she was actually murdered by Lauri, but nothing was ever proved. For Aileen, however, it was a signal that it was time to leave to make her own way in life. Living with Lauri was unthinkable. So, she took to the road, hitchhiking and earning some money from prostitution.

The next few years seemed to bring nothing but bad news into her already miserable life. Keith, her beloved brother, cruelly died of throat cancer, aged just twenty-one and Lauri committed suicide. Then, she had one of the few good things in her life happen to her. She met a man called Lewis Fell. He was the sixty-nine-year-old president of a Florida yacht club and it was love at first sight for him when he picked her up as she was hitchhiking one day. They were married but Aileen could not change her ways. She hung out in the wrong places, stayed out late and got into drunken fights in bars, eventually being jailed for assault. Fell realised he had made a huge mistake and had the marriage annulled after just a few months.

It had probably been the only chance Aileen Wuornos would ever have and she blew it. The next ten years were spent in a series of doomed relationships, drug-taking and criminal activity – forgery, prostitution and even armed robbery. When it all became too much to bear, she tried to kill herself.

As she hit rock-bottom, along came Tyria Moore, a twenty-four-year-old motel chambermaid whom she fell in love with. The two moved in together and Aileen took care of her new love, funding their life together from her earnings as a prostitute. Aileen's looks were fading, however, and it was getting harder to earn enough money. She had to find another way and seven dead men were going to provide her with the means of hanging on to her lover.

The first was middle-aged electronics repair business owner, Richard Mallory, who liked to party.

He often disappeared for days on end, out on an alcohol and sex binge and, therefore, when clients found his door locked one day in December 1989, no one was particularly worried. He would be back as soon as his money ran out. A few days later, however, his 1977 Cadillac was located outside Daytona. Then his body was found on a back road not far from Interstate 95, wrapped in a carpet. Three bullets from a .22 calibre pistol had been fired into him.

Police dug into Mallory's background of bars and strip-clubs, but they were unable to come up with anything that pointed to the killer.

Six months later, on 1 June 1990, another man was found shot dead. The naked body of forty-three-year-old David Spears turned up in woods forty miles north of Tampa. Spears, a heavy equipment operator, had last been heard of on 19 May when he let his boss know that he was on his way to Orlando. They found his truck with the doors unlocked on Interstate 75. There was a used condom close to his body and, once again, the weapon that had dispatched him was a .22.

Five days later, a third naked male body was found, also close to Interstate 75. The owner of the .22 had pumped nine bullets into Charles Carskaddon.

On 4 July, a car crashed off State Road 315, near Orange Springs, Florida and two women, later identified as Aileen and Tyria, were seen to clamber out, swearing at each other and obviously drunk. A by-stander asked if they needed help and the blonde, Aileen, begged her not to call the police. She told her that her father lived down the road and he would sort them out. They walked off.

When Marion County police officers later ran a check on the wrecked 1988 Pontiac Sunbird, they discovered that it was registered to sixty-five-year-old retired merchant seaman, Peter Siems, who had been missing from his home since 7 June. He had set out to visit family in Arkansas and had never turned up.

Troy Burress also failed to arrive at his destination on 30 July. A delivery man for a sausage manufacturer, he failed to make it back to his depot after his morning deliveries. They found his truck around dawn the next morning twenty miles east of the town of Ocala. It was unlocked and there was no trace of Burress. Five days later, however, a family picnicking in the Ocala National Forest stumbled on his badly decomposed body in a clearing just off Highway 19. He had been shot twice, once in the chest and once in the back. The bullets had come from a .22. Police were baffled. They picked up a drifter who had been seen hitchhiking on Highway 19 on the day in question, but he was quickly eliminated from their enquiries.

In the next two months she claimed her final two victims. Former police chief, Dick Humphries, now working for Florida's Department of Health and Rehabilitative Services celebrated his thirty-fifth wedding anniversary on 10 September. The following day, he disappeared and on 12 September, they found him, shot seven times with a .22.

A month later, trucker and security guard, Walter Gino Antonio's naked body was found on a logging road in Dixie County. He had died as a result of four shots from a .22.

Captain Steve Binnegar, commander of Marion County Sheriff's Criminal Investigation Department suspected that the perpetrator of the murders was more than likely a woman. Only non-threatening females would have been picked up by these men, he reasoned. He particularly suspected the two women who had crashed Peter Siem's car to be the killers. Sketches of them were circulated to the media and before too long they had names – Tyria Moore and a woman called Aileen. One lead, a motel owner in Tampa, named them as Tyria Moore and Susan Blahovec. Other pseudonyms for Aileen emerged – Lee Blahovec and Cammie Marsh Greene. The Greene identity led police to a pawnshop in Daytona where she had deposited a camera and radar detector belonging to Richard Mallory. Florida pawnshops require the person depositing items to provide a thumbprint. The thumbprint there plus another at a pawnshop in Ormand Beach, where she traded in a toolkit owned by David Spears, led investigators to fingerprints on an outstanding warrant against a woman named Lori Grody. Her prints had also been found in Peter Siems' car. The Blahovec, Greene and Grody aliases all led to one original source – Aileen Carol Wuornos.

On the evening of 8 January 1991, two undercover police officers posing as drug dealers located Aileen at a bar in Port Orange. She was almost arrested by diligent Port Orange cops, but they wanted to make no mistake and the two officers warned the officers off. They got into a conversation with her before she left for a biker bar, the Last Resort. The two undercover cops joined her there, drinking some more beers with her before leaving her to sleep the night away in an old car seat at the bar.

Next day when they hooked up with her again, they offered her the opportunity to have a shower in their motel room. As she left the bar, she was arrested on the outstanding Lori Grody warrant. The murders were not mentioned.

A day later, Tyria Moore was found visiting her sister in Pennsylvania. She was not charged with anything but began talking about the killings in the statement she made. She told how Aileen had arrived home one night in Richard Mallory's Cadillac, boasting that she had killed him. Moore claimed, however, that she had told her she did not want to know. If she did not know, she said, she would not have to report her lover to the police.

Back in Florida, they tried to trick Aileen into confessing in phone calls to Moore, reasoning that if Moore implied that they were trying to implicate her in the killings that Aileen would confess, rather than see Moore go to prison. Wuornos was no fool, however, and realised immediately what the police were trying to do. She was careful what she said.

Finally, however, on 16 January, she confessed, emphasising that Moore was in no way involved in the murders. She claimed they had all been carried out in self-defence, that all her victims had tried to rape her or had threatened her in some way. However, there was little consistency in her statements and she seemed to be embellishing them. She was convinced there was money to be made from the story of her life and a media frenzy had, indeed, broken out. Unfortunately, Florida does not allow felons to benefit financially from their crimes and she would not be getting rich quick.

Into the midst of all this emerged a born-again Christian, Arlene Pralle, who claimed that Jesus had instructed her to contact Wuornos. She became her defender on television and in magazines and newspapers and became very close to her. So close, in fact, that she and her husband legally adopted Aileen Wuornos, on the instructions of God, she claimed.

Wuornos received six death sentences and because of the cold-blooded nature of the way she killed and her cool, confident behaviour when interrogated, there was little doubt what the outcome would be. She herself said, 'I took a life. I am willing to give up my life because I killed people. I deserve to die.' Her reponse to the judge, prosecution and jury was less sanguine. When the jurors returned their verdict after only two hours, she screamed at them from the dock, 'I'm innocent! I was raped! I hope you get raped! Scumbags of America!' She later hissed at Ric Ridgeway, Assistant State Attorney, 'I hope your wife and children get raped in the ass!' She made an obscene gesture at the judge and shouted, 'Mother-fucker!' at him.

Aileen Wuornos's miserable life was brought to an end by lethal injection, which she had chosen over the electric chair, at 9.47 am on Wednesday 9 October 2002, more than ten years after her string of murders. Arguments still rage as to whether she was mad, as British broadcaster, Nick Bloomfield, who interviewed her, claimed, or whether, as the state claimed, she knew exactly what she was doing when she killed seven men.

MA BARKER

The name Ma Barker is probably familiar to most people due to the Roger Corman movie *Bloody Mama*. Her villainous actions and those of her four equally violent sons, earn a place in the annals of evil psychopaths. Together, Ma Barker and her boys terrorised midwest America in the 1930s, robbing banks and taking lives at will. There is no doubt that she was the driving force in the family and the bond was so strong, her sons were happy to follow where mother led.

Ma Barker was born in Springfield in 1872 and she was no stranger to the crimes of the Wild West. Her childhood hero was the outlaw Jesse James and it hit her hard when he was shot and killed in 1882. Kate, as she was known, was not a pretty teenager, and struggled constantly with her weight. She was flattered when she received the attention of a local farm labourer, George Barker, and even more thrilled when he asked her to become his wife.

They had four boys – Herman, Lloyd, Arthur 'Doc' and Freddie, who was the youngest and most definitely Ma Barker's favourite. The family lived in an impoverished state in a house which was little better than a shack. From an early age, Ma Barker started to hone her little criminals into shape. It wasn't long before the Barker boys caught the attention of the police, and Ma would have to use her very best persuasive skills to get her boys out of jail.

There was no doubt who wore the trousers in the Barker household, and by 1927, a very downtrodden George decided he couldn't take any more, and walked away from his family. Ma Barker decided she preferred the attention of women and it is rumoured that her boys all favoured homosexuality.

By the early 1930s, the Barker family had moved on to more serious crime, such as bank robberies. It wasn't until a sixth member of the gang arrived, Alvin Karpis, that their escapades took on a more serious nature. Already a hardened criminal, Karpis met Freddie Barker when they were both serving time in the Kansas State Penitentiary. Freddie was in prison for killing a policeman during an attempted theft of a car and, sharing a cell with Karpis, initiated the young Barker boy into more lucrative criminal activities.

When the pair were released, together with the remainder of the Barker family, they formed one of the most notorious criminal gangs of the 1930s – the Karpis-Barker gang. Not only did they start robbing banks on a regular basis, they also started hijacking mail deliveries and also turned to the more profitable business of kidnapping. The gang would not hesitate to kill anyone who got in their way, even if they turned out to be an innocent bystander.

They carried out their first kidnap in 1933, asking for an astonishing ransom figure of $100,000 for their victim, wealthy Minnesota brewer William Hamm. Flush with success, the gang upped their stakes and demanded $200,000 for their next kidnap victim, a banker by the name of Edward Bremer Jr. Ma Barker was the mastermind behind the snatch, and spent several months planning each stage. She worked out every precise detail and gave each of her boys a specific task. On 17 January 1934, Bremer dropped his daughter off at school and then headed off towards his office. His car was ambushed by Arthur Barker who held a gun to his head when he was forced to stop by red traffic signals.

The gang forced Bremer to sign the ransom demand, but attempts to retrieve the cash were botched on more than one occasion. Arthur became really frustrated and came close to killing Bremer. It was only his brother Freddie that talked him out of killing their victim, pointing out that they wouldn't receive any ransom if he was dead. The cash was eventually delivered on 17 February 1934 and Bremer was reunited with his family. He was one of the few men to escape from the clutches of Ma Barker and her gang.

This kidnap, however, turned out to be a big mistake, as Edward Bremer was a friend of President Franklin D. Roosevelt. The president was keen to stamp out this type of crime and instructed the FBI to deal harshly with any offenders. In response, the FBI employed highly trained 'flying squads' who specialised in hunting down public enemies, including the infamous John Dillinger.

The big mistake Ma Barker and her boys made was when they decided to eliminate George Ziegler. Ziegler was one of the masterminds behind the kidnapping of Bremer, but had become a problem to the gang by bragging about his exploits and drawing attention to himself.

On 22 March 1934, Ziegler was brought down by the Barker boys as he walked out of his favourite restaurant in Cicero, Illinois. The assassins were not careful when disposing of the corpse, they forgot to check Ziegler's pockets which contained valuable information about Ma Barker and her boys. This information was valuable to the FBI and they set about picking off each member of gang, one by one.

The first one of the gang to be apprehended was Arthur 'Doc', who was captured by the FBI on 8 January 1935. He was sent to Alcatraz where he was shot and killed when he attemped an escape.

The FBI managed to track down Ma and Freddie to a cottage they were renting in Lake Weir, Florida. Ma would not give up without a fight and managed to hold them off for four hours, using her favourite weapon, a machine gun. Ma Barker and her beloved Freddie were both killed, but they went out in a blaze of glory.

Lloyd served twenty-five years for murder but was freed in 1947. Shortly after his release he got married, but unfortunately for him his wife stabbed him to death in 1949.

Herman Barker was wounded in a gun battle with rival gang members, and rather than let them finish the job they started, he killed himself with his own gun.

Few people mourned the passing of Ma Barker and her boys. Many believed that she had given birth to sons of the Devil, but there is no doubt that she was an evil psychopath who passed on her love of killing and violence to her sons.